Essentials

of

Real Estate Finance

10th Edition
REVISED

David Sirota, PhD

Doris Barrell, CRB, GRI, DREI, Consulting Editor

Dearborn™
Real Estate Education

This publication is designed to provide accurate and authoritative information in regard to the subject matter covered. It is sold with the understanding that the publisher is not engaged in rendering legal, accounting, or other professional service. If legal advice or other expert assistance is required, the services of a competent professional person should be sought.

Senior Vice President and General Manager: Roy Lipner
Publisher and Director of Distance Learning: Evan Butterfield
Development Editor: Christopher Oler
Acting Editorial Production Manager: Daniel Frey
Senior Typsetter: Janet Schroeder
Creative Director: Lucy Jenkins

Published by Dearborn™ Real Estate Education Company,
a division of Dearborn Financial Publishing, Inc.®,
a Kaplan Professional Company®
30 S. Wacker Drive
Chicago, Illinois 60606-7481
http://www.dearbornRE.com

04 05 10 9 8 7 6 5 4 3

Library of Congress Cataloging-in-Publication Data

Sirota,David.
    Essentials of real estate finance/David Sirota; Doris Barrell, 10th ed., Rev.
      p. cm.
    Includes index.
    ISBN 0-7931-6084-7
    1. Housing—United States—Finance.   2. Mortgage loans—United States.   3. Real estate business—
United States.   I. Title: Real estate finance.   II. Barrell, Doris.   III. Title.
HD7293.Z9S55 2003
332.7'2'0973—dc21   2003003905

Contents

Preface

Welcome to the intriguing and always exciting world of real estate finance. Real estate markets in most areas of our country are enjoying extraordinary stability and growth. Based on relatively low interest rates, low unemployment, and controlled inflation, predictions are that this prosperity will continue at a steady pace through this decade.

Technology is shaping the ways in which real estate financing can be obtained. Although the traditional sources for loans are still available, electronic underwriting is providing borrowers with expanded opportunities to find affordable loans in a greatly reduced time-frame. With a relatively simple Internet connection, borrowers can not only find new sources for real estate finance, but they can also have the collateral property appraised and their credit checked in a fraction of the time required using traditional methods.

Large institutional owners of real estate continue to increase their real estate portfolios, creating new opportunities for pension funds and real estate investment trusts. These activities are accompanied by increasing equity and debt securitization.

Long-term, fixed-interest-rate loans are still the prevalent financing form, although lenders would prefer to make short-term, variable-interest-rate loans. However, costs for securing real estate loans have risen substantially. As a result, many principals involved in real estate transactions are designing new and different financing arrangements to meet their needs.

Participation loans, graduated-payment loans, less-than-interest-only (negative-amortization) loans, options, leasebacks, and other techniques are being used as lenders, builders, sellers, and buyers continue to struggle to succeed in the marketplace.

And succeed investors will, because the sturdy fabric of capitalism is woven from the strong and resilient threads of private enterprise. To a great extent, private enterprise depends on the ability of many individuals to comprehend and use real estate finance. Each investor need not know everything about all phases of financing real estate, but those who do understand the process are more likely to achieve success in their investments.

During the Great Depression, the U.S. capitalistic system was battered, torn, and generally worn threadbare. Safeguards for the government's security were woven carefully into the cloth, and the number and scope of these safeguards have continued to increase over the years.

The safety measures that secured our government also protected the people and their investments. People have depended, in ever-increasing numbers, on banks, thrift institutions, and life insurance companies to lend them the dollars with which to buy a piece of America. Some people bought large pieces, and some grouped together to buy even larger ones, but most people bought just the little piece they call home. The Federal Deposit Insurance Corporation (FDIC) stands resolutely behind everyone's deposits to the extent of $100,000 per account, guarding our savings.

This tenth edition has been revised to serve the needs of our ever-increasingly technological environment. We need to know the hard and fast rules and techniques of the industry, and we need them explained concisely and plainly with lots of examples as illustrations. This text has been updated to complement our readers' needs.

This textbook breaks down the study of real estate finance into two simple components: The principles of real estate finance are covered in the first half of the text, with the practices and applications included in the second half. What distinguishes *Essentials of Real Estate Finance* as a textbook is the clear and concise manner in which these components are described. Even the most sophisticated finance concepts become easy to understand and absorb with *Essentials of Real Estate Finance*. Each chapter begins with a list of key terms that is designed to help reinforce students' learning. This text's many charts and illustrations help students visualize key concepts along the way. Each chapter then concludes with a series of review questions that allow students to gauge their understanding of the material.

Every effort has been expended to develop this book in a logical, sequential format, with accurate, easily understandable language. The author welcomes all comments and questions about its contents and will answer them immediately. Address inquiries to D. Sirota, 564 Corpino de Pecho, Green Valley, AZ 85614, or call (520) 625-6417, e-mail dsirota@mindspring.com.

ABOUT THE AUTHOR

Dr. David Sirota has combined 40 years of field experience as a real estate agent, broker, appraiser, and consultant, plus an academic background culminating in a PhD from the University of Arizona in Area Development, in the writing of *Essentials of Real Estate Finance*. He says, "To be extraordinarily successful, it's not enough to know how the system works, but why it does. Then you can be in a position to utilize it for your own highest benefits."

Dr. Sirota taught real estate subjects at the University of Arizona in Tucson, the University of Nebraska in Omaha, Eastern Michigan University in Ypsilanti, National University in San Diego, and California State University in Fullerton. He held the Real Estate Chair at Nebraska and was a Visiting Professor at the University of Hawaii. He was involved as a consultant in the development of a congregate care center in Green Valley, Arizona, and acts in a consultant capacity for individuals and developers. He is a founding and continuing member of the Real Estate Educators Association, securing one of its first DREI designations. Dr. Sirota is the author of *Essentials of Real Estate Investment* and coauthor of *California Real Estate Finance.*

ABOUT THE CONSULTING EDITOR

Doris Barrell, CRB, GRI, DREI, has been in the real estate business for over 20 years, working first for a builder-developer, then as general brokerage agent, and for nine years as managing broker for a 60-agent office in Alexandria, Virginia. She brings this wealth of real-life experience into the classroom where she teaches finance, agency, fair housing, ethics, legislative and legal issues. Additionally, Doris serves as a regular consultant to Neighborhood Reinvestment Corporation and its training institutes all over the United States. Ms. Barrell is the author of *Real Estate Finance Today, Ethics and Real Estate,* and coauthor of the forthcoming *Reaching Out: The Financial Power of Niche Marketing.*

Acknowledgments

My gratitude must begin with the many students who have insisted through the years, "Dr. Sirota, you should write that down." To them I say, "Thank you for supplying the necessary motivation."

Thanks also to the following reviewers for their valuable assistance in the development of the tenth edition and tenth edition revised of *Essentials of Real Estate Finance:*

- Dr. Arthur Cox, University of Northern Iowa
- Bill Gallagher, DREI, GRI, CCDS, CBR, Mingle School of Real Estate, Bill Gallagher School of Real Estate
- Carl Hemmeler III, Columbus State Community College
- Rick Knowles, Capital Real Estate Training
- "Doc" Blanchard L. LeNoir, PhD, Cedar Valley College
- Dr. Wade R. Ragas, University of New Orleans
- Jerome D. Rutledge, Director of Education, North Texas Commercial Association of REALTORS®, Owner/Operator, Alliance Academy, and
- Nancy Seago, GRI, Nancy Seago Seminars

For their contribution to earlier editions of the text, thanks are also extended to Joseph L. Barrett, associate professor, Essex Community College; Bruce Baughman; W. Frazier Bell, Piedmont Virginia Community College; George Bell, DREI, George Bell Productions, Ltd.; Robert J. Bond; Lynn Brown, PhD, professor, Jacksonville State University; Thomas Cary, real estate instructor/coordinator, Wadena Technical Institute; Kelly W. Cassidy; Maurice Clifton, GRI, DREI, ERA West Wind—Boise; Gerald R. Cortesi, Triton College; Richard D. Cowan, North Carolina Academy of Real Estate; Lee Dillenbeck, real estate coordinator, Elgin Community College; Barbara Drisko, Real Estate Training & Education Services (RETES); Ed Elmer, Denver Financial Group; Calvin Ferraro, GRI, Coldwell Banker Real Estate; Gloria Fisher, Senior Loan Officer, Source One Mortgage Services, Green Valley, Arizona; Donald A. Gabriel; Arlyne Geschwender; Gerald N. Harris, Asheville Professional School of Real Estate; Janet Heller, Berks Real Estate Institute; Carl M. Hyatt; John Jeddeloh; Glenn Jurgens; F. Jeffery Keil, J. Sargeants Reynolds Community College; Mike Keller; John W. Killough, Blue Ridge Community College; Melvin S. Lang, National Institute of Real Estate; Craig Larabee, director, Nebraska School of Real Estate;

Thomas E. LoDolce, Financial Estate Institute; Lucy Loughhead; Jon C. McBride, Wake Technical Community College; Justin H. McCarthy, Minneapolis Technical Institute; Colin F. McGowan, Frederick Academy of Real Estate; Timothy C. Meline, Iowa Realty Company, Inc.; Stephen C. Messner; T. Gregory Morton; Henry J. Olivieri, Jr., Real Estate Education Company; Charles E. Orcutt, Jr., attorney at law and adjunct faculty, Babson College; Nick J. Petra, CFP, CRB, Priority One Education Systems; Paul R. Pope, real estate education consultant, University Programs, Inc.; Mike Rieder, Gold Coast School of Real Estate, A Gimelstob Company; John F. Rodgers III, Catonsville Community College; Charles V. Sederstrom, III, Randall School of Real Estate; Paul C. and Margaret E. Sprencz; Ronald Stark, Northwest Mississippi Community College; Phyllis Tonne, Dayton Area Board of Realtors, Audrey May Van Vliet, Academy of Real Estate Education, Inc.; Richard Zemelka, Maplewood Area JVS Branch, John Carroll University; and Roger Zimmerman, faculty, Polaris Career Center and Cuyahoga Community College.

To Ann Kennehan, my original indefatigable editor, counselor, corrector, and severest critic, my eternal admiration, affection, and respect.

To my loving wife, Roslyn, this book is dedicated with everlasting love.

CHAPTER 1

The Nature and Cycle of Real Estate Finance

▼ KEY TERMS

baby boomers
collateral
cycle
disintermediation
equitable title

FIRREA
hypothecation
leverage
mortgage-backed
securities (MBS)

primary market
secondary mortgage
market
Taxpayer Relief Act of
1997 (TRA '97)

There is no getting away from real estate! We farm on it, live on it, work on it, build on it, fly away from and return to it, and ultimately are buried in it. No one can question the importance of real estate in our lives.

Complementing its physical importance is the economic impact of real estate on our lifestyles. The industrial and commercial activities of our nation are completely dependent on the land and its natural resources for their very existence. Our society cannot function without food, lumber, minerals, water, and other parts and products of our land.

Many of us are involved, either directly or indirectly, in some activity concerning real estate. Salespersons, brokers, farmers, miners, engineers, surveyors, land planners, homebuilders, furniture manufacturers, and paint purveyors—all of these people and more depend on real estate and its use for their livelihood. Millions of persons are engaged directly in construction activities in the United States, with literally millions more providing them with the materials and peripheral services essential to their work.

THE NATURE OF REAL ESTATE FINANCE

The construction industry is vital to our country's economic well-being and thus is important in real estate finance. Any changes in its activities soon affect everyone. A building slowdown results in layoffs and cutbacks, while increased activity stimulates production and services in the many areas associated with the industry. Little construction is attempted that is not paid for by loans secured from the various sources of money for real estate finance. In fact, most real estate activities rely on the availability of borrowed funds.

Credit System Economy

We all recognize that our society is *credit oriented*. We postpone paying for our personal property purchases by using credit cards and charge accounts. Credit expands our ability to own goods that in turn enhance our lives.

The credit concept of enjoying the use of an object while still paying for it is the basis of real estate finance. Financing a real estate purchase involves large sums of money and usually requires a long time to repay the loan. Instead of revolving charge accounts or 90-day credit loans for hundreds of dollars, real estate involves loans of thousands of dollars, repayable for up to 30 years.

The long-term nature of real estate loans complements the holding profile of the major financial lenders. Furthermore, the systematic repayment of real estate loans, usually in regular monthly amounts, creates the rhythm that enables lenders to collect savings and redistribute funds to implement continued economic growth.

However, this rhythm can be interrupted when there is a prolonged period of **disintermediation;** that is, when more funds are withdrawn from financial institutions than are being deposited. This results in a net loss of deposits, a cutback in lending, and a slowdown in the economy. There is continuous, vigorous competition for the use of money among individuals, industry, and government. That is why we need the Federal Reserve (the Fed) and the secondary markets to redistribute funds nationally and provide a constant flow of cash.

Financing Relationships

The nature of the financing relationship can be described in three ways. In its simplest form, real estate finance involves pledging real property as **collateral** to back up a promise to repay a loan. As illustrated in Figure 1.1, a building and the land on which it stands are pledged to a lender as the borrower's guarantee that the terms of a loan contract will be satisfied. If a borrower defaults on repayment promises, the lender is legally able to foreclose on the real estate and sell it to try to recoup the loan balance.

A second way to describe real estate finance is **hypothecation.** The borrower remains the legal owner and retains rights of possession and control while the lender secures a "bare title," a "naked title," or an **equitable title** in the property. An equitable title confers no rights to the lender except after a loan default, when the legal title may be attained through foreclosure. In other words, under hypothecation, the lender has only a security, or equitable, interest in the collateral property, which ends when the loan is paid in full.

Hypothecation is found in other situations as well. A tenant may pledge leasehold rights as collateral for a loan. A lender may pledge rights in a receivable mortgage, deed of trust, or contract for deed as collateral for another loan. A life tenant can acquire a loan on beneficial rights as well as remainder rights. A farmer can pledge unharvested crops as collateral for a loan. In each of these cases, and others of similar design, the borrower retains possession, control, and use of the collateral but capitalizes on its value by borrowing against it.

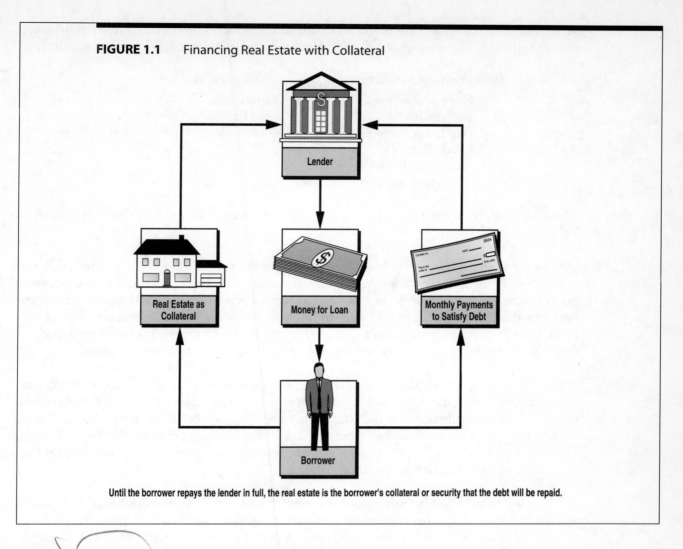

FIGURE 1.1   Financing Real Estate with Collateral

Until the borrower repays the lender in full, the real estate is the borrower's collateral or security that the debt will be repaid.

Leverage is the third way to describe real estate finance. Leverage is the use of a proportionately small amount of money to secure a large loan for the purchase of a property. Buyers invest a portion of their money as a down payment and then leverage by borrowing the balance needed toward the full purchase price.

The quality and quantity of leverage are important topics in this book. Some buyers may leverage 100 percent of the purchase price and not be required to invest any personal funds. Other buyers may have to invest 3, 5, 10, or even 20 percent of the purchase price before being eligible to borrow the balance. The degree of leverage depends on the specific situation and the type of loan desired. As we shall discover, these varying cash requirements dramatically affect a buyer's ability to purchase property. The use of leverage to purchase investment property generally increases the return on cash invested to an amount substantially higher than paying all cash.

MORTGAGE LENDING ACTIVITIES

Underlying and forming the foundation for mortgage lending is the concept of savings. These savings are loaned to borrowers from whom additional earnings are produced for the lenders in the form of interest. These earnings are then used in part to pay interest to the savers on their deposits.

Most loans for real estate are made by financial institutions designed to hold individuals' savings until they are withdrawn. These institutions include the following, among others:

Primary Market	Secondary Market
Commercial Banks	Fannie Mae �
Savings Banks	Freddie Mac
Life Insurance Companies	Ginnie Mae
Credit Unions	
Mortgage Brokers	
Mortgage Bankers	

[handwritten: Fannie Mae / Freddie Mac — For Profit corp.]
[handwritten: Ginnie Mae — Federal market Agency]

The scope of the mortgage lending activities of various sources of funds is shown in Table 1.1.

The total amount of mortgage loans outstanding at the end of the second quarter 2001 was more than $7 trillion. Included in the *Others* category in Table 1.1 are the indispensable government agencies involved in this field, as well as private finance and mortgage companies, real estate investment trusts, pension funds, credit unions, and individuals. Notice that more than 75 percent of all loans made are for one-family to four-family residential properties, a dramatic testimony to the importance of housing in the real estate market.

The price of real estate fluctuates over time, depending on changing market conditions. Most buyers do not have the cash required for real estate purchases. They must borrow to complete their acquisitions. If the sources for these loans were to be limited to any large extent, fewer properties would be developed and fewer would be sold. Shortages of funds for mortgage lending affect every level of the construction industry, with serious ramifications throughout the total national economy.

In the early to mid-1980s, interest rates on real estate loans were at double-digit levels, as shown in Figure 1.2. This effectively eliminated a major portion of the participants in the real estate market. To meet this emergency, a broad range of creative financing arrangements was invented to allow market continuity. These arrangements included partnerships between lenders and borrowers (participation financing), variable interest rate loans, and variable payment loans, all designed to relieve borrowers' burdens and permit lenders to stay in business. These financing techniques are still used today and will be described in later chapters.

TABLE 1.1 Mortgage Loans Outstanding, by Type of Property and Lender, End Second Quarter, 2001 (Billions of Dollars)

Lender	One-Family to Four-Family	Multifamily	Commercial	Farm	Total
Thrifts	616.5	63.1	71.3	.583	751.4
Banks	999.3	80.5	612.3	35.1	1,727.2
Life Insurance Companies	5.0	33.8	184.6	13.6	237.0
Others	3,859.7	261.4	380.8	63.9	4,565.6
Total	5,480.5	438.8	1,249.0	112.9	7,281.2

SOURCE: Federal Reserve Bulletin, March 2002, page A35.

FDIC - insurance on
your $$ up to 100k

FIGURE 1.2 30-Year Fixed-Rate Mortgage Interest Rates

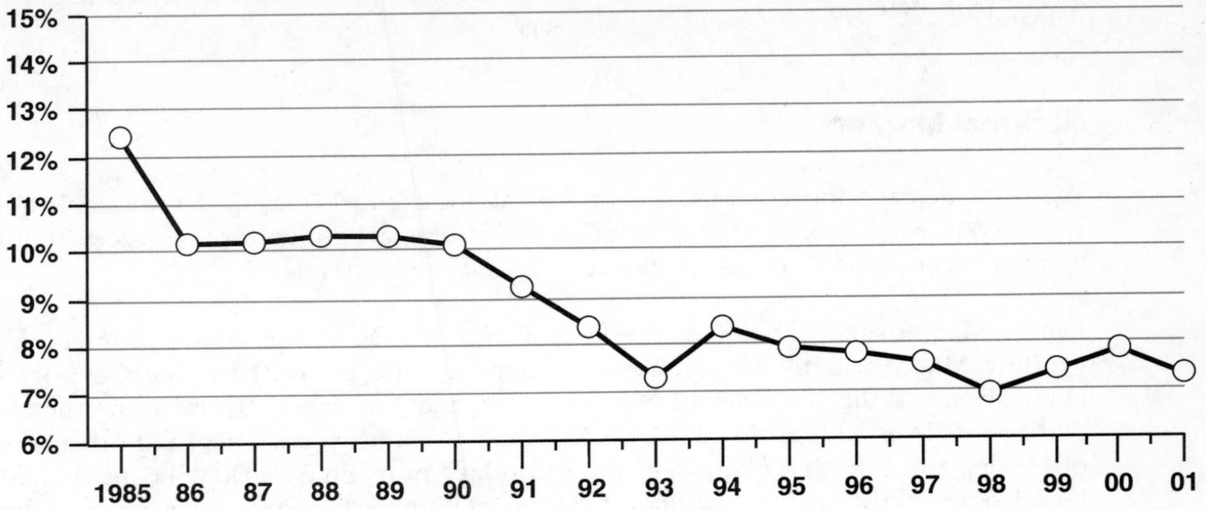

Source: Federal Home Loan Mortgage Corporation

As the decade progressed, interest rates fell almost as rapidly as they had risen and the demand for basic fixed-rate mortgages returned. This reduction in interest rates, to between 6 percent and 8 percent, resulted in a sharply increased demand for mortgage refinancing in the early 1990s. The focus of the lenders shifted from loans for purchasing property to loans for refinancing existing high-interest, adjustable-rate, and fixed-rate loans. In addition, these relatively low interest rates fueled a sharp rise in real estate activity that is expected to continue well into the first decade of this century. Real estate finance is a subject for constant analysis and monitoring as conditions often change over time.

Local Markets

Real estate is a local market in that it is fixed in place. It is impossible to move a parcel of land. As a result, any activities are done *to* and *on* the property. A building is constructed *on* the lot. Utilities are brought *to* the property and taxes are imposed *on* it. A real estate loan is made *on* a property, usually by a local lender or the local representative of a national lender.

The activities of the local real estate market, especially as they influence property values, are vital to the activities of the local real estate lenders. Regional, national, and international economic and political events have an indirect effect on specific real property values. However, the immediate impact of local activities on individual properties most directly affects their value.

For example, police power decisions involving zoning regulations can dramatically raise individual property values, while just as dramatically lowering neighborhood property values. Political decisions concerned with community growth or no-growth policies, pollution controls, building standards, and the preservation of coastline and wildlife habitats can significantly alter a community's economic balance and property values.

In times of economic distress, as evidenced by higher interest rates and/or unemployment, local financial institutions decrease their mortgage lending activities. This decrease adds to the downward cycle. In good times, their lending activities increase to serve the growing demand.

National Markets

When the demand for mortgage money is great, local lenders may deplete available funds. In an economic slump, these lenders may not have any safe outlets for their excess funds. A national mortgage market has developed to balance these trends.

Fannie Mae, formally known as the Federal National Mortgage Association (FNMA), Freddie Mac, formally known as the Federal Home Loan Mortgage Corporation (FHLMC), and the Government National Mortgage Association (GNMA) are the major participants in a viable national market for real estate mortgages. They, and other smaller operators, are collectively known as the **secondary mortgage market.** Loans created by local lenders, thrifts, banks, mortgage bankers, and others, known as the **primary market,** are purchased by these "second" owners who, in turn, often package these loans into mortgage pools. Proportionate ownership of these mortgage pools is then sold to investors in the form of securities called **mortgage backed securities (MBS).**

Sold to 2ND MARKET

In this manner, the secondary mortgage market participants act to stabilize the real estate market by shifting funds from capital-excess areas to capital-deficient areas. They provide safe investments for the purchasers of their securities. They allow lenders in slow-growth areas an opportunity to buy mortgages, and they purchase loans from lenders in the fast-growth areas. Thus, savings are pooled at the local level, then allocated according to needs at the national level. (See Chapter 4, *The Secondary Mortgage Market.*)

REAL ESTATE CYCLES

The ups and downs of real estate activities are described as real estate cycles. The word **cycle** implies the recurrence of events in a somewhat regular pattern. By studying past real estate market activities, researchers can develop prognoses for future investment plans.

Supply and Demand

As shown in Figure 1.3, real estate cycles are affected by many variables, all of which, either directly or indirectly, are influenced by the economic forces of supply and demand. Real estate cycles can be short term or long term. In the short-term cycle, the general business conditions that produce the earnings needed to create an effective demand usually trigger the real estate market's activity. In a growth area where business is good and demand is higher than the available supply of real estate, the prices of properties available for sale increase. This active demand generally encourages more building, and the supply of real estate tends to increase until there is a surplus. When the supply exceeds the demand, prices decrease. Any new construction becomes economically unsound. The cycle repeats itself as soon as the demand again exceeds the supply.

IN PRACTICE . . .

John and Martha are an elderly couple living in a small town in upper state New York. They have decided to sell their home of 34 years and move to a retirement community in South Carolina. Unfortunately, the only real industry in town—the Best Quality button-making factory—recently closed its doors, putting 300 people out of work. Most of the families who worked there are having to relocate as there are no jobs available in the immediate area, even at lower salaries.

Even though neither John nor Martha is directly affected by the factory shutdown, they will suffer the effects of a declining real estate cycle. Their home is now only one of many on the market at a time when there are very few potential buyers. The price they will be able to get for their property today is much less than they could have expected a year ago.

Another variable affecting the short-term real estate cycle is the supply of money for financing. Tight money circumstances develop when competitive drains on the money supply occur or the Fed takes certain actions to restrict the supply of money. The two largest competitors for savings are the federal government, with its gargantuan budgetary commitments, and industry, which taps the money markets to finance additional inventory or plant expansion. Any continuing deficits in its budget force the government into the borrowing market, reducing funds available for real estate finance.

In the short term, the market responds to current economic conditions, while in the long term, the time variables associated with real estate development prevail. It takes time to put a real estate project on the ground. From the creation of the idea to the acquisition of the land; through its possible rezoning, engineering, and preparation; during its construction, promotion, and sales, years sometimes pass. During this interval, the markets are fluctuating. The developer is lucky to enjoy any profits when all is completed.

FIGURE 1.3   Factors That Affect the Cycles of Real Estate

Housing Supply

Supply of Money for Financing

Business Activities

Population Growth and Characteristics

IRS Tax Rules

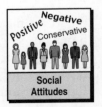
Social Attitudes

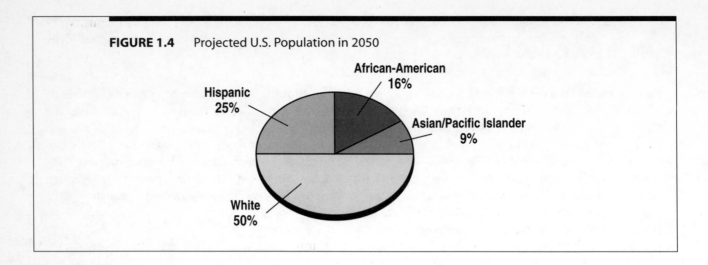

FIGURE 1.4   Projected U.S. Population in 2050

Short-term real estate cycles generally run from 3 years to 5 years. In the long term, they generally run from 10 years to 15 years. The ability to examine the causes of the cycles and to forecast their movements in order to anticipate the markets is important to a real estate investor's success.

Population Characteristics

An important factor involved in making real estate development decisions is the makeup of this country's population and how it changes over time. Past census information revealed that 80 percent of U.S. households live in officially designated metropolitan areas, mostly in the suburbs. The median house consists of 1,688 square feet and has 5½ rooms, 2.6 of which are bedrooms; and more than a third have two or more bathrooms. Two-thirds of these households have no children younger than 18. About 22 million persons live alone.

The 2000 census predicted a substantial increase in the total population to 394 million in 2050, up from 255 million in 1992. As shown in Figure 1.4, people from Asia and the Pacific Islands will increase from 3 percent to 9 percent of the population, while Hispanics will grow from 9 percent to 25 percent and African-Americans from 12 percent to 16 percent.

Our population is also aging. The 78 million **baby boomers** born between 1946 and 1964 are creating a middle-aged bulge in our population demographics. With fewer children being born and more people living longer, a higher proportion of the population is elderly. This creates a strong demand for nursing homes, congregate care centers, and other forms of housing for the elderly.

Our population is divided as follows:

- 25 percent married couples with children at home
- 25 percent single persons
- 30 percent married couples without children
- 10 percent single parents with children
- 10 percent nonfamily households (institutions)

The real estate trends of the late twentieth century have carried over into this century. The demand for real estate has continued to increase. The proportion of nontraditional households has continued to rise. The markets for trade-up homes are still strong. Throughout the United States the effect of the rising immigrant population continues to be strongly felt in the "gateway" cities. For more detailed demographic information for all areas of the country, see www.census.gov.

Social Attitudes

Changing social attitudes also influence real estate cycles. Historically, fast growth was the goal of many U.S. communities, and some even favor this approach today. Local governments often offer concessions to induce industry to move to their towns. Nevertheless, many communities promote an attitude of planned growth, legally limiting new construction activities to satisfy voters' demands.

Throughout the United States today, many communities are striving for "smart growth," with proper planning a prerequisite for allowing new development. A "no growth" policy leads to a downturn in the economy, but rampant "overgrowth" leaves communities lacking in schools, police and fire protection, and adequate transportation.

Tax Issues

The constantly changing federal income tax structure also affects real estate cycles. In 1986 Congress imposed dramatic restrictions on the use of excess losses from real estate investments to shelter other income under the Tax Reform Act of 1986 (TRA '86). Special treatment for capital gains and excessive depreciation deductions were also introduced.

Effective May 7, 1997, Congress again fine-tuned the income tax laws by passing the **Taxpayer Relief Act of 1997 (TRA '97),** providing home owners with broad exemptions from capital gains taxes on profits made from the sale of personal residences. Replacing the one-time exemption of $125,000 for sellers older than age 55, TRA '97 exempts up to $500,000 of profits from taxes for a couple (or up to $250,000 for a single person) who have lived in the property as a primary residence for more than two years in the five years previous to the sale.

TRA '97 eliminates the necessity to purchase another residence at a price equal to or higher than that of sold property. It also eliminates keeping records of repairs, additions, or other changes to the sold property's tax basis unless the gain from the sale exceeds the exemptions. These tax benefits may be taken every two years, and new IRS regulations now stipulate that if the property meets the entire exclusion, the transaction need not be reported at all. It is felt that TRA '97 has stimulated increased activities in the national residential real estate market and has effectively raised property values to new heights.

Investors in real estate may receive additional benefits from TRA '97. The maximum capital gains tax rate has been reduced from 28 percent to 20 percent, including a decrease from 15 percent to 10 percent for persons in the 15 percent tax bracket. Moreover, the depreciation recapture tax on the amount that has been depreciated over the years is charged at 25 percent. Note that the property must be held a minimum of 12 months.

The Internal Revenue Service Web site is very user friendly and provides a wealth of information on all tax issues. See www.irs.gov.

Property Value Fluctuations

Although some properties display a character of their own and run counter to prevailing trends, most properties are carried along in a cyclical action. Generally in the long run most real property values rise. In the short run, property values rise and fall.

The stabilizing influences of Fannie Mae, Freddie Mac, and GNMA have calmed some of the volatile short-term reactions of localized booms and busts. At the same time, the financial management policies of the Federal Reserve and the U.S. Treasury have largely soothed long-term reactions to these cycles. These latter federal government agencies largely control the supply of money in circulation. They attempt to anticipate any truly large-scale national cyclical variations in the economy. By adjusting the costs and amounts of money available, they tend to flatten the high peaks or low valleys of the cycles.

The hope that traditional real estate cycles can be moderated by better market information is currently being realized by increasing openness about real estate dealings, financing, and new construction. The following four key groups are largely responsible for providing this important market information:

1. Bond analysts and rating agencies submit highly detailed information to investors who participate in mortgage-backed securities, 14 percent of the real estate debt market.
2. Real Estate Investment Trust analysts provide full disclosure of the data in the field that now controls about 40 percent of the commercial real estate.
3. Bank and insurance analysts publish essential underwriting market data.
4. The Internet acts as an important conduit of the vast amount of data available instantaneously.

CHANGES IN REAL ESTATE FINANCE

We have seen real estate loan interest rates exceeding 20 percent in the early 1980s fall to less than 8 percent in the 1990s. An inflation rate of more than 13 percent has dropped to less than 5 percent. An exceedingly tight and structured banking system shifted, under deregulation, into financing excess construction activity. In some cases, free-wheeling banks and thrifts or savings associations made excessive loans on the basis of inflated appraisals. The havoc they created resulted in the passage of the Financial Institutions Reform, Recovery, and Enforcement Act of 1989 (**FIRREA**), which reinstituted stringent banking controls.

The Office of Thrift Supervision now controls our nation's savings institutions. It has limited the amount of loans that may be issued to one borrower to 15 percent of the net value of the borrower's assets, rather than 100 percent, which many developers enjoyed in the past. Current regulations limit thrifts to financing primarily single-family homes and allow only a few to provide money for apartment buildings.

The shrinkage of the thrift industry resulting from the many bankruptcies in the late 1980s has given rise to greater participation by other sources of real estate finance. Commercial banks, life insurance companies, pension funds, and credit unions have increased their lending activities. Strict underwriting rules are inhibiting commercial real estate lending, with only the most creditworthy and experienced developers securing new loans.

The economy is relatively stable and is projected to grow by 3 percent annually. Larger growth rates may not be achievable because of company restructuring (mergers and downsizing), and sluggish export growth.

Property values are expected to increase gradually. Despite fears that excess capital flowing into real estate may cause a market reversal, indications are that participants remain selective when buying or selling. The important question is whether this discipline can continue in the 2000s and prevent overbuilding, which greatly contributed to the recession of the 1980s.

SUMMARY

Real estate is pervasive in our lives. Not only do we depend on it for physical sustenance, it also provides us the materials for our economic well-being.

Millions of persons are involved in some form of activity related to real estate. When flourishing, the construction industry directly employs millions of people. Innumerable additional workers are engaged in providing this industry its materials and peripheral services.

Most real estate activities are financed. Monies accumulated by thrifts, banks, life insurance companies, pension funds, and other formal financial intermediaries are loaned to builders and developers to finance their projects. Other loans are made to buyers of already existing structures, thus providing the financial institutions a continuing opportunity for investments of their entrusted funds. These investments produce returns and new funds available for loans to stimulate additional growth.

These financing activities are based on the simple premise of real estate being pledged as collateral to guarantee the repayment of a loan. An owner of a property borrows money from a lender and executes a promise to repay this loan under agreed-upon terms and conditions. The real estate is pledged as collateral to back up this promise. The borrower continues to be able to possess and use the collateral real estate during the term of the loan. The ability to maintain control of the property while borrowing against it is called hypothecation. It is also a manifestation of leverage, by which a small amount of money can provide the means for securing a large loan for the purchase of property. If the promise to repay the loan is broken, the lender can acquire the collateral and sell it to recover the investment.

Generally the majority of loans on real estate are made by local financing institutions, using deposits accumulated by persons in the community. However, a national market for real estate finance operates under the auspices of Fannie Mae, Freddie Mac, and the Government National Mortgage Association (GNMA). These agencies maintain a secondary market for buying and selling mortgages on a national level.

The overall cycle of real estate economics and finance is modified by the forces of supply and demand. Excess demand normally leads to increased production, until excess supply reverses the cycle. Mirroring these forces of supply and demand is the availability of money for financing at reasonable costs. Other variables that affect real estate cycles include population changes in terms of numbers, age, and social mores; changes in political attitudes governing community growth policies; and changes in the federal income tax structure.

Complementing the secondary market activities that balance national level mortgage loan funding sources are the much broader controls exercised by the Federal Reserve (the Fed) and the U.S. Treasury. By controlling the amounts of money in circulation and the cost of securing mortgage funds, these agencies attempt to balance the fluctuations of the national money market.

WHAT IS MONEY?

Definition

Money allows us to convert our physical and mental efforts into a convenient method of exchange. Thus, we can define *money* as

- a medium of exchange or means of payment,
- a storehouse of purchasing power, and/or
- a standard of value.

In primitive societies, money is anything that is generally accepted as a means of exchange, such as beads, salt, shells, and so on. Money can also be represented by coins, bills, or checks, which are currently our convenient, acceptable, representative means for exchanging value.

Today's system of money is based on confidence. As long as the public can exchange symbolic paper money for commodities of like value, the system works. When that confidence is shaken, as in countries suffering economic or political turmoil, the ability of money to command commodities of like value diminishes.

Although some people seek to accumulate money for the sheer joy of possessing it, à la King Midas, most of us strive to acquire money for the goods and services it can purchase. Our efforts to acquire money are related directly to satisfying our need for food, clothing, and shelter. After we have acquired these essentials, we strive to accumulate money to satisfy our need for additional security, pleasure, and/or power, depending on individual motivations.

The Supply and Costs of Money

Economic stability is linked directly to the supply of money and the cost of money. As shown in Figure 2.1, the larger the *supply of money* in circulation, the greater the economic activity. When the economy is infused with more spendable cash, the possibility for an increase in spending activity is enhanced. Increased spending requires increased production to replenish depleted inventories. With increased production come more jobs. More people are employed and are spending money.

If this economic cycle is true, then the reverse condition, the withdrawal of funds from circulation, should result in a slowdown of economic activity.

The basic money supply is described as

- M1   cash in public hands, private checking accounts at commercial banks, credit union share accounts, and demand deposits at thrift institutions;
- M2   all of M1 plus money market mutual fund shares as well as savings deposits and time deposits of less than $100,000 at all depository institutions; and
- M3   includes M2 plus large time deposits at all depository institutions.

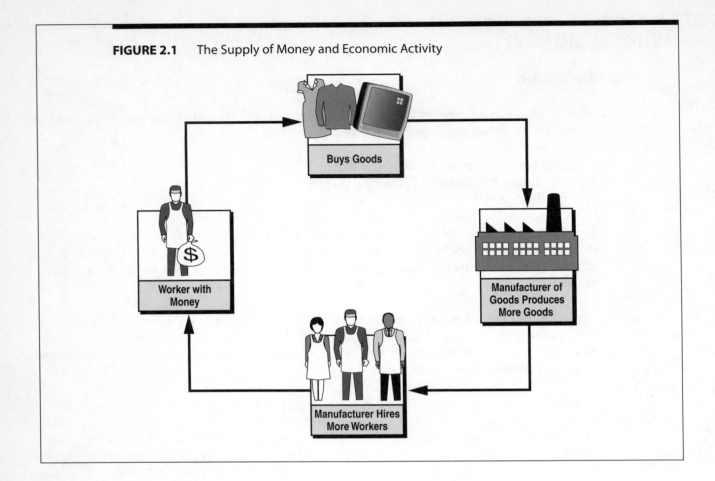

FIGURE 2.1 The Supply of Money and Economic Activity

Considering the *cost of money* in terms of the interest charged for borrowed funds, it would appear that the higher the cost, the lower the borrowing activity and the slower the economic activity. The reverse situation, the lowering of interest rates, should raise the demand for borrowed funds and produce increased economic activity.

Theoretically, then, manipulations of the supply and cost of money should result in economic balance. The reality is that a balanced economy is largely shaped by the federal agencies empowered to control the supply and cost of money: For example, the Federal Reserve System, the United States Treasury, and the Federal Home Loan Bank System. Although their efforts at balancing the national economy are not always successful, resulting in part from time lags and consumer resistance, these agencies have a profound effect on national real estate finance.

THE FEDERAL RESERVE SYSTEM (THE FED)

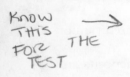

The **Federal Reserve System (the Fed)** is this nation's "monetary manager." The Fed is charged with the maintenance of sound credit conditions to help counteract inflationary and deflationary movements. It also has a role in creating conditions favorable to high employment, stable values, internal growth of the nation, and rising levels of consumption. The Fed keeps the public informed of its activities through its web site, as shown in Figure 2.2.

FIGURE 2.2   www.federalreserve.gov/

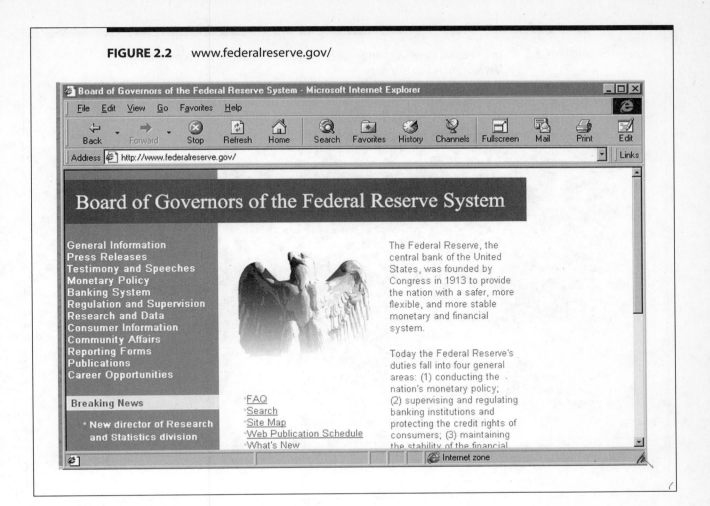

Purpose

The Fed was established in 1913 when President Woodrow Wilson signed the Federal Reserve Act. Its original purpose was to establish facilities for selling or discounting commercial paper and to improve the supervision of banking activities. Its full impact on our monetary system has broadened over time to include influence over the availability and cost of money and credit (interest rates).

As the central bank of the United States, the Fed attempts to ensure that money and credit growth over the long run is sufficient to provide a rising standard of living for all of U.S. citizens. In the short run the Fed seeks to adapt its policies in an effort to combat deflationary or inflationary pressures. And as a lender of last resort, it has the responsibility for utilizing policy instruments available to it in an attempt to forestall national liquidity crises and financial panics.

Organization

The Fed is a central banking system composed of 12 Federal Reserve districts. Each is served by a district Federal Reserve Bank, coordinated and directed by a single seven-member board of governors housed in Washington, D.C. These districts and their branch territories are shown in Figure 2.3.

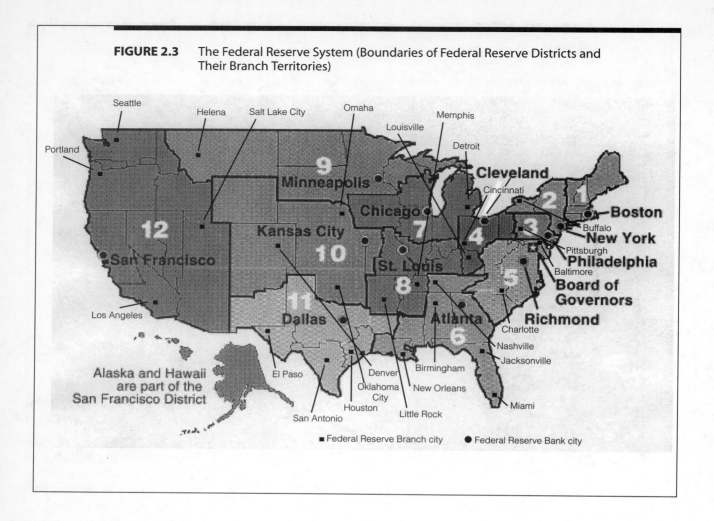

FIGURE 2.3   The Federal Reserve System (Boundaries of Federal Reserve Districts and Their Branch Territories)

■ Federal Reserve Branch city   ● Federal Reserve Bank city

The Federal Reserve banks are not under the control of any governmental agency, but each reserve bank is responsible to a board of directors. Each board is composed of nine members representing their Federal Reserve district. The organization of the Fed is shown in Figure 2.4.

Member Banks

All nationally chartered commercial banks must join the Fed, while state-chartered banks may also become members of the system. Each member bank is required to purchase capital stock in its federal reserve district bank to maintain sufficient monetary reserves to meet the Fed's requirements and to clear checks through the system. In addition, they must comply with other rules and regulations imposed by the Fed for governing loans made by member banks and maintaining the stability of our monetary system by insuring their deposits. Member banks may borrow money from their federal district bank when in need of funds, share in the informational systems available, and generally engage in all banking activities under the protective umbrella of the Fed.

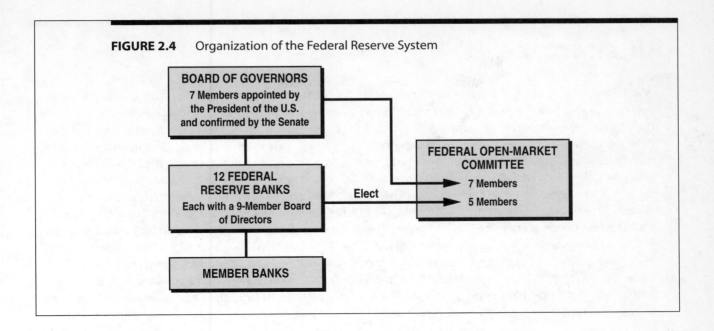

FIGURE 2.4   Organization of the Federal Reserve System

INSTRUMENTS OF CREDIT POLICY

The Fed has numerous functions, among which are issuing currency in the form of Federal Reserve notes (examine the paper money you have in your possession), supervising and regulating member banks, clearing and collecting their checks, and administering selective credit controls over other segments of the economy. Other functions include acting as the government's fiscal agent in holding the United States Treasury's principal checking accounts and assisting in the collection and distribution of income taxes. However, the four functions most closely related to real estate finance are

1. the Fed's regulation of the amount of its member banks' reserves,
2. determination of the discount rates,
3. open-market operations, and
4. supervision of the Truth-in-Lending Act (Regulation Z).   *KNOW THIS FOR TEST*

Reserve Requirements

Each of the Fed's individual member banks is required to keep reserves equal to a specified percentage of the bank's total funds on deposit with its federal district bank. These **reserve requirements** are designed to protect bank depositors by guaranteeing that their funds will be available when they need them. But even more important than this security for the banks' depositors is the Fed's ability to "manage" the national money market by adjusting the *amount* of reserves required from time to time. By *raising* the reserve requirement (and thereby limiting the amount of money available to the member banks for making loans), the Fed can frequently cool down a "hot" money market and slow the economic pace. By *lowering* the reserve requirements, the Fed can permit more money to enter a sluggish economy. Member banks can retain a larger percentage of their total assets, allowing more money to become available for loans. Managing the reserve requirements is one way the Fed serves its purpose of balancing the national economy.

IN PRACTICE . . .

What would happen if figures were released showing almost a 2 percent increase in inflation for the quarter plus a sharp drop in unemployment? Although this might seem like more "good news" than "bad," this combination would be a matter of concern to the Fed. The Fed is responsible for maintaining a stable economy and, ironically, the Fed must be as concerned when things are going too well as when things seem to be slowing down! The Fed must take quick action to prevent a spiraling effect into a run-away economy. If unemployment is low, employment is high. In order to attract good employees from a shrinking pool of job seekers, a company may have to pay higher salaries. In order to pay the higher salaries, the company raises prices. Higher prices lead to inflation.

The Fed has several tools it may use to slow things down, but the most likely one in this situation would be an announcement that the Federal discount rate will be increased. The discount rate is the interest charged by the Fed to its member banks. When this rate is increased, even if only by a quarter of a percent, there is usually an immediate reaction in the financial world. A slight "tap on the brakes" by the Fed can slow down the acceleration, heading off more serious problems later. Sometimes just a casual hint from the Fed's chairperson that rates may be going up will achieve the desired effect!

The amounts of reserves vary from 3 percent to 22 percent of the member banks' funds, depending on the type of these deposits and the location of the member banks. For instance, more reserves are required for checking accounts than for savings deposits, reflecting the short-term quality of the former versus the long-term quality of the latter. In addition, more reserves are required from a city bank than a country bank, because of the increased banking activities expected from numerous urban depositors as opposed to a smaller number of rural depositors.

Discount Rates

Commercial banks operate primarily to finance personal property purchases and short-term business needs. The loans they issue are referred to as *commercial paper*. The Fed operates a market for selling this paper at a discount, providing member banks with additional funds for continued lending activity. This is done at the "discount window," which is either open or closed to control the money supply. When the window is "open," money is added to the system, and vice versa.

Although discounting commercial paper may appear to have little significance for real estate finance, the process enables members to expand their lending activities. The banks actually *borrow* funds from their district federal reserve bank and pledge their commercial paper as collateral. In effect, the Fed charges the borrowing bank *interest* on its loan, interest that is considered to be the **discount rate,** which can also be interpreted as the cost of borrowed funds to the borrower bank. Thus, the individual bank has a basic or *primary interest rate* against which it can measure the interest it must charge its borrowers. As illustrated in Figure 2.5, the Fed discount rate is used by many major banks to set their **prime rate,** *prime* meaning simply the rate a commercial bank charges its most creditworthy customers or its "prime" customers. Now the implications for real estate finance become clearer. The higher the Fed's discount rate charged to the bank, the higher its prime will be and consequently the higher the rate of interest to the real estate borrower.

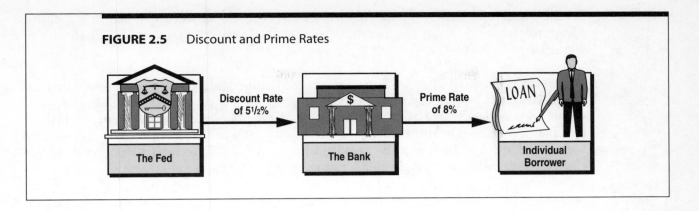

FIGURE 2.5   Discount and Prime Rates

In mortgage lending, these discounts establish the base interest charges for short-term mortgage loans. Borrowers, depending on their credit standings, can expect to pay the prime rate or higher, as circumstances dictate. For example, many construction loans are secured from commercial banks at "2 points above prime," or 2 percent above the prime rate. If the prime rate is 8 percent when the construction loan is made, the interest rate charged under this formula would be 10 percent. Thus, by adjusting the rate of its discount, the Fed exerts a great deal of control over the amount of money or credit available throughout the system.

When the Fed raises its discount rate, member banks slow their sales of commercial paper and obtain fewer additional funds. Therefore, less credit becomes available at the local level, and, theoretically, the economy is slowed. Of course, the reverse process occurs when the discount rate is lowered. The Fed's discount rate can be found daily in the *Wall Street Journal* and other financial publications.

Federal Funds Rate

The Fed also lends money to its member banks without requiring any collateral. These loans are usually made for short periods of time, and the rate of interest that is charged to the borrowing banks is known as the **federal funds rate.** It is the rate that banks charge each other for short-term funding, often overnight loans. The banks use this interbank borrowing to meet the Fed's requirements for cash liquidity in the bank's portfolio. The federal funds rate is published daily in financial journals and becomes another benchmark against which the banks can base interest charges to their customers.

Open-Market Operations

The Fed relies on its **open-market operations** as another important tool to achieve its goal of balancing the economy. These activities involve the purchase or sale of government securities in lots, which consist primarily of United States Treasury issues and also include securities issued by the federally sponsored housing and farm credit agencies, the Federal Home Loan Bank system, the Federal Housing Administration (FHA), and the GNMA, to name just a few.

Open-market bulk trading in securities generally averages several billion dollars per day. Special dealers authorized to handle these transactions "over the counter" manage the purchase and sale of these securities. Dealers and their customers are linked by a national communication system of services that facilitate the transfer of tremendous quantities of securities.

The Fed's open-market operations are directed and regulated by the system's Federal Open-Market Committee, which meets monthly to decide on current policies. This committee, also known as *FOMC,* is composed of 12 members. All 7 members of the Federal Reserve's board of governors serve on FOMC, giving them the majority. The president of the Federal Reserve Bank of New York and four other district reserve bank presidents are elected to serve one-year terms on a rotating basis.

A decision by FOMC to buy or sell securities has an immediate and important impact on the availability of money for economic activities. When FOMC *sells* securities, the economy slows down, as money available for credit is withdrawn from the market. When FOMC *buys* securities, it is in effect pumping money into the economic system, thereby encouraging growth and expansion. The impact of these procedures on the availability of money for real estate is quite similar to the impact caused by raising or lowering the discount rate.

Truth-in-Lending Act (TILA, Regulation Z)

KNOW FOR TEST!!

The Federal Reserve is responsible for supervising the **Truth-in-Lending Act (TILA),** Title I of the Consumer Protection Act of 1968. The Fed's board of governors was given the responsibility at that time to formulate and issue a regulation, called Regulation Z, to carry out the purposes of this act. Although enforcement of **Regulation Z** is spread over federal agencies, mainly the Federal Trade Commission, the Fed retains supervision over these agencies as part of its primary role as regulator of the U.S. national credit level.

Each of the following loans is covered by the act if the loan is to be repaid in more than four installments or if a finance charge is made:

1. Real estate loans
2. Loans for personal, family, or household purposes
3. Consumer loans for $25,000 or less

In the final analysis, however, Regulation Z is nothing more than a law requiring that lenders reveal total loan costs through the use of a standard measurement of interest rates, called an **annual percentage rate (APR)**. This is not an interest rate per se, but simply a rate that will reflect the effective rate of interest on a loan.

*F*OR EXAMPLE

Assume a borrower needs $1,000 for one year at 8% interest. If, at the end of the year, the borrower repays the $1,000 plus the $80 interest, the annual percentage rate (APR) and the interest rate will be the same ($80 ÷ $1,000 = 8%). However, if the lender collected a $25 service charge in advance, the borrower would receive $975 instead of $1,000 and pay $105 instead of $80. The APR would be calculated as follows: $105 ÷ $975 = 10.77%.

In addition to the finance charge and the APR, the Regulation Z disclosure statement must include the creditor's identity; the amount financed; the number, amount, and due dates of the payments; the notice of the right to receive an itemization of the amount financed; the late payment and prepayment provisions and penalties; a description of the security; and whether the loan can be assumed by a subsequent purchaser.

Advertising. Prior to the passage of the Truth-in-Lending Act, residential real estate lenders and arrangers of credit frequently included only the favorable loan aspects in ads, thus distorting the actual cost of obtaining credit. Now, advertising is strictly regulated by the law and advertisers are required to disclose *all* financing details if one item is disclosed. The advertising requirements apply to television, handbills, signs, and, as shown in Figure 2.6, newspapers.

Advertising terms that would require complete disclosure include: "Only 5% down!"; "Why pay the landlord when you can own for $550 per month?"; "30-year financing available"; or "Assume a 9.5% VA loan." Advertising terms that would not require complete disclosure include: "Low down"; "Easy monthly payments"; "10% APR loans available"; or "FHA and VA loans."

Right of Rescission

Under Regulation Z, if a consumer obtains a loan (refinancing, remodeling, or equity) that is secured by a principal residence, the borrower has the right to rescind the transaction up to three business days following the loan application or delivery of the disclosure statement, whichever comes later. Because borrowers have the three-day rescission period, lenders usually do not release funds until the rescission period has passed.

A major exception to the right of rescission applies to a loan that is used for the *purchase or initial construction* of the borrower's principal residence. Consequently, there is no right of rescission in a typical residential real estate purchase.

Any lender or arranger of credit who intentionally violates the requirements of the Truth-in-Lending Act is subject to a fine of up to $5,000 and/or imprisonment for up to one year. However, if the lender or arranger of credit unintentionally violates the law, the lender or arranger could be liable to the borrower for actual and punitive damages equal to twice the finance charge, up to a maximum of $1,000. A summary of the Fed's credit policy tools is shown in Figure 2.7.

THE UNITED STATES TREASURY

Although the Fed regulates money and credit, the United States Treasury is also involved in maintaining the nation's economic balance. Whereas the Fed determines monetary policies, the Treasury acts as the nation's fiscal manager. It is also responsible for controlling the daily operations of the federal government, including the management of the enormous federal debt and the supervision of the banking system through the Federal Deposit Insurance Corporation (FDIC). How effectively the Treasury balances the government's income against its long-term and short-term debt instruments has a direct effect on the monetary and credit climate of the country.

FIGURE 2.6   Newspaper Advertisement

Builders for You
Presents

Brand New Modern Tudor-Style Four Bedroom Ranch Homes

Enjoy this lovely home for only **$822** per month!

Based on sales price of $140,000 with 20% down payment,
1st mortgage of $112,000, 30 year loan at 8%, P&I payment $822,
taxes and insurance in addition, APR 8.35%.

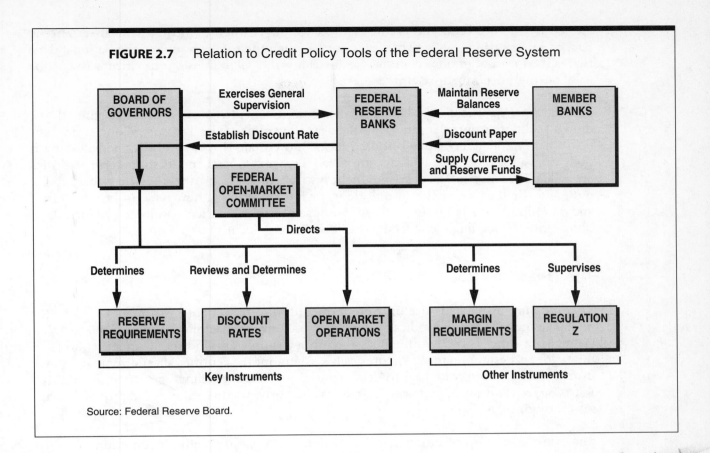

FIGURE 2.7 Relation to Credit Policy Tools of the Federal Reserve System

Source: Federal Reserve Board.

Office of the Comptroller of the Currency (OCC)   *Dont Need for test*

An important bureau of the U.S. Department of the Treasury is the **Office of the Comp-troller of the Currency (OCC).** It was organized in 1863 in large part to establish a national currency to finance the Civil War. The current role of the OCC is to charter, reg-ulate, and supervise all national banks. Its operations are funded primarily by assessments on the national banks with additional revenue from investment in U.S. Treasury securities. See www.occ.treas.gov.

The Nation's Fiscal Manager

The Treasury collects funds for government operating expenses from federal income tax payments, Social Security receipts, and other sources. These receipts are held on deposit in federal reserve banks and other insured domestic and foreign banks. Employers regularly send their payroll deductions for income tax and Social Security withholding tax to the nearest federal bank.

When federal revenues do not keep pace with federal spending, in either volume or timing, a deficit occurs. Often the amount of government funds on deposit in the nation's banks is not sufficient to make the payments required to keep the ongoing federal agencies in oper-ation. Then the Treasury has to borrow money to offset these shortages.

From time to time, short-term or long-term debt instruments, called **securities,** may be issued and sold by the Treasury to generate the cash it requires. These securities are guaranteed by the full faith and credit of the U.S. government, whose financial stability is backed by its taxing power. Thus, it is not so much the total amount of the national debt that is the measure of our economic health as it is the willingness of our citizens to pay for it by buying government security issues.

The national debt is composed of smaller component debts of varying denominations, drawn at different interest rates and due at various times. The Treasury's long-term debt instruments, called **Treasury bonds,** run for more than 10 years; its intermediate-length obligations, for 2 years to 10 years, are called **Treasury notes;** and its short-term securities are called **Treasury bills.** As existing debt instruments become due, they are either repaid, reducing the balance of the overall debt, or refinanced by a new issue of bonds, notes, and/or bills. At the same time, Treasury officials must meet their continuing regular fiscal obligations, which include federal payrolls and Social Security payments.

On TEST -

The Treasury's Role

The Treasury mixes its issues of short-term and long-term debt instruments to repay or refinance the securities periodically coming due. How it accomplishes this to keep the government in funds directly influences the money supply and indirectly affects sources of funds for real estate finance. Theoretically, issuing more securities should remove money from a "hot" economy and act to slow it down, just like the selling operations for FOMC. Likewise, repaying some securities issues as they become due should pump more money into a sagging economy.

Sometimes, because of purely fiscal pressure, the Treasury's efforts run counter to the Fed's goals. For instance, in an attempt to speed up a sluggish economy, the Fed will reduce its reserve requirements and discount rates to pump money into the economy. Simultaneously the Treasury will float a huge securities issue to meet unusually large deficits. By removing funds from the market, the Treasury is counteracting the Fed.

Historically the Treasury has assumed a continuing role as supplier of funds for practically all federal agencies. This role makes the Treasury a primary contributor to the success of many important national programs for real estate financing. The Treasury's participation in establishing Fannie Mae and GNMA created an indispensable national secondary mortgage market. Furthermore, the Treasury's funding of the federal land bank system has been of immeasurable and sustained help to farmers. Further discussion of the various roles of the Treasury Department may be explored on www.treasury.gov.

The Financial Institutions Reform, Recovery, and Enforcement Act of 1989 (FIRREA)

On August 9, 1989, **FIRREA** was signed into law to reform, recapitalize, and consolidate the federal deposit insurance system and to enhance the organizational and enforcement powers of the federal agencies regulating financial institutions. This action was taken in response to the failure of numerous savings and banking institutions and was an attempt to preserve the integrity of the U.S. banking system.

Under FIRREA, in 1989 the FDIC was moved from the Fed to the Treasury Department.

As outlined in Title I, Section 101 of the act, FIRREA has the following purposes:

1. To promote, through regulatory reform, a safe and stable system of affordable housing finance
2. To improve the supervision of thrifts or savings associations by strengthening capital, accounting, and other supervisory standards
3. To curtail investments and other activities of thrifts or savings associations that pose unacceptable risks to the federal deposit insurance funds
4. To promote the independence of the FDIC from the institutions holding the deposits it insures by providing an independent board of directors, adequate funding, and appropriate powers
5. To put the federal deposit insurance funds on a sound financial footing
6. To establish, under the Department of the Treasury, the Office of Thrift Supervision to manage this nation's savings associations

The Federal Deposit Insurance Corporation (FDIC)

The **Federal Deposit Insurance Corporation (FDIC)** was created by the Banking Act of 1933 to add stability to the failing U.S. bank system during the Great Depression. Its primary goal was to help reinstate the public's confidence in the commercial banking system by insuring the safety of deposits. Initially, insurance covered up to $5,000 for each account. This coverage climbed steadily over the years to its present level of $100,000 per title per account. The FDIC now insures all accounts in member depository institutions, including both banks and thrifts, up to this amount.

The FDIC is administered by a board of governors consisting of two permanent members—the U.S. comptroller of the currency and the director of the Office of Thrift Supervision—and three U.S. citizens appointed by the president, with the consent of the senate, to serve for a maximum of six years. No more than three members of the board may be from the same political party. The chair and vice-chair are designated by the president, with approval by the senate, from the three appointed members. Members so designated may not serve more than five years in either of these capacities. The FDIC supervises its member banks and thrifts by conducting regular examinations of their operations.

The FDIC is appointed receiver or conservator for the purpose of reorganizing or liquidating failed banks or thrifts. When acting in either of these capacities, the FDIC is not subject to the direction or supervision of any other agency or department of the United States or any state.

If a bank or savings institution fails, the FDIC can take any of the following actions to put the insured depository institution in a sound and solvent position:

- Appropriate funds to carry on the business of the failing institution
- Conserve its assets and property
- Place, if necessary, the insured depository institution in liquidation and proceed to dispose of its assets, having due regard for the conditions of credit in the locality
- Organize a new federal savings association to take over such assets or liabilities
- Merge the insured deposits of the failed institution with those of another insured depository organization

In the event of a liquidation, the payment of insured deposits will be made by the FDIC as soon as possible, either by cash or by a transferred deposit into another insured depository institution.

The Deposit Insurance Fund. Under FIRREA, the FDIC has been given increased powers through its independent control of its subagencies: the **Deposit Insurance Fund (DIF),** with its two subsidiaries, the **Bank Insurance Fund (BIF),** and the **Savings Association Insurance Fund (SAIF).**

The FIRREA changed the old federal deposit insurance system to the Deposit Insurance Fund (DIF). It eliminated the Federal Savings and Loan Insurance Corporation (FSLIC), which was unable to survive the burdens of the failed savings institutions. The DIF comes under the administration of the FDIC.

There are two separate insurance funds under the DIF, the Bank Insurance Fund (BIF), which insures deposits in member commercial banks, and the Savings Association Insurance Fund (SAIF), which insures deposits in member savings associations or thrifts. To fund these programs members pay an insurance premium of ½ of 1 percent of their annual average total of insured accounts.

The BIF reported an income of $1.6 billion for the year 2001 compared with a $198 million loss for 2000. The fund's reserve balance increased to $31 billion. The SAIF reported an income of $478 million for 2001 compared to an income of $441 million in 2000. The SAIF reserve balance increased to $10.6 billion at the end of 2001. Both funds are in a secure financial position.

THE FEDERAL HOME LOAN BANK SYSTEM (FHLB)

Organized in 1932 to bring stability to the nation's savings associations, the **Federal Home Loan Bank (FHLB)** was designed to provide a central credit clearing facility for all member savings associations and to establish rules and regulations for its members.

Organization

Patterned after the Fed, the FHLB includes 12 regional federal home loan district banks. These district banks are distributed throughout the states. The FHLB is directed by a three-member board, appointed for four years by the president with the approval of the senate. This board in turn appoints the Federal Housing Finance Board (FHFB) to supervise all mortgage lending by the 12 district banks.

Office of Thrift Supervision (OTS)

In the 1989 reorganization, FIRREA created the **Office of Thrift Supervision (OTS)** to replace the former Federal Home Loan Bank Board and to charter and regulate member savings associations. Similar to the way the OCC charters, regulates, and supervises the national banks, the OTS charters and regulates the member associations of the FHLB. The OTS is funded by assessments and fees charged to the thrifts it regulates.

In 1996 Congress gave thrifts increased flexibility in offering consumer loans. As a result, many of the new charters approved by OTS were issued to nonbanks such as insurance companies and other large financial entities. A federal charter from OTS preempts state laws and allows operations in all 50 states rather than having to be licensed in each individual state. For more detail see www.ots.treas.gov.

Although the Federal Home Loan Bank Board was disbanded by FIRREA in 1989, the new **Federal Housing Finance Board** now regulates the 12 Federal Home Loan Banks. The Finance Board is an independent regulatory agency of the executive branch of government that is charged with improving the supply of funds to local lenders in order to finance loans for home mortgages. See www.fhlb.gov.

Activities

A major function of the FHLB is to provide its members a national market for their securities. Although member associations may borrow money directly from their district home loan banks for up to one year *without* collateral, the longer-term loans necessary for real estate finance must have collateral pledged by the borrowing association. Acceptable collateral may include government securities or established real estate mortgages held in the association's investment portfolio. If thrifts capitalize on their stock in trade, real estate mortgages, they can obtain additional funds to expand their activities, just as commercial banks can discount their commercial paper with their Federal Reserve district banks.

The thrifts throughout this country have traditionally played an indispensable role in real estate finance. Despite their recent losses, they still play an important role in the single-family home loan market while participating in other forms of real estate loans. The intensity of their lending activities depends on the amount of accumulated savings, as well as reserve requirements set by the FHLB.

The FHLB is currently making a comeback in the real estate financing market, purchasing loans from its member banks and providing strong competition in the secondary market. In terms of total financial assets, the FHLB ranks second in the country, behind Fannie Mae and ahead of Chase Manhattan Corp.

SUMMARY

Our monetary system is based primarily on confidence rather than on gold or silver. Money is identified as a medium of exchange; its value is largely its ability to command the purchase of goods and services. When money is available at relatively low interest rates, the economy booms. The reverse is also true.

The federal government's role in mortgage lending permeates every phase of financial activity. The federal agencies charged with determining the quantity of funds circulating in our monetary system—and, as a result, the amount of credit available and the rates of interest in effect—are the Federal Reserve System (the Fed) and the United States Treasury. The Fed functions as a "manager" of money, regulating its member banks' reserves, determining discount rates, operating in the open market for buying and selling government securities, supervising the Truth-in-Lending Act, and regulating and controlling all facets of the country's commercial banking system. The actions of the Fed have a very strong influence on the number and dollar amounts of mortgage loans made.

The United States Treasury also plays an important role in real estate finance. The Treasury's primary purpose is to manage the national debt and balance the federal budget. Budget deficits are offset by issuing and selling government securities to raise funds. The amount of Treasury securities for sale determines to a large degree the quantity of money available for other investments, such as mortgages.

In addition, the Treasury is now involved in supervising all of this nation's depository institutions through the Office of the Comptroller of the Currency (OCC) and the Office of Thrift Supervision (OTS) plus the administration of the Federal Deposit Insurance Corporation (FDIC).

Participating with FDIC are the Bank Insurance Fund (BIF), which insures accounts in commercial banks, and the Savings Association Insurance Fund (SAIF), which insures savings institution accounts.

The Federal Home Loan Bank (FHLB) system, operating similarly to the Fed provides funds for both short-term and long-term needs of its members at favorable interest rates. The FHLB determines its members' reserve requirements and provides its members with an important secondary source of funds. The OTS regulates membership in the FHLB system.

CHAPTER 3

Additional Government Activities

▼ **KEY TERMS** * *Know these terms*

Community
  Reinvestment Act
  (CRA)
computerized loan
  origination
  (CLO)
Department of Housing
  and Urban
  Development (HUD)
Equal Credit
  Opportunity Act
  (ECOA)
Farm Credit System (FCS)
Farmer Mac

Farm Credit System
  Insurance
  Corporation (FCSIC)
Good Faith Estimate
  (GFE)
Home Mortgage
  Disclosure Act
  (HMDA)
HUD-1 settlement
  statement
industrial revenue bonds
  (IRBs)
Interstate Land Sales Full
  Disclosure Act

moratorium
mortgage revenue
  bonds
mortgage servicing
  disclosure statement
open-end mortgage
Real Estate Settlement
  Procedures Act
  (RESPA)
Section 8
tax increment financing
urban renewal
USDA Rural
  Development

HUD
FHA &
GNMA

Several federal departments and programs have been established to regulate trends in the U.S. housing market. These groups are responsible for the smooth and fair operation of various aspects of U.S. real estate.

This chapter examines the activities of the Department of Housing and Urban Development (HUD). HUD supervises the Federal Housing Administration (FHA), the Government National Mortgage Association (GNMA), and interstate land sales in addition to aiding a variety of housing programs focused on social improvement, including low-rent housing projects, urban renewal, and rehabilitation programs. This chapter likewise reviews current federal legislation that regulates the complex real estate marketplace. This legislation includes the Equal Credit Opportunity Act (ECOA), the Real Estate Settlement Procedures Act (RESPA), and various disclosure requirements. It examines the roles of various agencies that assist communities in attracting new industry, improving the housing of their citizens, and regulating the fair application of real estate loans.

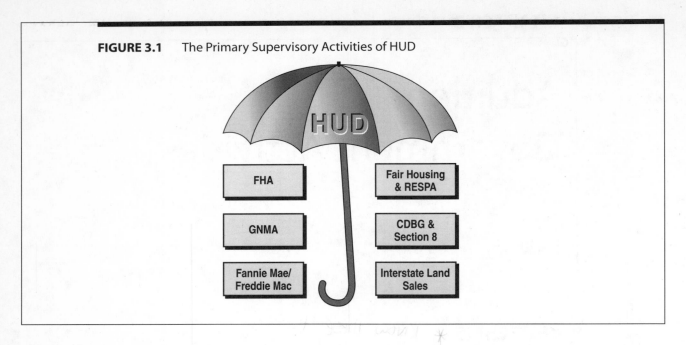

FIGURE 3.1   The Primary Supervisory Activities of HUD

The final section of this chapter reviews the contributions made to mortgage lending by the participants in the cooperative Farm Credit System (FCS). Designed to serve the particular financial needs of farmers and ranchers, the FCS agencies provide both direct and indirect funding for land acquisition, home and accessory buildings, equipment purchases, and general farm and ranch operations. Included in the Farm Credit System is the U.S. Department of Agriculture Rural Development. Formerly known as the Farmers' Home Administration (FmHA), this organization provides funds for farmers and ranchers who are unable to secure credit from other sources.

U.S. DEPARTMENT OF HOUSING AND URBAN DEVELOPMENT (HUD)

Under President Johnson's War on Poverty Program, the **Department of Housing and Urban Development (HUD)** was given cabinet status in 1965. It consolidated a number of older federal agencies.

HUD is the federal agency responsible for national policy and programs that address America's housing needs, improve and develop U.S. communities, and enforce fair housing laws. HUD's mission is to help create a decent home and suitable living environment for all U.S. citizens.

As illustrated in Figure 3.1, HUD's primary activities include

- supervising the Federal Housing Administration (FHA),
- directing the Government National Mortgage Association (GNMA),
- overseeing Fannie Mae and Freddie Mac operations,
- enforcing Fair Housing and RESPA regulations,
- managing Community Development Block Grant and Section 8 programs,
- managing the Indian Housing Act,
- regulating interstate land sales registration, urban renewal and rehabilitation programs, and
- supervising public housing projects.

FIGURE 3.2   www.hud.gov

One of the important functions of HUD is to provide information on home ownership to the public. The HUD Web site (Figure 3.2) is a tremendous resource for the public and for real estate practitioners. The introductory page, "Homes and Communities," guides the visitor to numerous other pages offering detailed information on home mortgage lending, FHA loan guidelines, and sources for home ownership education and counseling.

An important part of HUD 2020, the management reform plan, was the creation of Community Builders, whose task is to provide assistance and information to customers on economic development, homeownership, public housing, and other HUD programs. (The FHA and GNMA are covered in later chapters.)

Interstate Land Sales

The **Interstate Land Sales Full Disclosure Act,** passed by Congress in 1968, established the informational criteria for marketing residential land to potential buyers. Designed to reduce fraud in the sales of land by developers, the law requires that anyone selling or leasing 25 or more lots of unimproved land as part of a common plan in interstate commerce must comply with the act's provisions. The exceptions include subdivisions of five acres or more, cemetery land, commercial and industrial land, and any residential subdivision marketed exclusively in the state where it is located.

A developer must provide HUD with a *statement of record* that includes explanations and descriptions of existing and proposed encumbrances, improvements, utilities, schools, recreation areas, roads, and all services to be provided for the residents' use. A *property report* must be delivered to the buyer *prior* to the purchase of the property. The seller must have a signed receipt from the buyer indicating the buyer received the property report. If a property report is received within 48 hours prior to signing, the buyers have the right to change their minds within seven days, cancel their contract, and receive a return of any deposits made. However, if the report is *not* received within the allotted time, the buyers may legally rescind their contract at any time.

Urban Renewal

HUD sponsors **urban renewal** projects that encompass entire neighborhoods as well as specific properties. Neighborhood renewal involves large-scale planning, including site acquisition, site clearance, construction, and disposition. Urban renewal originates at the community level, where a workable plan is developed and then sent to HUD for approval and sponsorship.

In addition to providing funds for slum clearance, HUD makes loans and grants to owners and tenants in depressed areas for rehabilitating their properties. Grants are also available to demolish structures unfit for habitation.

Public Housing

HUD provides financial assistance to local authorities for acquisition and operation of properties for public housing programs. This assistance includes grant monies, housing subsidies, and other means of support.

IN PRACTICE . . .

Ever wonder how HUD funds are put to work?

Look no further than Tennessee where the Chattanooga Neighborhood Enterprise (CNE) organization helps develop, finance, renovate, and manage affordable housing for Chattanooga's low-to-moderate income citizens. Take for example the Chattanooga Police Officer Program, that created affordable housing opportunities for police officers in specific neighborhoods.

Under this program CNE provided sworn police officers with a second mortgage of 40% of the sales price (up to a maximum of $40,000) to be used for down payment and closing costs. The second mortgage payments were deferred for three years with no payments and no interest accrual. At the beginning of the fourth year, the police officer was required to make payments at a rate of 2%. In all respects, this was a win-win program.

Community Development Block Grants (CDBG). The CDBG program helps communities with economic development, job opportunities, and housing rehabilitation. CDBG funds have been used to construct and improve public facilities such as water, sewer, streets, and neighborhood centers; to purchase real property, and to assist private businesses.

HUD has distributed more than $80 billion to the CDBG programs, with 70 percent going to communities with more than 50,000 people and 30 percent to smaller communities. Seventy percent of these funds must benefit low-income and moderate-income families.

Under the Section 108 loan guarantee component of the CDBG program, communities can obtain financing for economic development, housing rehabilitation, and large-scale physical development projects.

Subsidized Housing. The subsidized housing program assists low-income households with rental subsidies in the private sector through **Section 8** Certificates and Vouchers. Families seeking assistance apply through their local public housing agency. Tenants have the freedom to select housing where they want to live within a standard rent range. The rent subsidies are paid to owners and consist of the difference between what the tenant can pay and the contracted rent.

Under legislation passed in year 2001, individual Public Housing Authorities (PHAs) now have the option to use a portion of their Section 8 funding to assist first-time home buyers. Each PSA makes the determination of how much of their funding they wish to allocate to this program. FHA sets minimum income and employment requirements but other eligibility requirements are set by the PHA. For example, recipients must attend a homeownership and housing counseling program.

Other Programs. HUD also provides funds for public housing agencies to develop and operate housing for low-income families. HUD has more than 3,500 public and American Indian housing authorities that provide public housing and services to more than 1.5 million households.

HUD helps finance public housing agency projects to integrate public housing into surrounding communities and provide residents the skills to contribute to their communities. It offers monetary support to state and local governments and nonprofit organizations to assist homeless individuals and families to move from the streets to temporary shelters to supportive housing—and, ideally, back into the mainstream of American life. HUD also helps fund cooperative housing for low-income persons, housing for the elderly, mortgage interest subsidies, relocation assistance, college housing, disaster area reconstruction, and housing in isolated areas.

HUD also provided special "Officer Next Door" and "Teacher Next Door" programs to encourage police officers and teachers to purchase and live-in homes in the area in which they worked. In both cases a HUD-owned property could be purchased at a 50 percent discount with a down payment of only $100. A second mortgage was placed for the discount amount which required no interest or payments as long as the officer or teacher lived in the property for at least three years. Because of the discovery of some misrepresentations, this program is presently on hold. For full details on all of HUD's special programs, see www.hud.gov and check on the appropriate program.

HUD and the Mortgage Bankers Association have entered into a joint homebuyer education program called "Passport to Homeownership." They have allocated a $1 million budget for advertising and brochures to explain how the FHA automated loan underwriting system works and how consumers can maintain good credit.

OTHER FEDERAL LEGISLATION

In the past, real estate transactions were virtually unregulated, and each party was assumed to be knowledgeable about the facts and conditions surrounding the sale and financing of a property. As the marketplace evolved and became more complex, it also became clear that many purchasers or sellers were not well informed. As a result, some significant federal legislation was passed that has become standard practice in every real estate transaction.

The Federal Equal Credit Opportunity Act (ECOA)

The **Equal Credit Opportunity Act (ECOA)** is Title VII of the Consumer Protection Act. It prohibits lenders from discriminating against credit applicants on the basis of race, color, religion, national origin, sex, marital status, age, or dependency on public assistance. The basic provisions of the act include the following:

- The lender may not ask if the applicant is divorced or widowed. However, the lender may ask if the borrower is married, unmarried, or separated. The term *unmarried* denotes a single, divorced, or widowed person and, in a community property state, is of particular interest to local lenders.
- The lender may not ask about the receipt of alimony or child support unless the borrower intends to use such income to qualify for the loan. The lender may ask about any obligations to pay alimony or child support.
- The lender may not seek any information about birth control practices or the childbearing capabilities or intentions of the borrower or coborrower.
- The lender may not request information about the spouse or former spouse of the applicant unless that person will be contractually liable for repayment or the couple lives in a community property state.
- The lender may not discount or exclude any income because of the source of that income.
- The lender must report credit information on married couples separately in the name of each spouse.
- The lender may ask about the race or national origin of the applicant, but the borrowers can refuse to answer without fear of jeopardizing their loan.

The ECOA also prohibits lenders from discriminating against credit applicants who exercise their rights under the Truth-in-Lending laws. In addition, lenders and other creditors must inform all rejected applicants in writing of the principal reasons why credit was denied or terminated. The focus of the ECOA is to ensure that all qualified persons have equal access to credit.

Both the Justice Department and HUD are charged with protecting borrowers from discrimination in lending practices under the fair housing laws and ECOA. An example of ECOA's effectiveness is the case against the Chevy Chase Federal Savings Bank in Washington, D.C., which was accused of violating the racial discrimination standards. The bank denied all allegations but agreed to invest $11 million to open at least one new branch in African-American areas of the city. The bank also agreed to provide eligible borrowers discounted interest rates and grants equaling 2 percent of the loan down payments.

The Real Estate Settlement Procedures Act (RESPA)

← Very Important to know for test

Administered under the FHA, the **Real Estate Settlement Procedures Act (RESPA)** is designed to protect the participants in a real estate transaction by providing closing cost information so they better understand the settlement procedures. RESPA covers the sale of residential properties and the acquisition of mortgage loans, including home equity loans, second mortgages, and refinancing loans on residential properties.

Disclosures under RESPA. In order to protect participants in a real estate transaction, RESPA requires all service costs to be disclosed at various times during the process. Disclosures must be made during the time of a loan application, before settlement closing, at settlement, and after settlement.

Disclosure at the Time of a Loan Application. At the beginning of the mortgage loan process, the lender must provide the borrower three items:

1. a special information booklet containing information on real estate settlement services;
2. within three business days, a **Good Faith Estimate (GFE)** of settlement costs listing the charges the borrower is likely to pay at closing and indicating whether the borrower has to use a specific settlement service;
3. a **mortgage servicing disclosure statement** informing the borrower whether the lender intends to keep the loan or transfer it to a different lender for servicing in addition to information on how the borrower can resolve complaints.

Disclosures before Settlement Closing. Prior to settlement, the lender must inform the borrower whenever a settlement service refers the borrower to a firm with which the servicer has any connection, such as common ownership. The service usually cannot force a borrower to use a connected firm. A preliminary copy of a **HUD-1 settlement statement** is required if the borrower requests it 24 hours prior to closing. This form estimates all settlement charges that must be paid by the participants. The borrower must also receive a copy of the Truth-in-Lending statement prior to closing that discloses the annual percentage rate and total costs of credit involved in the transaction.

Disclosures at Settlement. The HUD-1 settlement statement is distributed at closing and shows the *actual* charges incurred by the participants. In addition, an initial escrow statement is required at closing or within 45 days of closing. This statement itemizes the estimated taxes, insurance premiums, and other charges that must be paid from the escrow account during the first year of the loan. It is now federal law to include a lead-based paint disclosure on all properties built before 1978.

Disclosures after Settlement. After settlement an annual escrow loan statement must be delivered by the loan service to the borrower. This document enumerates all escrow deposits and payments during the past year. It indicates any shortages or surpluses in the escrow account and informs the borrower how to remedy them. If the loan service is transferred to another servicer, a servicing transfer statement is delivered to the borrower.

Revised RESPA regulations have reinforced the prohibition against kickbacks. Generally, the payment or receipt of a fee for the referral of business related to settlement without rendering a service violates RESPA. If a service is given and a fee is paid or received, there must be full disclosure. RESPA, under Section 8, prohibits the payment of referral fees or

IN PRACTICE . . .

Sam Smith recently represented Ann Jones as her buyer agent for the purchase of a new town house. Sam recommended three different loan officers for Ann to contact regarding obtaining a home mortgage loan. Ann picked Jim Brown and was very happy with him until this morning when she received a Truth-in-Lending statement in the mail. She immediately called Sam, obviously very upset, saying:

"You and Jim both assured me that I was getting an 8% loan and that I was going to be able to borrow $100,000. Today I get this statement in the mail saying that the interest rate will be 8.45% and that I am only borrowing $97,000! Now I don't know what or who to believe!"

This is not an uncommon reaction to receipt of the Truth-in-Lending statement. Fortunately Sam has dealt with this many times before and was quickly able to calm Ann down. He then explained to her that the Truth-in-Lending Act requires the lender to disclose exactly how much they are earning on the loan, including any loan fees and discount points that may have been charged. Because there were three points on this $100,000 loan the lender only sends a check for $97,000 to the settlement table (they receive the other $3,000 in points, paid by the buyer, seller, or both). When the discount points and additional loan fees are calculated, the lender's actual yield becomes 8.45%.

fee-splitting between affiliated entities in a real estate transaction (e.g., a real estate broker refers a buyer to an affiliated mortgage company). Nevertheless, RESPA does allow a controlled business arrangement between affiliates when referral fees are not paid.

The Federal Reserve Regulation X does permit **computerized loan origination (CLO)** networks. The use of a CLO network allows brokers and others to offer consumers direct access to mortgage lenders through a computer terminal. RESPA allows fees to be paid for providing this access, but the fees must be reported to the consumers.

The Community Reinvestment Act (CRA)

The **Community Reinvestment Act (CRA),** passed by Congress in 1977, ensures that financial institutions pursue their responsibilities to meet both the deposit and the credit needs of members of the communities in which they are chartered. Each institution is required to delineate its community, specify the types of credit services it offers, post a public notice stating that the institution is being reviewed by a federal supervisory agency and prepare a community reinvestment statement to be made available to the public.

The act provides that an appropriate federal supervisory agency assess the institution's record in meeting the credit needs of the community, including low-income families. The act covers the majority of U.S. financial institutions; the term *federal supervisory agency* includes the comptroller of the currency, board of governors of the Federal Reserve System, Federal Deposit Insurance Corporation, and the Office of Thrift Supervision.

When assessing an institution's compliance with the CRA, the agency must prepare a written evaluation that includes a section for filing in the records and a section to be made public. The public section includes the agency's rating of the institution, ranging from "outstanding" to "substantial noncompliance" in meeting community credit needs.

Failure to comply with the act's provisions can result in denial by the institution's regulatory authority of any request for a change in rating.

Under the impetus created by the Financial Institutions Reform, Recovery and Enforcement Act (FIRREA), an amendment to the CRA provides that a portion of the net profits of banks be set aside each year to help provide affordable housing and financing programs to assist lower-income families to acquire suitable shelter. Major participants like Fannie Mae and Freddie Mac, as well as private mortgage insurance companies such as Mortgage Guaranty Insurance Corporation (MGIC) and GE Capital Mortgage Insurance Company, offer complete programs of assistance to lending institutions. These programs include modified loan qualification guidelines, lower down payments and educational programs on the responsibilities of home ownership. Most programs are limited to families with incomes of 80 percent or less of the median income for the local area. Some programs exclude private mortgage insurance premiums, others have no loan limits. CRA loans are increasing in popularity.

The Home Mortgage Disclosure Act (HMDA)

Under the **Home Mortgage Disclosure Act (HMDA),** all mortgage originators are required to report information relating to income level, racial characteristics, and gender of mortgage applicants. This includes loans originated as well as applications rejected.

STATE FINANCING AGENCIES

Various states have established agencies to provide financial assistance at the community level for special real estate developments. These agencies are grouped into categories—one to assist local communities in attracting new industry and another to improve the housing of its citizens.

Industrial Development Agencies

Under legislation from the state government, communities have organized industrial development agencies empowered to purchase and improve land for industrial and office parks. These activities are funded by **industrial revenue bonds (IRBs)** backed by a state's bonding credit. Some funds are also raised through voluntary contributions from citizens interested in expanding the economic base of their community.

Community growth is the ultimate goal behind the development of industrial land. By offering preplanned industrial park sites, as well as other amenities and incentives, a community can attract new industrial activities. This can create new jobs and more commercial activity in the local area, with commensurate increases in profits for businesses and tax revenues for the community. Theoretically these additional revenues would offset much of the bonds' costs, although the primary sources for monies to repay the bonds would be building rentals and sales of the improved industrial sites.

Many U.S. communities have used the IRB approach to achieve growth and have been successful in attracting new industries. The interest paid on these bonds is federally income tax free to the bond purchaser, thus providing a lower borrowing interest rate to the developer.

Mortgage Insurance Programs

Some states have developed special real estate mortgage insurance programs of their own, funded by the state itself. The state sells either general obligation bonds repaid from state income tax collections or, more frequently, revenue bonds repaid from the mortgage insurance premiums collected. The funds raised from the sale of these bonds are used primarily as reserves for backing specific development projects. For instance, if a community wished to embark on a rehabilitation project, money could be secured from private sources to pursue this objective. If the project were approved, the state would issue insurance for repayment of the funds so the work could proceed.

Money raised from the sale of state bonds might also be used for direct loan purposes, such as special loans for the purchase of farm or ranch land. The states of California and Texas have such loans available—the former for its eligible veterans, the latter for anyone meeting the qualifications for the loans. Other states have special programs for veterans and for low-income housing projects, as well as other socially oriented programs.

Community Redevelopment Agencies

Local governments may establish community redevelopment agencies for expansion of the supply of low-income housing. These agencies are supervised by city council members and can acquire property by eminent domain. Any building program must agree to allocate 30 percent of the rental units for low-income tenants before it can be approved. Replacement housing must be provided within or outside the redevelopment area for every person displaced by the project.

Tax Increment Financing. Projects of community redevelopment agencies are funded in large part with **tax increment financing.** This technique allocates the increased property tax revenues derived from redevelopment to pay the debts incurred in improving the area. It requires that property taxes be frozen as of the date the redevelopment plan is adopted, with any excess taxes applied directly to satisfy the debt or used as security for the sale of bonds. After the debts have been satisfied, the taxes may rise to current levels, offsetting additional community costs brought about by the improvements.

Mortgage Revenue Bonds. Some community redevelopment agency projects are financed by issuing tax-exempt **mortgage revenue bonds.** The proceeds are utilized to make below-market-interest-rate loans to developers in the project area.

AGRICULTURAL LENDING

Farm loans have special cyclical requirements. The values of farm and ranch lands depend on productivity, and productivity in turn depends on management expertise and climatic conditions. Although management skills can be evaluated based on past experience, nobody can estimate the effect of nature on each season's crops, and farm and ranch loans acquire a unique risk factor.

Agricultural loans have to be designed with as much flexibility as possible. Rather than following a rigid payment pattern, their design must allow the farmer-borrowers the opportunity to pay when they *can*. It is essential, for instance, that the principal amount not come due in a bad crop year. The terms of the loans need to be lengthened, up to 40 years in some cases, to allow for those years when crops may fail and no payments can be made. Farmer-borrowers also need an opportunity to pay larger portions of the principal, in addition to the interest required, during a good year so that they can repay their loans in full over the longer time period.

Farmer-borrowers need to be able to extend, expand, and otherwise adjust their loans depending on unforeseen circumstances. The extension and expansion techniques designed to satisfy the special problems of the farmers are defined as **open-end mortgages.** As a last resort for a distressed farmer-borrower, a **moratorium** on payments occasionally is used to offset imminent foreclosures brought on by situations outside the borrower's control. Open-end mortgages and moratoriums will be discussed later in this book.

THE FARM CREDIT SYSTEM (FCS)

The **Farm Credit System (FCS),** inaugurated under the Farm Loan Act of 1916 and as amended from time to time, provides much of the credit used by U.S. farmers, ranchers, and cooperatives. It also serves the credit needs of rural homeowners, electric and telephone cooperatives, and rural water systems.

The FCS is a network of borrower-owned cooperative financial institutions and related organizations that serve all 50 states and the Commonwealth of Puerto Rico. These institutions specialize in providing credit and related services to farmers, ranchers, and producers or harvesters of aquatic products. FCS loans may finance certain processing and marketing activities of these borrowers. Loans may also be made to rural homeowners (for housing); certain farm-related businesses; and agricultural, aquatic, and public utility cooperatives. FCS banks do not take deposits.

The Farm Credit Administration (FCA) is an independent federal regulator responsible for examining and ensuring the soundness of all FCS institutions. The FCA Web site (www.fca.gov) provides easy access to data submitted by each of the FCS institutions.

Participants in the Farm Credit System

The FCS comprises various banks, associations, and corporations. These include the following:

- Six Farm Credit Banks (FCBs), which make direct real estate loans through Federal Land Bank Associations (FLBAs), Production Credit Associations (PCAs), Agricultural Credit Associations (ACAs), and Federal Land Credit Associations (FLCAs). PCAs make short-term loans; ACAs make intermediate-term loans; and FLCAs make long-term loans.
- One Agricultural Credit Bank (ACB), which has the authority of the FCB and provides loan funds for agricultural, aquatic, and public utility cooperatives. The ACB is also authorized to finance U.S. agricultural exports and provide international banking services for farmer-owned cooperatives.
- The Federal Farm Credit Banks Funding Corporation, an entity owned by FCS banks that markets debt securities the banks sell to raise loan funds.
- The Farm Credit System Financial Assistance Corporation chartered in 1988, provides needed capital to the system. It obtains monies by purchasing preferred stock issued by system institutions that have received financial assistance authorized by the FCS Assistance Board.

- The Federal Agricultural Mortgage Corporation (**"Farmer Mac"**), created to offer a secondary market for agricultural and rural housing mortgages. Farmer Mac guarantees the timely payment of principal and interest on securities representing interests in, or obligations backed by, groups of agricultural real estate loans.
- The Farm Credit Leasing Services Corporation, which provides equipment-leasing services to eligible borrowers, including agricultural producers, cooperatives, and rural utilities.
- The FCS Building Association, which acquires, manages, and maintains facilities to house the headquarters and field offices of FCA. The FCSBA was formed in 1981 and is owned by FCS banks; oversight of its activities is vested in the FCA Board.

Farm Credit System Insurance Corporation (FCSIC)

The Farm Credit System Insurance Corporation (FCSIC) was established by the Agricultural Credit Act of 1987 to ensure the timely payment of principal and interest on insured notes, bonds, and other obligations issued on behalf of FCS banks. It also acts as conservator or receiver of FCS institutions. By ensuring the repayment of FCS securities to investors, FCSIC helps maintain a dependable source of funds for farmers, ranchers, and other FCS borrowers.

The Farm Credit Council

The Farm Credit Council is a national trade association representing the interests of the Farm Credit System. The council addresses the system's legislative and regulatory concerns and provides services to its membership in human resources, training, insurance, credit, and risk management. Its membership is derived from the Farm Credit District Councils and CoBank National Bank for Cooperatives. These member councils, in turn, draw their membership from Farm Credit banks and associations, as well as other cooperative farm lenders and cooperatives.

The U.S. Department of Agriculture Rural Development Program (USDA Rural Development)

The activities of the Farm Credit System are complemented by the **USDA Rural Development** agency. This governmental unit was created in 1994 to combine the Farmers Home Administration, the Rural Development Administration, the Rural Electrification Administration, and the Agricultural Cooperative Service.

The USDA Rural Development Program is forging new partnerships with rural communities to reverse the downward spiral of rural job losses, out-migration, and diminishing services. The program funds projects that bring housing, community facilities, utilities, and other services to rural areas. The USDA also provides technical assistance and financial backing for rural businesses and cooperatives to create quality jobs in rural areas.

Each year these programs create or preserve thousands of jobs and improve thousands of units of rural housing. The USDA works with state, local, and American Indian tribal governments, as well as private and nonprofit organizations and user-owned cooperatives. (The USDA Web site is www.rurdev.usda.gov.)

(**Munie Mae**); and the many private **Real Estate Mortgage Investment Conduits (REMICs)** that use **Mortgage-Backed Securities (MBS)** to collateralize their own securities.

The structure of the mortgage lending market has undergone dramatic changes over the past years. The changes started in the mid-1980s when the savings associations and thrifts found themselves burdened with long-term, low-interest-rate mortgages while, at the same time, paying high interest rates on savings deposits. In many cases, these institutions found their costs for deposits exceeded their income from loans, resulting in serious losses.

To turn these circumstances around, many lenders attempted to sell their loans to the participants in the secondary market. Those who did sell had to accept deep discounts, adding to their woes. Those who did not sell found themselves facing bankruptcy. As a result, many lenders were forced out of business in the late 1980s.

Today the financial market for real estate loans is based on the ability of loan originators to dispose of their new loans as quickly as possible in the secondary market as they need to replenish funds and strive to manage the interest rate risk that arises from long-term, fixed-rate mortgages. This results in loan originators having to follow closely the loan guidelines established by Fannie Mae and Freddie Mac.

The trend toward selling real estate loans has led to the development of a major new group of investors. Based on the concept of collateralization—the pooling together of homogenous types of mortgages to use as collateral for issuing marketable securities—private companies have emerged to challenge the dominant positions of Fannie Mae and Freddie Mac. Operating as real estate mortgage investment conduits (REMICs), these life insurance companies, pension funds, and other mortgage companies are creating new loans for their own portfolios, as well as buying and selling loans from other originators.

This chapter examines the participants in the secondary mortgage market and how their activities facilitate the national distribution of funds to the primary markets. See Figure 4.1 for a simplified diagram of the process.

FANNIE MAE

Fannie Mae is a New York Stock Exchange Company and the largest non-bank financial services company in the world. It operates pursuant to a federal charter and is the nation's largest source of financing for home mortgages. Over the past years, Fannie Mae has provided nearly $2.8 trillion of mortgage financing for over 34 million families. Now officially named Fannie Mae, the Federal National Mortgage Association was organized as a U.S. government agency in 1938 to establish a secondary market for the purchase of FHA-insured mortgages. The scope of Fannie Mae's operations was broadened in 1944 to include purchasing VA-guaranteed loans. The purchases of FHA and VA loans were made at **par;** that is, Fannie Mae paid mortgage holders *full face value* for their securities. They could not have been sold in the marketplace for full value, so Fannie Mae became a most important provider of funds for the real estate mortgage market.

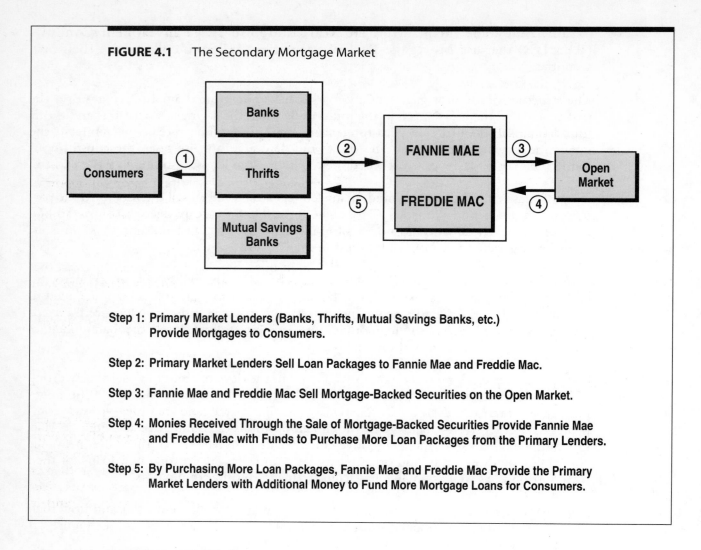

FIGURE 4.1   The Secondary Mortgage Market

Step 1: Primary Market Lenders (Banks, Thrifts, Mutual Savings Banks, etc.)
Provide Mortgages to Consumers.

Step 2: Primary Market Lenders Sell Loan Packages to Fannie Mae and Freddie Mac.

Step 3: Fannie Mae and Freddie Mac Sell Mortgage-Backed Securities on the Open Market.

Step 4: Monies Received Through the Sale of Mortgage-Backed Securities Provide Fannie Mae
and Freddie Mac with Funds to Purchase More Loan Packages from the Primary Lenders.

Step 5: By Purchasing More Loan Packages, Fannie Mae and Freddie Mac Provide the Primary
Market Lenders with Additional Money to Fund More Mortgage Loans for Consumers.

Secondary Market

In 1954 Fannie Mae was rechartered as a national secondary mortgage market clearinghouse to be financed by *private capital*. Fannie Mae was now empowered to *sell* its mortgages as well as purchase new FHA and VA loans. Fannie Mae's purchases were no longer made at par but at whatever discounted price would develop a reasonable rate of return. This profit attitude was consistent with the reorganizational goal of private ownership. Fannie Mae did not have to purchase every mortgage submitted to it, only those mortgages that met its standards for marketability.

In other words, Fannie Mae imposed its own criteria for acceptance of mortgages submitted for sale, which sometimes created animosity among mortgage originators. It was argued that one federal agency should accept another's standards. Fannie Mae countered with the argument that the FHA and VA standards for credit and appraisal were *minimum* standards and insisted that all mortgages submitted to Fannie Mae would have to meet its own standards for quality, yield, and risk. The quality and level of stability of guaranteed and insured loans were raised in order to meet these new requirements.

When Fannie Mae *purchased* mortgages, a servicing agreement was usually executed allowing the loan originator-seller to act as a collection agent for a specified fee. This fee, a rate of approximately one fourth to three eighths of one percent of the mortgage balance, created a substantial source of income for the originator, depending on the size of its mortgage loan portfolio.

Loan originators derive a large portion of their mortgage investment income from origination and collection fees. In many cases, especially with the mortgage bankers who issue the bulk of FHA and VA loans, the more loans that can be created, the higher the potential profits. Thus, the Fannie Mae secondary mortgage market allowed loan originators an opportunity to "roll over" their money. By selling their mortgages, these originators could secure more funds for making additional loans, thereby collecting more origination fees. When retaining the service rights on the old loan, originators also earned a new collection fee.

When Fannie Mae *sold* its mortgages, it did so in open-market transactions in which the purchasers were required to pay current prices for the securities. This confirmed the private ownership profit motives of this quasi-government agency. Sales of Fannie Mae mortgages have fluctuated through the years, with peak sales occurring when other investment opportunities were minimal.

Organization

The Housing and Urban Development Act of 1968 changed the Fannie Mae organization once again. Based on its successful operation in preceding years as a quasi-public, profitable corporation, Fannie Mae was reorganized as a fully private corporation. All Treasury-owned stock was redeemed, and a like amount of over-the-counter common stock was offered to the general public. Fannie Mae became a separate, privately owned corporation subject to federal corporate income tax, and exempt from state income taxes, and it retained the benefit of government "sponsorship."

Fannie Mae is administered by a 15-member board of directors serving one-year terms, ten of whom are elected by Fannie Mae stockholders. The remaining five are appointed by the President of the United States from various segments of the construction, real estate, and financing industries. In addition, the board of directors seeks advice from the 8-member General Advisory Committee, also composed of representatives from the housing and mortgage lending industries. The secretary of HUD must approve Fannie Mae policies on borrowing capital, maintaining financial liquidity, and paying appropriate stock dividends.

The 1968 reorganization was meant to enhance Fannie Mae's ability to participate in the secondary market and to encourage new money to enter the real estate mortgage market, both of which it continues to do successfully. Fannie Mae could now purchase mortgages at a **premium (in excess of par)**. Fannie Mae was also allowed to expand its own borrowing ability by floating securities backed by specific pools of mortgages in its portfolio.

The Emergency Home Finance Act of 1970 gave Fannie Mae the additional authority to purchase mortgages *other than* FHA-insured or VA-guaranteed loans, mostly conventional loans. This further expanded Fannie Mae's impact on national real estate finance.

Administered Price System

In the past, Fannie Mae's mortgage purchasing procedures had been handled under a free-market-system auction. Lenders offered to sell Fannie Mae their loans at acceptable discounts, with Fannie Mae buying the lowest-priced loans, those with the deepest discounts. This system has been replaced by an **administered price system** in which Fannie Mae adjusts its required yields daily in accordance with market factors and its financial needs.

Under the administered price system, lenders call a special Fannie Mae rate line to secure current yield quotes and then a separate line to place an order to sell. Lenders may order a mandatory commitment whereby delivery of loans to Fannie Mae is *guaranteed* or a standby commitment in which the lender retains the *option* to deliver the loans or not, depending on the price at time of delivery.

Underwriting Standards

Lenders wishing to sell their conventional loans to Fannie Mae must subscribe to their guidelines, which are revised from time to time. These include the following guidelines:

- Any conventional loan with an loan-to-value (LTV) ratio of more than 80 percent must have private mortgage insurance (PMI) coverage on the amount of the loan exceeding 80 percent. This insurance must be issued by a company outside of the lender's control.

- Fannie Mae requires the borrowers' debt-to-income ratio to be 36 percent of their combined total gross monthly income. This debt includes the total monthly housing expenses plus any long-term installment debt payments. Under special circumstances for low-income or first-time home buyers, this ratio can be raised to 43 percent or even as high as 50 percent for a Fannie Mae Streamlined Purchase Money Mortgage Option 2.

- Buydowns are allowed, except for adjustable-rate mortgages. Buydowns involve extra cash payments made at the inception of a loan to reduce the monthly payments by reducing the interest rate.

IN PRACTICE . . .

Reliable Savings Bank has just closed on five million dollars worth of home mortgage loans. The loans are all for 30 years and at an interest rate of 8%. Although these loans will provide Reliable a steady stream of income for many years, the bank is now faced with a dilemma—no more funds available to make additional mortgage loans.

One way to achieve more capital would be to sell the mortgages to Fannie Mae or Freddie Mac. Of course, Reliable would have to make sure that it fol-lowed the Fannie Mae/Freddie Mac guidelines with regard to the current maximum loan amount, down payment of at least 3% of sales price, qualifying ratios up to 36% for affordable loan products, seller contribution to purchaser's closing costs, and any private mortgage insurance requirements. As long as these guidelines are met, the five million dollar package of loans can be sold but there will be a discount on the total. Reliable can maintain the level of yield it desires, however, by passing along the discount to the borrowers in the form of discount points.

- Gift funds are allowed on LTV ratio loans greater than 80 percent, but the borrower must make at least a 5 percent investment. For loans of 80 percent LTV or less, all funds can be from gifts. All gift funds in the donor's account must be verified and evidence of withdrawal and receipt and deposit to the borrower's account must also be verified. Some programs prohibit the use of gift funds.

- Usually, coborrowers, guarantors, or cosigners do not take title to the property. However, their income may be counted for qualifying purposes if they sign the promissory note. If the coborrower's income is used for qualifying a loan of greater than 90 percent LTV, the coborrower must occupy the property.

Conforming and Nonconforming Loans. The terms *conforming* and *nonconforming* are used by lenders to define loans that conform to the Fannie Mae/Freddie Mac qualifying guidelines. Loans that do not meet the conforming guidelines, including maximum loan amount and down payment requirements, are called *nonconforming*.

The loan limits are adjusted each January by a formula specified in the Housing and Community Development Act of 1980. The limits are indexed to the October-to-October change in the national average house price as reported by the Federal Housing Finance Board. This average house price is based on single-family houses financed by conventional loans. For example, in 2003 the following conventional loan limits prevail:

Single-family house	$322,700	359,600 *359,650*
Duplex	413,100	*460,400*
Triplex	499,300	*556,500*
Fourplex	620,500	*691,600*

Limits as of 2005

These limits are 50 percent higher in Alaska, Hawaii, Guam, and the U.S. Virgin Islands.

Although these are conforming conventional loan limits, buyers may pay any price for a property, making up the difference in cash. Maximum loan limits are established to set a standard for these types of loans so that they become homogeneous packages for securitization in the secondary market. Loans issued in excess of these amounts are nonconforming. They are called **jumbo loans** and are usually made by lenders for their own investment portfolios.

Automated Underwriting System. The mortgage financing industry is undergoing dramatic changes as new technology is being applied. Leading these changes is an **automated underwriting system** that can quickly, objectively, and accurately predict multiple risk factors in a loan application.

Need to know these two terms for TEST

Fannie Mae provides two versions of its automated system: the **Desktop Underwriter**® and the **Desktop Originator**® for lender services and independent mortgage broker-agents respectively. Lenders access Fannie Mae's sophisticated loan analysis system through the software they offer their customers. Estimated loan approval time runs 60 seconds on the average. *Fannie Mae uses*

Information on Fannie Mae's electronic underwriting systems, Desktop Underwriters® and Desktop Originator®, can be obtained on www.fanniemae.com.

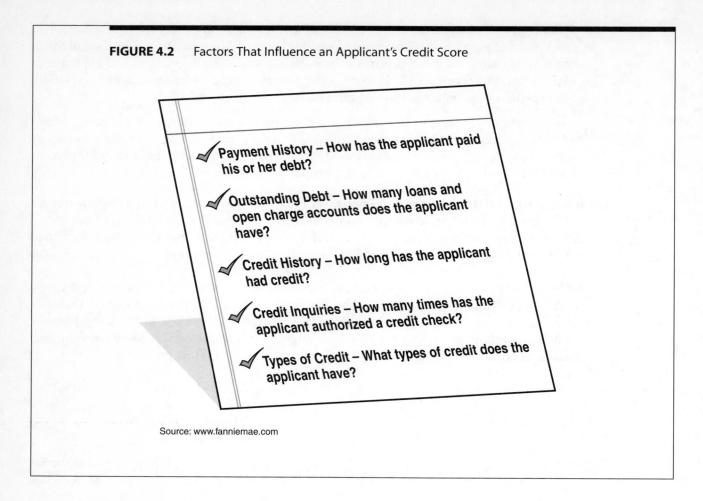

FIGURE 4.2 Factors That Influence an Applicant's Credit Score

✓ Payment History – How has the applicant paid his or her debt?

✓ Outstanding Debt – How many loans and open charge accounts does the applicant have?

✓ Credit History – How long has the applicant had credit?

✓ Credit Inquiries – How many times has the applicant authorized a credit check?

✓ Types of Credit – What types of credit does the applicant have?

Source: www.fanniemae.com

Included in the automated underwriting process is **credit scoring,** an objective method of assessing credit risk based on the statistical probability of repayment of the debt. The applicant's score is based on data included in one or more of the national repository files maintained by Experian (formerly TRW), Equifax, or Transunion.

Credit scores reflect the combination of many risk factors. In some instances a borrower who has had a bankruptcy with an otherwise "clean" history of making payments may have a better credit score than another borrower who has not had a bankruptcy but has a long history of delinquent payments.

Credit scores are *not* based on age, race, gender, religion, national origin, marital status, current address, or receipt of public assistance. As shown in Figure 4.2, credit scores are based on factors such as how you pay your bills, how much outstanding debt you have, what type of credit and how long you have had established credit, and how many times you have had inquiries relative to extending credit.

The scores on the FICO test (named after Fair, Isaac & Co., the San Rafael, California-based firm that created the test) assign relative risk rankings to applicants based on statistical analyses of their credit histories. As shown in Figure 4.3, the applicants who always pay their bills on time and make moderate use of their credit cards receive the highest scores, 700 to above 800. The applicants who are late in paying bills present greater risks and get lower scores from 400 to 620.

FIGURE 4.3   Credit Scoring and Applicant Characteristics

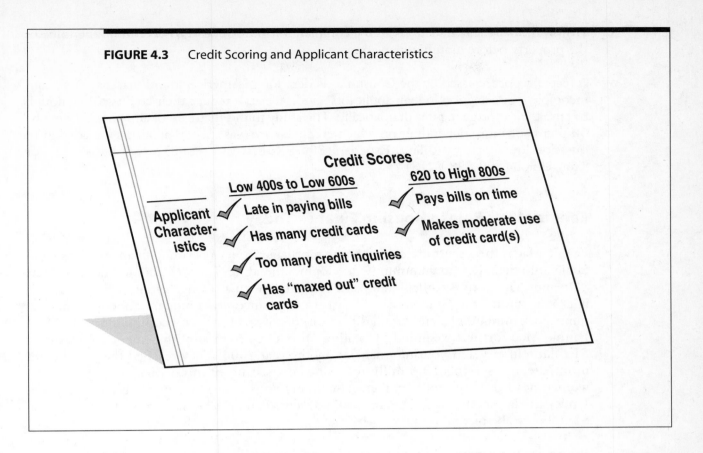

The Fair, Isaac & Co. predicts that the next generation of scoring programs will be so advanced as to allow better scores for the homebuyers now treated by lenders as marginal or rejected. Potential borrowers may check their own credit scores for a fee on www.myfico.com.

Lenders may order credit scores electronically at relatively low cost from credit repositories or bureaus. Credit scoring speeds up the loan approval process. Most lenders today order a **tri-merge credit report** containing information from all three of the major credit repositories. In most cases the numerical credit score will be different on all three reports due to variations in time and content from creditors. Generally, the lender will use the middle score, not an average.

Potential misuse of credit scoring has prompted the following rules on their use:

- Never automatically disqualify anybody because of a subpar credit score (credit scores may not "single out" or prohibit low-to-moderate-income borrowers from becoming homeowners);

- Be aware of potential errors in electronic credit files;

- With a subpar score, look hard at the score factor codes and work with the applicant to clear "fixable" items.

In some cases today the property is never viewed as to condition or external factors. Rather, the property is appraised by a collateral assessment that uses statistical analysis, including regression analysis, and compares property features with others that have recently been sold.

However, many lenders still require a complete on-site appraisal to determine the value of the property before granting loan approval.

A recent report released by the Consumer Federation of America, found that inaccurate and incomplete information in loan applicants' credit files can reduce their credit scores enough to raise their mortgage rates dramatically. The study found that 31% of all scores differed by 50 points or more depending on which credit service was used. Applicants are advised to question low scores by calling, Experian (800-EXPERIAN), Equifax (800-685-1111), or TransUnion (800-888-4213).

Fannie Mae's Role in Housing Finance Today

Fannie Mae is the largest investor in home mortgages today providing financing for single-family, multifamily, and community development lending. In 1991 Fannie Mae started its "Opening Doors to Affordable Housing" initiative with a strong commitment to providing financing for the "underserved" market of low-income to moderate-income families, minorities, immigrants, and families living in distressed inner-city communities. In 1994 Fannie Mae further expanded "Opening Doors" with an announcement to provide a $1 trillion in targeted housing financing by the year 2000. They reached their goal eight months early, serving 10.6 million families consisting of minorities, young families, women head-of-household families, new immigrants, and others needing consideration. Under the latest American Dream Commitment, Fannie Mae has pledged an additional $2 trillion to be placed in the next decade.

Information on many of these targeted financing products may be found on the Fannie Mae Web site under American Dream Commitment. See www.fanniemae.com.

Affordable Housing Loans

The first of these affordable loan products was the **Community Home Buyer®** program, the first loan program to allow for a 5 percent down payment with an additional requirement that the borrowers attend a homebuyer education class. Today there are at least ten different loan products, each tailored to meet the needs of a specific group of potential home buyers. In most cases, there are certain income limitations based on HUD's median income figures and a requirement for homebuyer education counseling.

The newest of Fannie Mae's affordable housing loans was made available nationwide in June 1998. The **Flex 97** requires a minimum down payment of 3 percent but allows the borrower to provide this money from gifts, loans from family members, cash assistance from an employer, or from other sources. This is in contrast to other conventional loan low down payment programs where the down payment must come from the borrowers' own personal cash resources.

The Flex 97 also allows the home *sellers* to contribute up to 3 percent of the mortgage amount toward the homebuyers' closing costs. The interest rates on these loans are the market rates for 30-year, fixed-rate mortgages. The loans have a high maximum dollar ceiling, currently $300,700 but no maximum income limitations or requirements for homebuying counseling.

Fannie Mae also offers the Flexible 100, which allows borrowers to put a zero down payment but requires a 3 percent contribution to closing costs, which may come from the same sources as under the Flex 97.

The Flex 97 and Flexible 100 are a result of the advances in computer technology allowing lenders to analyze a borrower's application and predict the true risk of default with exceptional accuracy. Fannie Mae uses its Desktop Underwriter® system to evaluate borrowers for the Flex loans. There are no exact credit score levels to qualify for this program, but the borrower needs to demonstrate responsible use of credit in the past and the ability to pay future monthly mortgage debt for the property being purchased. The intent of the flexible loans program is to provide low down payment opportunities to families with moderate or lower incomes who, despite good credit, might not otherwise be able to purchase a home. For more information call Fannie Mae at 1-800-732-6643, or see www.fanniemae.com.

Fannie Mae's Web site includes information on its home improvement loans, Homestyle™ mortgages, and energy conservation loans. The site has a list of lenders who provide loans for purchasing and renovating older homes or enlarging and improving current housing.

To maintain the flow of funds available for the purchase of mortgage loans from the primary market, Fannie Mae issues securities backed by pools of mortgage loans called mortgage-backed securities (MBSs), which are sold on the open market.

FREDDIE MAC

The credit crunch of 1969 and 1970 gave rise to the Emergency Home Finance Act of 1970, which created, among other things, the Federal Home Loan Mortgage Corporation, now officially known as *Freddie Mac*. Freddie Mac was organized specifically to provide a secondary mortgage market for the U.S. savings associations and thrifts that are members of the Federal Home Loan Bank System.

Organization

Freddie Mac was established with an initial subscription of $100 million from the 12 Federal Home Loan district banks and placed under the direction of three members of the Federal Home Loan Bank Board. Freddie Mac was given the authority to raise additional funds by floating its own securities, which were backed by pools of its own mortgages. Since 1989, Freddie Mac has become an independent stock company in direct competition with Fannie Mae.

Since the elimination of the Federal Home Loan Bank Board, Freddie Mac is now governed by an 18-member board of directors, 13 elected by the stockholders and 5 appointed by the President of the United States. It has a line of credit with the U.S. Treasury for $2.5 billion, giving it equal status with Fannie Mae. Freddie Mac, like Fannie Mae, remains under HUD oversight as a Government Sponsored Enterprise (GSE). More recently the **Office of Federal Housing Enterprises Oversight (OFHEO)** was charged with insuring that proper reserves are maintained by both of the "super powers" of the secondary market.

Operations

Freddie Mac is empowered to purchase conventional loans, as well as FHA-insured and VA-guaranteed loans, from lenders all over the country. It also accepts convertible mortgages, loans established at an adjustable rate that may be changed to a fixed rate. Its commitments to purchase are issued at designated discounts and/or specific interest rates for various types of mortgages, with fees charged accordingly. It buys loans for its own pools to collateralize its **participation certificates (PCs),** which in turn, it guarantees to the security buyers.

Underwriting Standards

Following Fannie Mae's underwriting requirements, Freddie Mac stipulates borrower's income qualifications as 28 percent and 36 percent with private mortgage insurance to be purchased on conventional loans with more than an 80 percent LTV ratio. However, with some programs the debt-to-income ratio can be raised to 43 percent or as high as 50 percent. Allowed are buydown loans, gift funds, and conventional loans on single-family homes up to $322,700.

Freddie Mac ✕
Loan Prospector ↑

Electronic Underwriting System. Freddie Mac provides its own electronic underwriting service, called **Loan Prospector®**, to participating lenders, mortgage insurers, mortgage bankers and brokers, and others in the real estate market.

The Loan Prospector® computer program evaluates a borrower's creditworthiness using statistical models and judgmental rules. The credit evaluation indicates the level of underwriting and documentation necessary to determine the investment quality of a loan. It includes the borrower's credit reputation and financial capacity as well as the estimated value of the property. The credit analysis uses information from the loan application and credit searches. The value of the property is derived from statistical models or from a traditional appraisal.

Loan Prospector® provides an assessment of a loan's risk profile and estimates accurate pricing commensurate to the risk. A jumbo loan is a mortgage exceeding Freddie Mac's conforming loan limits. A **subprime loan** is a mortgage that does not meet Freddie Mac's investment quality standards. Often referred to as B, C, or D paper, there is a definite market today for these loans that generally require a larger down payment and higher rate of interest.

Risk-Based Loan Pricing. Both Fannie Mae's Desktop Underwriter® and Freddie Mac's Loan Prospector® provide information allowing lenders to price each loan according to its individual factors. Historically, real estate loans are made on the basis of average pricing. If the market indicates interest rates for 30-year, fixed-rate loans to be 7 percent with a 2 point placement fee, then most 30-year loans will be made for this price. With the advent of advanced computer technology, lenders will be able to identify the risk associated with each specific loan and charge the borrower an interest rate and placement fee accordingly.

It is anticipated that this technique will provide borrowers more liberal loan underwriting requirements such as higher debt ratios and loan-to-value guidelines. However, lenders still are generally not impressed with **risk-based pricing** as credit risk is only one factor involved in a mortgage loan. It will continue to be difficult to quote rates and costs without actually evaluating the property with an appraisal and analyzing the borrower's credit history.

Although lenders have been implementing risk-based pricing for years in the secondary mortgage market, it has not yet become popular for primary mortgage lending. Probably the mortgage industry is currently simply too busy to worry about it right now. Spokespersons for the industry indicate a struggle with how to implement risk-based pricing. They do agree, however, that it is imminent and will be a part of the general real estate finance spectrum in the near future. Currently it is being used by lenders making jumbo loans in excess of $252,700 and subprime loans that have a less than A rating. The following case study is an example of a *subprime loan*.

FOR EXAMPLE

Joe and Susan Martin are really anxious to purchase their first home. Unfortunately, their credit history is not good and their credit scores are quite low. When they married five years ago right after graduating from college they got caught up in the "credit card" frenzy and soon found themselves with almost as much in credit card debt as their combined annual salaries! It will take at least two years for them to "clean up" their credit. Are they stuck with renting or is there some way they could purchase now?

They could consider taking a "B" paper loan. They might have to look to parents for a gift to be used towards a down payment, or perhaps consider withdrawing funds from their IRAs. They will have to be prepared to pay a higher than market interest rate. Nevertheless, they would be in a home of their own, receiving tax benefits, and building equity. After some period of time, they could apply for refinancing at a more favorable rate.

Affordable Housing Loans

Affordable Gold® is the counterpart to Fannie Mae's Community Home Buyer® program, following the same general qualifying guidelines. Numerous other special programs are available through Community Development Lending Initiatives, including rehabilitation financing.

Freddie Mac offers a parallel mortgage plan to Fannie Mae's Flex 97. It is called **Alt '97** and allows alternative methods for making the 3 percent down payment, similar to Flex '97. More than 680 lenders using Freddie Mac's Loan Prospector® are able to provide the Alt '97 nationwide for conventional loans up to the current maximum loan amount.

Freddie Mac also offers a 100 percent mortgage that requires no down payment but does require that the borrowers have excellent credit and funds equal to 3 percent of the sales price to cover closing costs. All of Freddie Mac programs are described in great detail on the Web site www.freddiemac.com.

New Credit Standards

Freddie Mac has instituted a new credit standard for qualifying loan applicants. Called the "Gap Ratio," it offers a valuable test for consumers anticipating buying a home or applying for a mortgage. The gap ratio is the difference between the applicants' monthly debt-payment-to-income ratio and the monthly housing-expense-to-income ratio. The new standard suggests that the gap between these two debt ratios generally should not exceed 15 percentage points. This places greater emphasis on an applicant's current credit card balance, auto loan payments, student loans, and other revolving credit payments.

For example, if the applicant's mortgage expenses total 33 percent of monthly income and the total monthly revolving credit payments are an additional 17 percent of monthly income, the total monthly-debt-to-income ratio is 50 percent. That alone is not always sufficient to deny a loan, but in this case, the fact that the total revolving debt load is more than 15 percent above the housing debt load is enough to deny the loan.

Potential Competitive Difficulties

Both Freddie Mac and Fannie Mae are currently under attack from this nation's banks and other large lenders fearful that their own loan-making abilities will be usurped by these large secondary mortgage market operators moving directly into the loan origination business.

HUD has been encouraging the expanding number of mortgage loan originators to use the FHA automated underwriting system as a way of providing more competition and making such loans widely available. Banks and other big lenders are now concerned that Fannie and Freddie are preparing to take a further step by becoming primary lenders themselves and taking over the home loan business. The Federal Reserve Bulletin of May, 2001 shows that Fannie and Freddie control about 37 percent of the over $5 trillion of one-family to four-family and multifamily mortgage loans outstanding.

Congress has been examining new bills designed to reign in the activities of Fannie and Freddie but to date have not passed any legislation to this effect.

THE GOVERNMENT NATIONAL MORTGAGE ASSOCIATION (GNMA)

Created in 1968 as a wholly owned *government* corporation under the Urban Development Act, the Government National Mortgage Association (GNMA), or "Ginnie Mae," is under the direction of the Department of Housing and Urban Development (HUD). Ginnie Mae is responsible for providing financing for special assistance programs, urban renewal projects, housing for the elderly, experimental housing, and other housing programs deemed important by HUD but difficult to finance in the normal market. In addition, Ginnie Mae is responsible for the operation of the mortgage securities pools. See www.ginniemae.com.

Securities Pools

Most significant for real estate finance is Ginnie Mae's role in its *mortgage-backed securities program*. Backed by the credit of the U.S. government and funded by the immense borrowing power of the United States Treasury, Ginnie Mae has developed a comprehensive plan for guaranteeing timely payments of principal and interest by issuers of securities to the holders of these securities. This guarantee from Ginnie Mae allows qualified mortgage originators of FHA-insured and VA-guaranteed loans to secure additional capital for lending purposes by *pledging a pool of their existing loans as collateral* to back up a securities issue. This guarantee is an alternative to the *sale* of the mortgages. The loan originators still collect their own servicing fees, but now they have the use of additional funds to lend, and the securities buyers have Ginnie Mae's guarantee that they will receive their shares of the monthly mortgage payments.

Under one Ginnie Mae mortgage-backed securities program, mortgages have to be homogeneous in interest rates and types of properties financed and must be pooled together in sums of no less than $2 million to back up a securities issue totaling the same amount. Thus the collateral pool contains a number of specific eligible mortgages, each no more than one year old (or two years for multifamily mortgages), covering identifiable properties and executed by real persons who make regular monthly mortgage payments.

In another program, the mortgages in the pool do not have to be homogeneous. They may have differing interest rates within a 1 percent range. The securities backed by these various mortgage pools are registered, issued in requested denominations, and guaranteed by Ginnie Mae.

The three general types of mortgage-backed securities are:

[handwritten: Know this →]

1. straight **pass-throughs**, *[handwritten: Payments to be made to buyer as payments recvd.]*
2. modified pass-throughs, and *[handwritten: – Payments to be made Timely]*
3. fully modified pass-throughs. *[handwritten: Guarantee monthly principal & interest.]*

The straight pass-through securities provide for payments to be made to the securities buyer as they are received from the mortgages in the pool. The modified pass-through securities provide for a guaranteed monthly interest payment to the securities owner, regardless of whether the entire payment of principal and interest was received from the mortgage pool. The fully modified pass-through securities guarantee a monthly principal and interest payment, regardless of actual payments collected.

In addition to a $500 application fee, Ginnie Mae charges the issuer of the securities a premium for its guarantee, based on the balance of the securities outstanding at the end of each month.

OTHER GOVERNMENT PARTICIPANTS

Federal Agricultural Mortgage Corporation (FAMC)

Also known as "Farmer Mac," the Federal Agricultural Mortgage Corporation (FAMC) was created by the Agricultural Credit Act of 1987 to establish pools of agriculture loans. FAMC cannot purchase loans, but it approves loan poolers and the types of loans they can accept. It underwrites securities backed by pools of mortgage loans, much as Ginnie Mae does.

Municipal Mortgage Enhancement

A program initiated in 1984, known as Municipal Mortgage Enhancement (Munie Mae), allows AAA-rated mortgage-backed securities to be exchanged for underlying mortgages on tax-exempt, multifamily projects. This gives an AAA rating to the mortgage revenue bonds used to fund the developments and enables developers to secure money at the lowest market rates.

REAL ESTATE MORTGAGE INVESTMENT CONDUITS (REMICS)

A real estate mortgage investment conduit or REMIC is basically a conduit, holding fixed pools of mortgages that back securities collateralized by the mortgage cash flows. It is now the basic structure for the securitization of real estate mortgages and has achieved its goal of opening the general capital markets to real estate borrowers.

The REMIC structure offers issuers a flexible tool with which to design classes (**tranches**) of ownership interests to meet investor needs and respond to market conditions. A series of tranches are established with the payments from the mortgage pool allocated sequentially to each class. A specified tranch receives principal payments only after the principal on the previous class has been paid. Thus, the higher the class the shorter its maturity.

Some tranches are "stripped" into *interest-only (IO)* or *principal-only (PO)* components offering trading and hedging opportunities arising from the uncertain repayment feature of mortgage securities. The strips are created by dividing the cash flows from a pool of mortgages. The IO strips receive all the interest portions of the payments while the PO strips receive all the principal payments. When interest rates fall and mortgage payments accelerate, the IO strips drop in value because their holders will receive less interest than expected over the life of the securities. Likewise, the PO strips will increase in value because their holders will receive principal payment at a faster rate. When interest rates rise, the reverse is true.

An increasingly popular REMIC is the Commercial Mortgage-Backed Securities pool (CMBS). Prior to the development of this REMIC, commercial loan originators had no option but to keep these loans in their own portfolios. Very large loans were divided among several lenders. The CMBS industry has entered its ninth year with 20 percent ($300 billion) of the commercial and multi-family U.S. mortgage loan market.

SECONDARY MARKET FOR JUNIOR FINANCING LOANS

The idea of short-term, high-yield investments in junior mortgages, deeds of trust, and contracts for deed has attracted many private investors, real estate holding companies, and industrial corporations with surplus capital to invest.

The most active participants in the arena of junior real estate finance are small private lending companies that originate new junior loans and buy and sell existing second liens. Included are real estate brokers, numerous mortgage brokers, and mortgage bankers who operate on lines of credit. They make up an active and effective secondary junior loan market.

Real estate finance companies that have organized specifically to make junior loans also contribute to this market's strength. These companies issue a new junior loan to a qualified property owner who pledges equity in exchange for cash. Another source for the finance companies is a creditworthy property buyer who needs to raise funds to satisfy the cash demands of the seller. These mortgage finance companies also purchase existing second mortgages from their owners, but usually at a discount to enhance the yield.

Many states require that private mortgage finance companies dealing in financial securities be licensed and that they post bonds with their licensing agencies to protect the public from any illegal activities. Some states regulate these dealers so stringently that they are even required to submit their advertising for approval to the state's real estate commissioner to prevent the possibility of misleading the public. Accurate records must be maintained, lending laws observed, Regulation Z enforced and, in general, just and equitable procedures followed by the securities dealers in watchful states.

A growing secondary market for the sale of land contracts has emanated from the successful activities of land promotion companies. Large numbers of land contracts are created from sales of lots in subdivided desert areas of Arizona and New Mexico, the mountains and plateaus of Colorado and Texas, and the lowlands of Florida. The lots sold in these "retirement" or "second-home" communities are usually financed by a junior contract for deed drawn between the developer and the buyer, who invariably makes only a very low down payment. These contracts then become the property of the land developer. They are capitalized by being pledged at commercial banks as collateral for cash loans or are sold at a discount to buyers who are interested in the return these investments produce.

Over the years some illegal activities have been associated with the sale of these land contracts. In some instances it was found that the actual value of the collateral land backing up the contracts was much less than the discounted price paid by the investor. Contracts written for $3,995 might actually have been drawn against property worth only $1,500. If there was a default on the part of a land purchaser and a subsequent foreclosure sale, the buyer of such a contract would lose a substantial portion of the investment. In some cases it was discovered that there were *no real property buyers* at all, only some unscrupulous promoters who were defrauding the public. In other cases there was not even any real land involved in the original sale, just a series of phony contracts prepared to fleece unwary consumers. Under these schemes, a contract buyer received a few initial payments and then the selling company declared bankruptcy, leaving the contract holders high and dry. When investing in this very speculative area of contracts for deed on land developments, buyers must exercise much caution.

Fannie Mae and Freddie Mac also participate in the junior loan market by buying and selling junior securities from approved lenders. These lenders must be experienced junior financiers, maintain a net worth of $250,000 as well as a reserve fund of $\frac{1}{5}$ of 1 percent of all outstanding principal balances of their junior loan portfolios, be licensed, and agree to service the loans sold to Fannie Mae and Freddie Mac.

SUMMARY

This chapter examined the roles of the various major agencies involved in the secondary mortgage market for real estate finance. These agencies are Fannie Mae, Freddie Mac, and the GNMA.

Based on electronic procedures that are uniform in the evaluation of credit and collateral, a huge market for trading in securities has evolved. Local originators of loans sell them to second owners throughout the country as investments, thereby freeing local capital for making more loans. In addition to FHA and VA loans, the secondary mortgage market has expanded to include conventional loans on homes, condominiums, multifamily projects, and commercial developments. Operating as warehousers of money, Fannie Mae and Freddie Mac effectively redistribute funds from money-rich areas to money-poor areas.

Fannie Mae was organized originally in 1938 as a federal agency involved primarily in purchasing and managing FHA-insured loans. The association has evolved into a private, profit-making corporation dealing in every type of residential real estate mortgage loan.

To raise funds for the purchase of these mortgages, Fannie Mae charges fees and has the authority to borrow from the U.S. Treasury. More recently, however, Fannie Mae has been authorized to market its own securities and is expanding its strategies to meet the pressures created by an active real estate market.

Freddie Mac was created in 1970 to provide a secondary mortgage market for the nation's savings associations. Through the years it has evolved into a private corporation, buying and selling all types of loans and adding immeasurably to the effectiveness of the secondary market.

Created as a wholly owned government corporation in 1968, the GNMA is under HUD. It finances special assistance programs and participates in the secondary market through its mortgage-backed securities pools.

By pooling homogeneous mortgages into prescribed amounts, qualified mortgage originators can issue securities against this pool and sell like amounts to investors. These securities are designed to deliver a reasonable return on the investment and are guaranteed not only by the mortgage pool itself but also by GNMA which insurers, for a fee, the timely payment of principal and interest to the holders of these securities.

In addition to the three major participants in the secondary market, other public and private agencies and companies are developing under the concept of collateralization. This concept pools existing mortgages together in homogeneous packages that are then pledged as collateral to issue mortgage-backed securities (MBS). These MBSs are, in turn, sold to investors.

Included in this list of secondary market participants are the Federal Agricultural Mortgage Corporation (Farmer Mac), which deals in farm and ranch loans; the Municipal Mortgage Enhancement Program (Munie Mae), which exchanges securities for underlying mortgages on tax-exempt multifamily projects; and the various real estate mortgage investment conduits (REMICs) introduced in 1988.

CHAPTER 5

Sources of Funds:
Fiduciaries

▼ **KEY TERMS**

construction loans   fiduciary   participation financing
credit unions   financial intermediaries   principals
demand deposits   interim financing   thrifts
equity loans   mutual savings banks

Money available to finance real estate emanates from a long list of traditional and not so traditional lenders. The range of loan sources extends from the banks, thrifts, life insurance companies through the mortgage bankers and brokers to the private lending companies and finally to the sellers who carry back loans to sell their own properties.

Sometimes, depending on market activities, real estate lending loses its normally conservative perspectives as it did in the late 1980s. A frenzy of lending coupled with lax mortgage underwriting resulted in a huge banking crisis in this country. As a result of the bankruptcies of banks and thrifts and federal government takeovers, new sources for real estate finance have emerged. Nonbank lenders such as General Motors Acceptance Corporation, General Electric Capital Mortgage Corporation, and others have entered the market as lenders placing loans through their servicing agencies.

This chapter examines the real estate lending activities of the institutions that hold individual deposits—banks, thrifts, life insurance companies, pension funds, and credit unions. Collectively they are called *fiduciaries*.

ON
TEST ⟶ A **fiduciary** is an entity acting as an agent on behalf of other persons or organizations, called **principals.** A fiduciary relationship is founded on the trust and confidence of one person or organization in the integrity and fidelity of a representative agent. Thus a fiduciary must represent the principal honestly and with the highest ability.

Organizations that collect money from depositors or premium payers and lend these funds to borrowers are called *financial fiduciaries* or **financial intermediaries.** These fiduciary organizations manage and guard entrusted funds over a period of time. The funds must be protected so they are available to their owners, dollar for dollar, when called for according to established arrangements. Because of certain characteristics, such as value, durability, and fixity, real property attracts much of this capital.

COMMERCIAL BANKS

As the name implies, commercial banks are designed to be safe depositories and lenders for a multitude of commercial banking activities. Although they have other sources of capital, including savings, loans from other banks, and the equity invested by their owners, commercial banks rely mainly on **demand deposits,** better known as *checking accounts,* for their basic supply of funds. Commercial banks are also among the most active issuers of loans.

Mortgage Loan Activities

Commercial banks are designed primarily to make loans to businesses to finance their operations and inventories. Depending on market conditions, they often diversify into loans on real estate. In the past, they concentrated on industrial and commercial property real estate loans. But commercial banks are also active in the one-family to four-family home loan market.

Most of their realty loan activities include **construction loans,** also known as **interim financing,** home improvement loans, and mobile home loans. These loans are all relatively short term and match the bank's demand deposit profile.   Construction loans run from three months to three years, depending on the size of the project. Home improvement loans may run up to five years and include financing the cost of additions, modernization, swimming pool construction, or other similar improvements. Mobile home loans are usually carried for ten years, but many have been extended for longer periods to serve the increasing demand for this form of housing. These longer mobile home loans usually include insurance from the Federal Housing Administration (FHA) or guarantees from the Department of Veterans Affairs (VA).

Some commercial banks also serve their select customers by providing them with long-term mortgage money on their homes. Other banks participate to some degree in the secondary money market by either selling home loans that they originate or buying packages of home loans to round out their own investment portfolios. Most of these home loans are either FHA-insured or VA-guaranteed. Some commercial banks make loans to farmers for the purchase or modernization of their farms or for financing farm operations.

Loans to borrowers based on the equity in their homes, **equity loans,** are a popular product for commercial banks. The IRS has eliminated tax deductions for interest paid on consumer loans but preserved the deductions for interest paid on home loans. As a result, banks compete vigorously for equity loan business to offset their diminished consumer loan business. Borrowers may use the monies generated by equity loans to purchase personal property, pay for education expenses or vacations, and even buy additional real estate. Commercial banks also participate in real estate financing through at least three other avenues: by operation of their *trust departments;* by acting as *mortgage bankers* (including the ownership of mortgage banking companies); and by direct or indirect ownership of *other lending businesses.*

Commercial banks' trust departments supervise and manage relatively large quantities of money and property for their beneficiaries. They act as executors or coexecutors of estates, as conservators of the estates of incompetent persons, as guardians of the estates of minors, as trustees under agreements entered into by individuals or companies for specific purposes, and as trustees under insurance proceeds trusts. They also act as escrow agents in the performance of specific escrow agreements, as trustees for corporations in controlling their bonds, notes, and stock certificates, and as trustees for company retirement or pension funds.

In keeping with their fiduciary responsibilities to obtain maximum yields at low risks, trust departments usually take a conservative approach when making investments with funds left in their control. The primary role of the trustees is to preserve the value of the property entrusted to their management. Real estate loans made from these trust accounts are only one possibility in a long list of investment opportunities.

In addition to acting as originating and servicing agents for their own mortgages, many commercial bank mortgage loan departments originate and service loans for other lenders. Acting in the role of mortgage bankers, commercial banks represent life insurance companies, real estate investment or mortgage trusts, or even other commercial banks seeking loans in a specific community. In this capacity, a mortgage loan department secures an origination fee and a collection fee for servicing the new account, adding earnings to its overall profit picture.

Finally, some commercial banks participate, either directly or indirectly, as owners of real estate mortgage trusts (REMTs) or as members in a regional bank holding company. These expanded investment opportunities add great flexibility to the real estate mortgage loan activities of commercial banks. Some larger banks make loans on commercial real estate developments, such as apartment projects, office buildings, or shopping centers. These larger loans usually are placed through bank holding companies or subsidiary mortgage banking operations.

Despite a movement toward the consolidation of banks, there currently is a countermovement of small bank start-ups. More than 200 new small banks were chartered in 1998-1999, mostly organized by bankers who lost their jobs through mergers. These new banks are seeking business from the customers generally overlooked by the larger banks—small business owners, elderly depositors, and persons disenchanted with large bank anonymity.

On November 12, 1999, the Financial Services Modernization Bill, also referred to as the Gramm-Leach-Bliley Bill for the congressmen who introduced it, was signed into law. It ended severe banking restrictions imposed by the 1933 Glass-Steagall Act. The act prohibited banks from marketing a range of financial products, a practice many believed led to the severity of the Great Depression. The new law allows banks to market annuities, stocks and bonds, and title insurance in addition to certificates of deposit and other financial services. The Bill prohibits banks from acting as real estate brokers and it also prohibits the sale of savings associations (thrifts) to commercial firms.

However, the banking world continues to fight for the right to conduct general brokerage, arguing that brokerage falls within the definition of "financial services." New legislation may be required to clarify this issue.

MUTUAL SAVINGS BANKS

Formed to provide savings services for the emerging class of thrifty workers in the U.S. industrial expansion of the mid-19th century, **mutual savings banks** are concentrated in the eastern United States. Although a few of these financial institutions are located in the states of Alaska, Oregon, and Washington, most are found in Connecticut, New York, and Massachusetts. Others are located in Delaware, Indiana, Maryland, Minnesota, New Jersey, Ohio, Pennsylvania, and Wisconsin.

These banks are organized as mutual companies in which depositors-owners receive profits as interest or dividends on savings accounts, and leading local business people make up the board of directors. The boards maintain their integrity and continuity by controlling the appointments of new directors. They generally take a strongly conservative investment attitude, reflecting the safety requirements of their depositors.

Mutual savings banks play an active and important role in *local* real estate financing activities, providing long-term mortgage loans. This is a natural consequence of the nature of their organization, for these banks are actually savings institutions. More than 70 percent of their assets are derived from savings accounts, which by definition have a long-term quality.

Mutual savings banks prefer to make real estate loans on properties located near their home offices so that the loans can be supervised efficiently. In those instances where a bank's funds exceed local mortgage market demands, out-of-state mortgage outlets are sought, mostly through mortgage bankers.

Mutual savings banks generally are limited in their lending activities by their charters. These limitations vary from state to state and are also further affected by specific bank policies. Usually, only 60 percent to 70 percent of total savings deposits may be invested in real estate mortgages, and then mostly within restricted lending boundaries and predominantly in residential properties. These area restrictions were originally imposed to ease loan servicing requirements, among other purposes. However, with the increasing scope and safety of the national mortgage market through the activities and services of Fannie Mae, Ginnie Mae, and Freddie Mac, some mutual savings banks are beginning to relax their territorial restrictions. In addition, relaxed regulations are allowing them to expand their activities to include more commercial banking services.

Although mutual savings banks play a relatively small role in actual dollar amounts in the total national real estate loan market, they do provide important local real estate loan support, and they were the prototype for the savings associations/thrifts.

SAVINGS ASSOCIATIONS/THRIFTS

Legend has it that the savings and loan associations, now known as savings banks or **thrifts,** were born when ten friends got together, each of them contributing $1,000 to a pot. Each contributor then drew a number from a bowl, with number one having the use of the $10,000 for a prescribed time period, then number two, and so on. This legend is not too far from the truth, because the early institutions were established as *building and loan associations,* having as their specific purpose the provision of loans to their depositors for housing construction.

IN PRACTICE . . .

Jim Smith, a local builder, wishes to obtain financing to build six houses. He first checks with his own credit union—it is a fairly small credit union and they do not finance construction or home mortgage loans.

Jim then calls his insurance agent and finds that they are only interested in much larger projects—in which they might actually acquire some ownership interest. His own home mortgage loan is with a local savings bank so he meets with a loan officer there. He finds that the savings bank would be interested in providing loans for the eventual buyers of the six properties, but the savings bank is not interested in construction financing.

Jim finally goes to a large commercial bank and is successful in acquiring a construction loan. In fact, the commercial bank offers him a construction/permanent loan product that will provide the construction financing now, and guarantee the availability of permanent financing for the mortgage loans required by the buyers of the finished properties.

Thrifts are organized as either stock or mutual companies. Many mutual associations have converted to stock companies to attract more capital. These thrifts were relatively free from public regulation until the creation of the Federal Home Loan Bank System (FHLB) in 1932. Paralleling the Federal Reserve System for the commercial banks, the FHLB was chartered to regulate member organizations, determine their reserve requirements, set discount rates, and provide insurance for their depositors.

The FHLB operates the 12 district banks which are regulated by the Federal Housing Board. The member savings associations are chartered and regulated by the Office of Thrift Supervision (OTS). The accounts are insured up to $100,000 per title per account by the Savings Association Insurance Fund (SAIF) under the Federal Deposit Insurance Corporation (FDIC).

All savings banks must be chartered, either by the OTS or by the state in which they are located. All federally chartered savings banks are required to participate in the federal FDIC insurance program.

Mortgage Lending Activities

Of all the financial fiduciaries, savings banks still have the most flexibility in their mortgage lending operations. Although some limitations are imposed by federal or state regulations, savings banks can make conventional mortgage loans for up to 100 percent of a property's value. More commonly, though, the loans are based on an 80 percent loan-to-value ratio with private mortgage insurance (PMI) required for any loan with higher than an 80 percent LTV (loan-to-value). Any limitation on the area in which loans can be made has been virtually eliminated by the ability of savings banks to participate in the national mortgage market through Freddie Mac and Fannie Mae. Savings banks also participate in the FHA-VA loan market, but only to a limited extent.

Paralleling the growing movement in small commercial bank start-ups is a marked increase in applications to the OTS for charters to operate new savings banks. The only way for companies that aren't commercial banks to enter into the full service banking business is to secure a savings bank charter. This charter can be owned by any type of company and a federal charter enables the new savings bank to operate in all 50 states. The OTS is currently reviewing applications from insurance companies and securities dealers as well as applications from manufacturers, retailers, and others.

LIFE INSURANCE COMPANIES

Life Ins. Co.'s ARE NOT A Primary Lender

In the United States a large portion of the savings is in the hands of life insurance companies. Until the growth of savings banks, life insurance companies were the most important depositories of institutional savings in the United States. They control about 12 percent of all savings, second only to the savings banks, and they predominate commercial realty loans. Life insurance companies have always played a major role in the real estate mortgage market. Approximately 30 percent of their assets are invested in all types of real estate loans.

Although there are no national laws concerning life insurance or casualty insurance companies, each state regulates these companies under their departments of insurance. Life insurance and casualty companies can raise premium rates with permission from these state agencies—based on the amount needed to pay current claims and the earnings of the portfolio for future claims.

Life insurance companies are less concerned with the liquidity than with the safety and long-term stability of an investment. As illustrated in Figure 5.1, they prefer to finance larger real estate projects like shopping centers, leaving to other lenders smaller loans such as home mortgages and construction financing.

Today, however, they are also active in financing single-family homes, filling a gap created by the troubled savings and loan industry. Many of these smaller loans are made through the services of mortgage brokers and bankers.

Many life insurance companies try to enhance the profitability and safety of their positions by insisting on equity positions in any major commercial project they finance. As a condition for such a loan, the company requires a partnership arrangement with the project developer. This type of financing is called **participation financing,** and it serves to expand the life insurance companies' investment portfolios. Life insurance companies also purchase blocks of single-family mortgages or securities from the secondary mortgage market.

The continuing popularity of term insurance provides life insurance companies billions of dollars on which they do not pay dividends. This allows these companies to participate competitively in the real estate mortgage market, and life insurance companies play an indispensable role in providing funds for real estate developments.

PENSION AND RETIREMENT PROGRAMS

Monies held in pension funds have similarities to the premiums collected and held by life insurance companies. Pension monies are collected routinely, usually from payroll deductions, and are held in trust until needed at retirement. They are not usually distributed in a lump sum but in regular payments, mostly on a monthly basis. This gives the pension fund managers a substantial amount of fixed funds together with a continuous flow of new monies.

Historically, pension monies were invested in government securities and corporate stocks and bonds, with little going into mortgage lending. Since the advent of the secondary

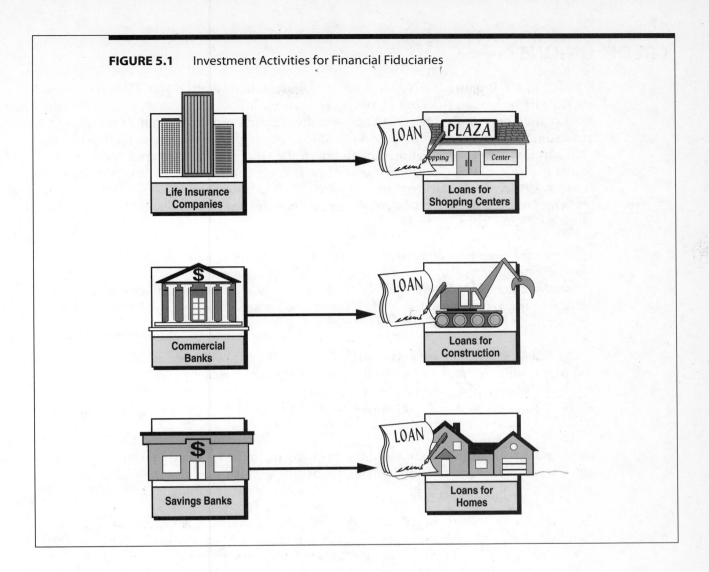

FIGURE 5.1   Investment Activities for Financial Fiduciaries

mortgage market, pension fund managers have increasingly been purchasing blocks of mortgage-backed securities.

Pension funds form a considerable potential source of capital for the nation's financial markets. Their direct participation in real estate mortgages clearly has increased, although it seems that government-administered plans are less likely than private plans to invest in mortgage lending. The former are geared to purchasing government securities; the latter could take advantage of the mortgage banking system and the opportunities for mortgage investments.

Currently, pension funds comprise about 24 percent ($177 billion) of the total real estate equity market. Generally loan-to-value ratios do not exceed 50 percent, and investments range between $75 million to $150 million. Some funds joint venture with other large lenders, and a few place loans on more specific projects such as student housing, senior living facilities, and self-storage projects to generate higher yields.

CREDIT UNIONS

more flexible than banks—

Created in 1970 under the National Credit Union Administration (NCUA), the 11,000-plus **credit unions** in the United States are non-profit financial organizations into which worker members deposit their savings, usually through regular payroll deductions. The attraction of these organizations is their ability to pay higher interest rates on deposits than conventional savings associations. In addition, they offer their members a wide variety of loans, at interest rates often below that of their competitors. Credit union members may borrow money—on their personal property, such as autos and furniture; for home improvements; on their real estate equity; to purchase real estate; on second mortgages; and on participation loans.

Until recently, credit unions were prohibited by court rulings to reach out for new members beyond their existing membership base. Congress reversed this ban with the Credit Union Membership Access Act effective January 1999. Now credit unions may solicit new memberships. In addition, the NCUA board of directors expanded membership eligibility to household occupants of existing members.

These changes have allowed small business groups to join credit unions as well as any person who resides in a member's household including unmarried couples, live-in housekeepers, nursing care professionals, or anyone who contributes support to the household. Moreover, all immediate family members may also be eligible to join, greatly expanding credit union growth potential.

Credit unions are serious competition to the banking industry. They generally are not governed by federal, state, or local banking regulations, which provides them great flexibility in making loans. They have been aggressively marketing their equity and real estate loans.

Although credit unions specialize in personal property loans, it is expected that they will continue to expand their participation in real estate finance as they offer highly competitive interest rates and low loan placement fees. The credit unions are also involved in the secondary markets by pooling their mortgage loans into various real estate mortgage investment conduits (REMICS).

SUMMARY

The organizations designed to hold deposits are called financial fiduciaries. The fiduciary relationship includes an obligation on the part of the institution to represent and serve its depositors with professional responsibility and integrity. The major financial fiduciaries, also known as financial intermediaries, are commercial banks, mutual savings banks, savings associations or thrifts, life insurance companies, pension and retirement funds, and credit unions. Because these organizations are fiduciaries, they usually display conservative investment attitudes compatible with their roles as guardians and protectors of their depositors' and premium payers' money.

Commercial banks participate in real estate finance mainly as short-term lenders, preferring to maintain their liquidity while at the same time maximizing their earnings by trading in commercial paper. Through their mortgage loan departments, however, commercial banks are also active in construction loans, home improvement loans, and mobile home mortgages—all relatively short-term investments. In addition, through their trust departments,

Sources of Funds: Semifiduciary and Nonfiduciary

▼ KEY TERMS

bearer bonds
combination or hybrid
    trusts
correspondents
cosign
coupon bond
debentures
equity trust

vs.

general obligation bonds
industrial revenue bonds
junior financing
line of credit
mortgage bankers
mortgage brokers
mortgage revenue
    bonds

municipal bonds
real estate investment
    trusts (REITs)
real estate mortgage
    trusts (REMTs)
warehouse of funds
zero coupon bonds

SEMIFIDUCIARY LENDERS

The second general source of funds for real estate finance is a group known as *financial semifiduciaries*. This group is composed of real estate mortgage brokers and bankers, real estate mortgage and investment trusts, and real estate bond dealers. Some semifiduciaries arrange mortgages between the major fiduciary lenders and borrowers, while others make direct loans using their own funds.

Unlike banks, thrifts, life insurance companies, pension funds, and credit unions, which are directly responsible to their depositors and premium payers, the semifiduciaries are removed from a first-person relationship. The *quality of a fiduciary relationship* is somewhat implicit in their actions, but the semifiduciaries' responsibilities are directed either internally, to their owner-partners, or externally, to the primary fiduciaries they represent. They are never directly responsible to any depositors or premium payers. Although a semifiduciary is expected to invest entrusted funds with sound judgment, no guarantee is given that the money will be returned dollar for dollar, as is the case in a primary fiduciary relationship. The distinction is quite fine, but it allows the semifiduciaries to take more risks than the primary financial fiduciaries.

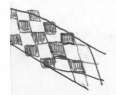

Mortgage Brokers and Bankers

Often financial fiduciaries lack the monetary capacity to expand beyond their local markets. However, various commercial banks and thrifts do accumulate assets that exceed local needs. When this occurs, these institutions look to the regional and national mortgage markets provided by Fannie Mae, Ginnie Mae, and Freddie Mac for expanded investment opportunities. These institutions also use the services of mortgage brokers and mortgage bankers.

Likewise, life insurance companies and pension fund managers enlist the aid of mortgage brokers or mortgage bankers to originate and service some of their real estate loans at the local level, rather than maintain an expensive network of branch offices. Similarly, investment trusts and individuals make mortgage loans with the aid and services of these local mortgage brokers and mortgage bankers.

Mortgage Brokers.   Much as a stockbroker or a real estate broker acts to bring buyers and sellers together to complete a transaction for which the broker is duly compensated, a mortgage broker joins borrowers with lenders for a real estate loan. The successful completion of the loan entitles the mortgage broker to earn a placement fee. The successful placement of a $1 million loan at a 2 percent fee would result in a mortgage broker earning $20,000. Because the larger the loan, the larger the fee, most **mortgage brokers** specialize in loans for large residential and commercial realty projects. More recently mortgage brokers have also become active in the single-family home loan market.

Unlike the major fiduciary lenders, a mortgage broker seldom invests capital in a loan and does not service a loan beyond its placement. After a loan "marriage" is completed, specific arrangements are made for the collection of the required payments. Usually these payments are made directly to the lender, but often they are collected by a local escrow collection service. The mortgage broker fulfills all obligations when the loan is completed.

Although mortgage brokers are semifiduciaries, it is important that they assume a large part of the responsibility for qualifying borrowers and investigating the soundness of an investment. In fact, their very business lives depend on the quality of the loans recommended. Thus, an informal fiduciary relationship occurs when mortgage brokers conscientiously qualify loans before submitting them to lenders.

A borrower seeking the services of a mortgage broker depends on the broker's access to the many fiduciary institutions that participate in real estate lending. A mortgage broker's success is a function of two things: accessibility to the offices of the major real estate lenders and the ability to "sell" the loan to these lenders. If the loan appears initially to be a poor risk, a broker would be destroying his or her long-run effectiveness with a recommendation.

The National Association of Mortgage Brokers, located at 8201 Greensboro Dr., Suite 300, McLean, VA 22102, 703-610-9009, www.namb.org, is the first trade organization for this group. Emphasizing adherence to a strict code of ethics, this association promotes a full range of educational programs for its members. In addition, it endorses the licensing of mortgage brokers.

The scope of mortgage brokerage activities ranges from the plush offices of the large national firms, to the commercial banks' mortgage loan departments, which often originate loans for other fiduciary lenders, to the real estate broker, who arranges a loan between a property buyer and a lender. Regardless of the operation's size, however, if the

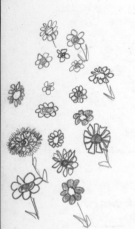

[handwritten margin notes]

Mortgage Banker
Has a primary responsibility to the depositor

Mortgage Broker
has a primary responsibility to the lender. considered a semifiduciary

intermediary receives a fee for mortgage placement services, he or she is acting as a mortgage broker.

Mortgage Bankers. Many lenders seek to make real estate loans on properties located far from where they can personally supervise the loans. However, it is desirable to observe the physical condition of the collateral carefully, as well as to be available in the event of loan collection difficulties. Therefore mortgage lenders, also known as *investors,* seek the services of local semifiduciary intermediaries, called **mortgage bankers,** or **correspondents.** These intermediaries not only originate new loans but also collect payments, periodically inspect the collateral involved, and supervise a foreclosure, if necessary. Mortgage bankers literally *manage real estate loans.*

Operation. Mortgage banking is not "banking" in the traditional sense. There are no tellers, cashiers, checking accounts, savings accounts, safe deposit boxes, or depositors. Mortgage bankers sometimes lend their own money or borrow from a commercial bank, which is why they are called mortgage "bankers." This is one important distinction between mortgage lenders and mortgage brokers. Some banks and bank holding companies own subsidiary mortgage banking companies to expand their latitude in creating and servicing their loans. Some larger companies are even going public, but most mortgage banking companies are privately owned. As private entrepreneurs, they derive income from fees received for originating and servicing real estate loans. The more loans they place in their books, the greater their income. Therefore, the mortgage banker is under constant pressure to secure new business with which to earn substantial origination fees and increase service collection accounts.

Most mortgage bankers maintain a high community profile, taking active roles in social, political, and humanitarian efforts within their geographic regions. They also cultivate friendships with local land developers, builders, and real estate brokers to establish mutually beneficial associations. At the same time, most successful mortgage bankers develop a large retinue of mortgage loan investment companies, which they represent in a specific locale. Thus, the mortgage banker assumes the role of an intermediary, searching out and developing new mortgage business, originating loans, selling the loans to investors, and collecting the payments on the loans for the benefit of the investors. Some of the larger mortgage banking companies maintain hazard insurance and escrow departments in addition to their loan origination and servicing divisions. Some also write life insurance and act as real estate brokers, appraisers, and investment counselors.

Although the mortgage banking industry is regulated under specific state laws, it is less regulated than banks because, in effect, mortgage bankers are not lending depositors' monies. In fact, mortgage bankers most often lend their own monies, or monies that they borrow from banks, to place new loans. These loans are then pooled into homogeneous "packages" that satisfy the requirements of specific loan investors as to loan amounts and property locations. Such packages are then sold to these investors, while the mortgage banker retains the servicing contract.

Mortgage bankers are involved with every type of real estate loan. They can finance every stage of a real estate development—from providing funds to a developer to purchase, improve, subdivide the land, and construct buildings thereon to providing the final permanent long-term mortgages for individuals to buy these homes. In fact, a mortgage banker provides the expertise, money, and commitment necessary for the success of many real estate projects, both residential and commercial.

IN PRACTICE . . .

Mary is a loan officer for Adams Home Lending Company, which is a subsidiary of Adams Mutual Savings Bank. Mary is currently working with a young couple who are trying to purchase their first home. Unfortunately, they have run up some rather large amounts on their five credit cards and their overall credit picture is not too good.

However, Mary feels that there are some significant compensating factors that should make it possible for them to get their loan approved. Because Mary is a loan officer for Adams Home Lending Company, mortgage bankers representing Adams Mutual Savings Bank, she is well aware of the qualifying stand-ards required by the investor and will be able to work directly with the underwriter to try to make this loan work. If Mary was a loan officer for a company acting as a mortgage broker, she would not have such direct access to the source of funding for the loan and might not be as successful in working with the underwriter. On the other hand, as the mortgage banker is limited to its primary source of funding, there might not be as wide a range of programs available as there would be if Mary worked for a mortgage broker where she would be able to "shop around" to find a loan product that would fit the young couple's needs.

The mortgage banker's financial activities are based largely on the investors' commitments as to the quantity and required yields of mortgages to be placed in a particular community. For example, Metropolitan Life Insurance Company may want to invest $50 million in multiunit apartment projects in a specific community. The company may specify a certain interest rate and that no single mortgage may be less than $10 million or more than $20 million. Its representative mortgage banker would then seek to lend these funds on economically feasible projects to qualified borrowers. The mortgage banker must first negotiate, document, appraise, analyze, submit, and seek approval for a particular loan from Met Life, who, in turn, issues a mortgage commitment to the mortgage banker who then issues a commitment to the developer.

The mortgage banker in this example typically might begin by making a commitment to a builder for a permanent loan on the apartment buildings to be built. This commitment would be based on the value of the property as estimated from the builder's plans and specifications. The banker would stipulate that a certain sum of money be loaned under the specific terms and conditions of payment, interest, and time.

On the strength of this commitment, the builder would be able to obtain a construction loan from a fiduciary lender, usually a commercial bank. This construction loan would be repaid from the permanent loan proceeds when the project was completed. When the total of these loans satisfied the $50 million commitment of Metropolitan Life, they would be sold as a package to this investor, who would then reimburse the mortgage banker. The banker would probably retain the responsibilities of collecting and supervising the loans.

Mortgage bankers often lack the financial capacity to lend the monies necessary to develop a "package" for their final investors because these investors will not send the mortgage banker any funds until the packages are accumulated. The mortgage banker will usually seek the aid of a *commercial banker*, who will, in turn, make a commitment to the mortgage banker to lend certain sums of money during the construction period until funds are received from the investors for mortgage settlements. This is called a **line of credit**. These short-term loans fit perfectly into the commercial banks' requirements, and essentially

these banks become "warehouses" for mortgage money. Now the mortgage banker can draw down on the committed **warehouse of funds,** paying the commercial bank's interest requirement until the final funding from the investor satisfies the warehouse commitment. For example, the mortgage banker could borrow the monies from a commercial bank to close the loans with various borrowers until such time as Met Life took delivery of the loans and funded them. Thus, the financial fiduciaries and semifiduciaries complement each other's activities.

There is substantial and constant competition in the mortgage lending business. Depending to a great degree on the status of the money markets, the mortgage bankers compete with local savings banks, commercial banks, real estate investment trusts, and other mortgage bankers for a share of the market. The Mortgage Bankers Association (MBA) is headquartered at 1919 Pennsylvania Avenue, Washington, DC, 20006-3438, and is active in promoting homebuyer education, often cooperating with local or state housing organizations. (Call at 800-793-2222 or on the Internet at www.mbaa.org.)

Real Estate Trusts

Born under the provisions of the Real Estate Investment Trust Act of 1960, real estate trusts are designed to provide vehicles by which real estate investors can enjoy the special income tax benefits already granted to mutual funds and other regulated investment companies. The earnings of regular corporations are taxed at the corporate level and then again at the individual level when distributed as dividends to stockholders. The real estate trusts have only a single tax, imposed at the beneficiary level. There are three types of real estate trusts: (1) the real estate investment trust (REIT), also known as an equity trust; (2) the real estate mortgage trust (REMT); and (3) the combination or hybrid trust, which is a mixture of the investment and mortgage trusts.

To qualify as a trust, the following eight basic requirements must be met:

1. The trust must not hold property primarily for sale to customers in the ordinary course of business.
2. The trust must be beneficially owned by at least 100 investors.
3. The trust must not have fewer than five persons who own more than 50 percent of the beneficial interest.
4. The trust's beneficial interests must be evidenced by transferable shares or certificates of interest.
5. 95 percent of the trust's gross income must be derived from its investments.
6. 75 percent of the trust's gross income must be derived from real estate investments.
7. No more than 30 percent of the trust's gross income may result from sales of stocks and securities held for less than 12 months or from the sale of real estate held for less than four years.
8. 95 percent of the trust's gross income must be distributed in the year it is earned, in the form of dividends, and thereby the trust does not owe federal income taxes at the corporate level.

Real estate trusts are classified as semifiduciaries in real estate finance because their investment decisions are generally entrepreneurial in design. As with a mutual fund in the stock market, where the value of the stock is primarily a reflection of the success of the fund's managerial decisions, the value of a beneficial interest in an investment trust is also a measurement of the profitability of that enterprise. If the investment trust is a successful entity, the beneficiaries profit accordingly. However, if the investment trust fails, the beneficiaries' investments are lost. Thus, although the quality of a fiduciary relationship is implicit between the investment trust managers and the beneficiaries of a trust, investment decisions are made in a relatively unregulated manner, and high risks ride in tandem with potentially high-profit investments.

Real Estate Investment Trusts (REITs). Designed to deal in equities, **real estate investment trusts (REITs)** are owners of improved income properties, including apartments, office buildings, shopping centers, and industrial parks. As an **equity trust**, the REIT can offer small investors opportunities to pool their monies to participate as owners of larger and, hopefully, more efficient and profitable real estate investments. The REIT's income is derived from two sources: (1) the net profits secured from its rental investment properties and (2) the capital gains made when these properties are sold. All profits are subject to income tax but only at the participant's level.

REIT is a mutual fund

As REITs are designed as a form of "mutual fund," it passes rental income directly through to shareholders with no tax imposed at the REIT level. In exchange for avoiding the double income taxes paid by business corporations and their stockholders, REITs are expected to be strictly passive investors.

However, some more ingenious REIT executives have found a way to overcome the limitations on active business operations. They have created the "stapled" or "paired-shared" REIT structures involving the combination of two separate entities, one a regular (C) Corporation and the other a REIT, trading the two as a single unit.

Under this technique, the REIT can acquire active property investments such as hotels, which normally cannot be operated directly by REITs. The REIT then leases the property to the (C) Corporation to operate without limitations. Alternatively, the (C) Corporation may own and operate such active income investments and pay the REIT a portion of the profits in the form of interest on a loan made by the REIT, secured by the investment property.

Continued exploitation of this process has forced Congress to pass legislation providing that stapled or paired entities must be treated as a single company when it comes to qualifying under the REIT rules. It is expected that more stringent legislation will be approved to force the REITs to observe the passive investment requirement.

REITs have grown to be a significant participant in the real estate market, acquiring billions of dollars in commercial property equities. After building up prices around the country for the past few years, REIT's activities have recently been curtailed by their declining stock prices. They are no longer viewed as growth stocks as a result of rising acquisition prices, stable occupancy levels, and new supply and demand concerns. Not willing to issue stock at depressed prices, nor able to borrow more and increase their debt ratios to dangerous levels, the REITs have settled into being known as good dividend payers. Analysts predict a relatively stable future for the REITs in the 2000s. However, if new investor capital fails to flow into the industry, REIT viability may be threatened.

Real Estate Mortgage Trusts (REMTs). More significant to mortgage lending are the **real estate mortgage trusts (REMTs)**. Attracting millions of dollars through the sale of beneficial shares, REMTs expand their financial bases with strong credit at their commercial banks and make mortgage loans on commercial income properties. Many of these are properties constructed for the investment portfolios of REITs. In fact, many REMTs are owned by either a parent company REIT or a commercial bank.

The REMTs' main sources of income are mortgage interest, loan origination fees, and profits earned from buying and selling mortgages. Although these trusts participate in long-term permanent financing, they are more inclined to invest in short-term senior and junior loans, where higher potential profits prevail.

Combination (Hybrid) Trusts. **Combination or hybrid trusts** join real estate equity investing with mortgage lending, thus earning profits from rental income and capital gains as well as mortgage interest and placement fees. REITs chartered today seek approval to invest in real estate *and* finance real estate whether or not they intend to do both.

Real Estate Bonds

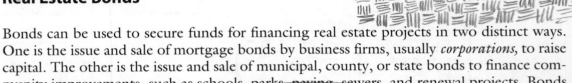

Bonds can be used to secure funds for financing real estate projects in two distinct ways. One is the issue and sale of mortgage bonds by business firms, usually *corporations,* to raise capital. The other is the issue and sale of municipal, county, or state bonds to finance community improvements, such as schools, parks, paving, sewers, and renewal projects. Bonds in the latter group are termed collectively **municipal bonds.** Figure 6.1 illustrates various types of bonds used in mortgage lending.

The administration of funds raised by a bond sale is left in the hands of a *trustee,* who acts as an intermediary between the borrower (issuer) and the bond owners (purchaser-lenders). The trustee supervises the collection of payments from the borrower and makes disbursements to the appropriate bondholders.

If the borrower defaults on a real estate bond, the trustee files a notice with the borrower that the entire balance and the interest are immediately due in full. At the same time, upon declaration that the borrower cannot or will not satisfy the debt, the trustee may enter the property, dispossess the borrower, and manage or sell it. All income or sales proceeds will apply to the benefit of the bond owners because, in effect, the trustee is their semifiduciary representative.

The Nature of Bonds. Corporate bonds are credit instruments used to raise long-term funds. When these bonds are backed by a mortgage on specifically described real property, they are called *secured bonds.* When a company issues bonds that are a claim against its general assets, they are called *unsecured bonds* or **debentures.**

Corporate bonds are also classified according to their method of payment. **Coupon bonds** have interest coupons attached, which are removed as they become due and are cashed by the bearer. Interest is paid to the person possessing the coupon, so these bonds are also called **bearer bonds.** *Registered bonds* are issued to a specific owner and cannot be transferred without the owner's endorsement. Under this form of bond, interest is paid to the last registered owner.

Bonds can be classified further as to the nature of the issuer—for instance, railroad bonds, industrial bonds, or corporate bonds. They are often described by the nature of their security, such as mortgage bonds, income bonds, or guaranteed bonds, or by their

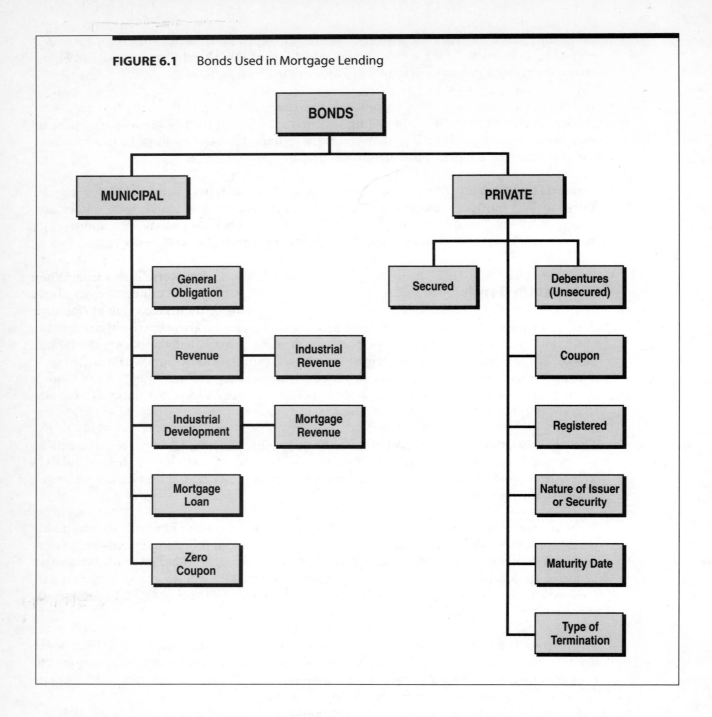

FIGURE 6.1   Bonds Used in Mortgage Lending

maturity date, as in long-term, short-term, or perpetual bonds. In addition, bonds may be classified by their type of termination—for instance, convertible, redeemable, serial, or sinking fund bonds. Finally, they may be classified by their purpose—for example, refunding, construction, equipment, or improvement bonds.

The issue of corporate bonds to raise funds for real estate capital improvements, such as plant expansion or new equipment acquisition, is a relatively costly approach when compared to the use of mortgages. To float a new bond issue successfully, a corporation must secure the services of an investment banker or broker, print bonds (usually in $1,000 denominations), and pay fees in advance to the appropriate regulating agencies as well as to the issuing brokerage house. The success of a new bond issue is usually underwritten by the investment company because, in effect, it promises to buy all the bonds not sold. The effectiveness of a bond sale depends on the yields designated to be paid to the purchasers, as well as the available supply of investment money. Underlying the entire process are the financial credibility of the issuing company and the value of the collateral property involved.

A large company, such as General Motors, could easily float a debenture or unsecured bond issue, while smaller companies would have difficulty even in issuing secured bonds. The investment broker is responsible for advising which bonds to market, what interest rates to pay, and what prices the bonds should have, according to specific money market conditions.

After the bonds are sold, their values fluctuate with the money market. For instance, if market interest rates rise, the value of the bonds issued at a lower interest rate decreases accordingly. To compete with higher market interest rates, the face value of these bonds would be discounted if the bond owner wished to sell them. The reverse is also true. When interest rates drop below those being paid on existing bonds, their value increases above their face amount. Thus, bonds may be worth 95 percent of their face value at one time and 105 percent at another, depending on market conditions. This effectively changes the yield on bonds to more or less than the stated rate of interest, depending on the bonds' sales price.

Bonds are rated according to the financial security of their issuers. Investment rating services, such as Standard and Poor's, Moody's, and Fitch's, constantly watch the major companies and report their financial conditions as they reflect on the companies' ability to pay their debts when due. Bonds with the highest ratings are considered by buyers to be safe investments and thus are not discounted to any major degree. Bonds with lower ratings usually are traded at greater discounts to reflect their higher risks.

Municipal and Private Bonds. A popular use for real estate bonds is to finance municipal improvement projects. By issuing **general obligation bonds,** guaranteed by the taxing power and the full faith and credit of the community, governments can raise funds for financing schools, street improvements, sewer installations, park developments, and other civic improvement projects.

A variation on this theme is the issue of *revenue bonds* to fund a specific community improvement project. These bonds will be repaid from the revenues generated by the improvements. For instance, a toll bridge could be constructed using the money raised from the sale of revenue bonds, and the repayment of the bonds would be designed to match the revenue secured from the tolls collected.

An illustration of the role of such revenue bonds in mortgage lending is their possible use in developing employment centers for a community. For instance, a city could float revenue bonds to develop an industrial park or construct buildings that might be leased to commercial tenants. These bonds are known as **industrial revenue bonds.** The rental income from the buildings would be adequate to repay the bonds over a long period of time. By this process new jobs are created, new taxes are generated, and generally an impetus of growth is infused into the community. Additional revenue bonds and other incentives can then be used by these growth-oriented communities to attract more businesses to their industrial parks.

Industrial Development Bonds. Unlike industrial revenue bonds, which are issued by a municipality for public improvements, *industrial development bonds* allow private investors an opportunity to finance apartment and commercial developments by using tax-exempt, and thus relatively inexpensive, funds. The developer prepares an application for approval by a local city or county Industrial Development Authority (IDA). This application includes the plans for the apartment or commercial development and a statement describing the need for these units to enhance the community's welfare. The bond attorney for the IDA reviews the application and makes a recommendation to the all-volunteer board.

If approval is secured, the developer hires a bond broker and floats a new issue. The interest rate is determined by the broker as a function of the market with the earnings exempted from federal, and often state, income taxes.

Mortgage Revenue Bonds. Mortgage revenue bonds are a form of industrial development bond. The bond issue is tax exempt because it is offered by state and local governments through their housing financing agencies. Use for the proceeds of the bond sales are limited to financing segments of the housing markets, such as low-income buyers, first-time buyers, and so on. Other limitations are imposed as well, such as the prices of homes eligible for participation in the bond program and the income of the borrowers.

The government agency transfers the proceeds of the bond sale to the lender, who then makes a mortgage loan to the developer of the project. Because of the tax exemption on income derived by the bondholders, interest to the borrower is lower than market rates, and rents can be lowered accordingly. In addition, 20 percent of the units must be allocated for low-income renters for ten years or half the life of the loan, whichever is longer.

A significant portion of the senior housing market, assisted living care facilities, can now be financed with tax-exempt revenue bonds so long as the project does not provide continual or frequent medical or nursing services according to IRS rule 98-47. The ruling states that these are residential rental properties and eligible for the bonding finance.

Zero Coupon Bonds. Also known as *zero treasuries,* **zero coupon bonds** represent an old approach to bond buying that has been introduced into the money market. They are patterned after World War II savings bonds, which were sold for $18.75 and redeemed after ten years for $25. A buyer writes a check for a bond at a discounted price and holds this bond until maturity or until it is sold, with interest compounding regularly. Interest must be reported each year for tax purposes even though it is not collectible until the bond matures. This is called an *original issue discount (OID).*

Some housing developers offer such bonds as gifts to entice the hesitant to buy a home. By holding the bond until the loan is paid in 30 years, the owner can recover the entire cost of the house in cash. For example, a 30-year, 10-percent $60,000 face value bond can be purchased for $3,420 today and will yield $60,000 in 30 years.

Mortgage Loan Bonds. Some states issue income-tax-free bonds to secure funds for relatively low-cost mortgage loans. These loans are available to eligible persons to help them acquire homes and condominium apartments. The interest income from these bonds is tax exempt at both the federal and state levels, so their purchasers can buy them at lower rates than would be required on taxable investments. These savings are passed along to the borrowers, who will pay slightly higher interest rates on their loans than are paid to the bondholders to cover operational costs. Thus, although the entire program is designed to be self-supporting, it does pass the subsidizing effect over the entire country and the state involved through the loss of income tax revenue.

NONFIDUCIARY LENDERS

Another group of lenders that provides funds for mortgage lending are the *financial non-fiduciaries*. This group includes individuals and private loan companies. Little precise data are available about the overall impact of nonfiduciary lenders in the realty money market because of the relatively private nature of the participants' transactions. Because these nonfiduciaries invest their own funds in real estate finance, they owe no duty to others and can maintain complete discretion over their activities.

Despite this comparative freedom to make all final decisions, nonfiduciaries observe certain limitations. Nobody invests to lose money, so good underwriting practices must be followed. Nevertheless, of all the lenders in the field of mortgage lending, the nonfiduciaries have the most flexibility and can take the most risks. This often makes them the only source available to finance certain real estate transactions.

Individuals

When other financing is not available, the sellers of property often have to provide the funds to close the deal. Arrangements for seller-financing are usually made in the negotiations directly between the buyer and seller.

Sellers as Lenders. The single most important source of nonfiduciary finance funds consists of the sellers who finance a portion of the sales price with carryback loans. In fact, seller financing has become the only way many sales can be consummated. Using junior loans, contracts for deed, wraparounds, and other creative financing devices (described in later chapters), sellers often help finance a portion of a property's sales price.

Some loans made directly between buyers-borrowers and sellers-lenders involve first mortgages. For instance, when the property being sold has been held free and clear of any debt, the seller might carry back a new first mortgage from the buyer for most of the purchase price. If a free and clear house sold for $80,000, and the buyer made a $20,000 cash down payment, the seller could carry back the balance of $60,000 with a new purchase-money first mortgage, executed according to agreed-upon terms and conditions.

However, most individual financial agreements involve junior financing where the seller carries back a *portion* of the equity in the property. For example, if a house is selling for $80,000 and the current balance on the existing mortgage is $55,000, the seller might agree to carry back $15,000 of the $25,000 equity as a second mortgage if the buyer agrees to pay $10,000 as a cash down payment.

Sellers agreeing to carry back a portion of their equity as a junior loan subject to an existing senior loan must be aware of the risk that the buyers may not keep up the payments on the senior loan. This would put the sellers in jeopardy of losing their junior loan equity. To offset this risk, a collection escrow should be established at the time of the sale and the buyers should be required to send both the senior and junior loan payments to the collection agent with directions for immediate notification to the sellers if these payments are not forthcoming.

Family Members as Lenders. Homebuyers, especially those with small children, may find they do not have the funds necessary to meet down payment requirements. They invariably look to their parents or other family members for help. Under these circumstances, a letter from the "donors" indicating the amount of the "gift" is delivered to the loan officer who is preparing the new loan package. In some cases, the donors are required to **cosign** the mortgage documents in order to include their own financial resources as additional collateral.

These arrangements often can be established as partnerships in which the parents, as co-owners, make the down payment and the "children" agree to make all the monthly payments on the mortgage. If the property is refinanced or sold in the future, the partners will share in the proceeds.

Based on the 2002 tax law that allows anyone to make an annual tax-free gift of up to $11,000, some parents can greatly aid their children in purchasing a home. Thus, a married couple could accept up to $44,000 in tax-free gifts: $11,000 from each parent to each of the children.

Private Loan Companies

Privately owned loan companies are proliferating throughout this country. They range from the large national company with branches in almost every city to the individual entrepreneur who may personally buy and sell loans. These private lenders deal primarily in **junior financing** arrangements that use a borrower's equity in real property as collateral. This type of junior financing is often used to raise funds for consumer purchases, such as automobiles and furniture.

Although the consumer goods financing companies technically do participate in real estate finance, their activities are too peripheral and sporadic to make them important in this field. However, there are numerous other private loan companies designed to deal exclusively in real estate finance. These companies make loans from their own funds or monies borrowed from their commercial banks, act as mortgage brokers in arranging loans between other lenders and borrowers, and buy and sell junior financing instruments, usually at a discount. In this latter capacity these private real estate loan companies help create a market for investment in junior loans.

Private real estate loan companies usually charge more than other lenders. They attempt to offset the risks inherent in their junior lien position by charging the maximum interest rates allowable by law and imposing high loan placement fees. Many states have developed laws regulating the activities of private lenders. Besides requiring loan companies to obtain licenses and performance bonds, some states limit the amount of fees that these lenders can charge for their services.

OTHER LENDERS

The various foreign funding sources for mortgage lending activities in the United States have not yet been identified clearly. Japan and countries of the Middle East and Europe have billions of dollars on deposit in U.S. banks. Although these monies substantially increase the capacity of these banks to enlarge their loan portfolios, the quality of these funds is still unknown. If they turn out to be relatively short-term funds, they will have little impact on mortgage lending. But if these funds are left on deposit for relatively long periods of time, they may have a profound effect on the monies available for mortgage lending.

SUMMARY

Mortgage brokers act as catalysts in the process of matching borrowers and lenders, a service for which they earn a finder's fee. Fees on residential loans are related to an origination fee and compensation for the servicing of the loan. Fees on commercial loans are related to the time and effort expended in the loan's successful presentation. Once a loan has been finalized, the broker's responsibilities are usually completed.

Mortgage bankers, on the other hand, not only generate new mortgage loans between the major fiduciary lenders and individual borrowers but continue to function as intermediaries. They collect mortgage payments, inspect the condition of collateral, counsel delinquent borrowers, and foreclose when necessary. In addition, mortgage bankers often invest their own funds or borrow money from their banks to finance site acquisitions, land improvements, construction costs, and permanent mortgages in order to complete a full development program. Mortgage bankers also serve as representatives or correspondents for large real estate mortgage investors, such as major insurance companies. These investors rely on mortgage bankers to place new loans and group them into packages that are then sold to the investors while the mortgage bankers retain the service contracts. Thus, the mortgage bankers provide a vehicle for the national distribution of mortgage money.

The real estate trusts, much like the stock market's mutual funds, are depositories for small investors who pool their monies for greater investment flexibility. The investors take a passive role in management and allow the trust's directors to decide on the investment policy.

Some real estate trusts are involved exclusively in equity holdings. These equity trusts are described as real estate investment trusts (REITs), and they purchase property for its income and potential growth in value. Other real estate trusts, defined as real estate mortgage trusts (REMTs), invest primarily in short-term real estate mortgage loans. Some real estate trusts are hybrids that combine equity participation and mortgage investments.

The issue and sale of real estate bonds is an additional source of funds for mortgage lending. Corporations issue bonds to secure money for plant expansion, equipment purchases, and operational expenses. Various governmental bodies issue bonds to raise funds for improvements, such as schools, parks, streets, industrial developments, and sewage plants, to name just a few. The administration of funds raised by a bond sale is left in the hands of a trustee, who supervises the collection of payments from the borrower-issuer and the distribution of dividends to the investors-purchasers.

Stepping in to fill the gaps created by the conservative and quasi-conservative financing attitudes of the fiduciaries and semifiduciaries, the private lenders, both companies and individuals, often provide the funds required to close many real estate transactions. Without their ability to make independent decisions and take extra risks, many real estate transactions would be impossible to complete.

Mon

Instruments of Real Estate Finance

▼ KEY TERMS

acceleration clause
assumed
beneficiary
carryback loans
contract for deed
covenants
cross-defaulting clause
defeasance clause
due-on-sale clause
encumbrance
equitable rights
equity loans
exculpatory clause

junior loans
legal description
lien
lien theory
lifting clause
mortgage
mortgagee
mortgagor
non-recourse clause
note
novation
power of sale
predatory lending

know the difference 100%

prepayment clause
release clause
second mortgage
statutory redemption periods
subject to
subordinate
title theory
trustee
trustor
usury
vendee
vendor

Although many aspects of mortgage lending change frequently, the instruments for executing a real estate loan have remained basically the same. This chapter reviews the broad legal aspects of pledging real estate as collateral for a loan, and examines the form and content of the three instruments used to finance real estate. Actual copies of a *note and deed of trust,* a *note and mortgage,* and a *contract for deed* are reproduced for a more precise understanding of their formats. Standard forms are shown because each state usually has its own statutes stipulating the form and content of these instruments. It is always good practice to consult the laws of the state in which property is located before deciding which finance instrument to employ.

This chapter examines a number of special provisions that can be included in financing instruments to serve the needs of both borrowers and lenders. The final section reviews the instruments used to establish junior financing relationships.

ENCUMBRANCES AND LIENS

[handwritten margin notes: Encumbrance 1) easement 2) public & private restrictions 3) Encroachment]

An **encumbrance** is a right or interest in a property held by one who is not the legal owner of the property. Encumbrances that affect the physical condition of a property may be imposed on a parcel of land without destroying the owner's estate. These physical encumbrances do not prevent the owner from using the property or transferring it. Encumbrances of this type include *easements,* public and private *restrictions,* and *encroachments.*

Almost every parcel of real property has some form of physical encumbrance imposed on it. Most common is the utility easement that provides the accessibility, both under and over the land, for the installation of water, gas, electric, telephone, and sewer services. These easements are recorded agreements between the property owner, usually the original subdivider, and the appropriate agency responsible for the services indicated. These recorded physical encumbrances become "**covenants** that run with the land" and follow the title through its various owners.

A property's title may also be affected by a financial encumbrance called a **lien.** A lien is a charge against a specific property where the property is made the security for the performance of a certain act, usually the repayment of a debt. Thus, deeds of trust, mortgages, and contracts for deed are all forms of liens.

Unlike physical encumbrances, liens are personal in quality, relating owners' economic situations with their real property. Liens can be either *voluntary liens,* such as financing instruments, or *involuntary liens* imposed by law, such as liens for taxes or assessments, mechanics' (construction) liens, and judgment liens. *General liens* apply to all nonexempt property, while *specific liens* apply only to a single property of the debtor.

IN PRACTICE . . .

Sam and Sally are purchasing their first house for $150,000. They are making a down payment of $15,000 with a mortgage loan of $135,000. The mortgage establishes a financial encumbrance on the property. This encumbrance is called a *lien.* Prior to settlement they are informed by the title company handling the closing that there are several other encumbrances on the property:

- The local electric utility company has an easement across the front edge of the property where they have power lines buried that serve that entire block.
- The homeowners association has restrictions against any fencing in the front yard of the house.

- The next door neighbor's fence is encroaching on the property by four inches on one side of the property.

Should any of these be of concern to Sam and Sally? The title company agent explains that the electric company's gross easement and the homeowner association's private restriction are covenants that "run with the land"; in other words, they have been previously granted and automatically transfer along with the conveyance of the property. The question of the neighbor's fence encroaching on their property may need to be resolved before title insurance will be issued.

A mortgage loan secured by a parcel of real estate becomes a specific voluntary lien against the subject property at the time it is recorded at the courthouse of the county where the property is located. Deeds of trust, mortgages, and contracts for deed will be signed by all appropriate parties, acknowledged by a notary, and usually recorded. This recording process is designed to give public notice that a lender has certain lien rights in the property described in the loan instrument.

Lenders' rights are invariably superior to the rights of other subsequently recorded lienholders, with certain special exceptions. These exceptions include the specific liens imposed by local, state, and federal governments for nonpayment of property or income taxes. Otherwise, based on the doctrine of "first in time, first in right," lenders establish a priority lien position on the date their loan document is recorded. In the event of a foreclosure and sale of the collateral, the proceeds of the sale are distributed per the priority of the liens existing against the subject property. Lenders whose loans have the earliest recording dates are said to be in senior lien positions, and their rights take priority over those of all subsequent lienors.

LOAN SECURED BY A REAL ESTATE INTEREST

Any interest in real property can be security for a real estate loan. Most common to real estate finance is the pledge of a fee simple ownership as collateral to back up a promise to repay a money debt. Real property can also be pledged as collateral to secure financial lines of credit or ensure the specific performance of a contract. Fee simple ownership can be enjoyed by individuals, corporations, and various forms of partnerships. Individuals, their assigns, and their heirs can pledge their titles and interests in real estate in exchange for loans. Corporations, as legally created entities, may own real property and can pledge it as collateral for financing purposes. Likewise, various combinations of individuals and corporations that have joined into partnerships to own real properties can pledge their interests in these properties in order to borrow money.

Less-than-freehold interests, such as rental income from property or the leasehold rights of a tenant, can also be used as collateral for a loan. The parties to a life estate can pledge their interests for loans, even though these interests are not fully vested when the loan is secured. Most lenders are aware of the risks involved with such loans.

Other interests in real property can be owned independently from the land itself. Rights to the use of the airspace over a parcel of property fall into this latter category, as do the rights to the use of water and the extraction of oil and minerals from the earth. These rights can be pledged as collateral for a loan, either singly, collectively, or jointly with other properties.

In some instances, personal property is required as additional security to real property pledged as collateral for a loan. Thus, loans for houses might include furnishings as collateral, in addition to the real estate. Commercial property loans might include trade fixtures as mortgage loan collateral.

Title, Lien, and Intermediate Theories

Originally most real estate loans were designed to allow the *lender* to take actual physical possession of the land until the principal sum of the loan and any agreed-upon interest was obtained from the proceeds of the land's production. For all intents and purposes the lender was the owner of the land until the debt was satisfied, at which time ownership and possession were returned to the borrower. Simply put, the lender held title to the collateral.

As the system evolved, the procedure was changed to allow *borrowers* to remain in possession of the land, so long as they kept the terms of the loan agreement. However, the borrower was still required to transfer legal ownership to the lender by placing title to the property in the lender's name. Thus, the lender secured legal title and the borrower retained **equitable rights** in the property.

Concern about who held title to collateral property stemmed from lender demand for guarantee of the return of funds loaned or, at least, a property with value adequate to substitute for funds lost. Here the rights of a lender were superior to the rights of a borrower. The lender could dispossess the borrower *without notice* at the first default of the loan agreement. No compensation was made for any monies already paid to the lender. This concept has evolved into the **title theory** of mortgage lending, which has been adopted in some states.

As time progressed, the laws were modified to reflect the borrower's legal right to redeem property within some reasonable time *after* default. This right, called an *equitable right of redemption,* gave defaulting borrowers time to protect their interests, but it ceased when the property was sold at a foreclosure sale.

To complement these equitable redemption rights, more than half the states have adopted periods for redemption *after* the foreclosure sale. These **statutory periods of redemption** vary from three months to two years, depending on the state.

Through the years, the competition between lenders' and borrowers' rights has shifted dramatically to borrowers. Most states have adopted the **lien theory,** which recognizes the rights of lenders in collateral property as *equitable* rights, while borrowers retain their *legal* rights in their property. Thus, a borrower maintains legal interest in property while pledging it as collateral to a lender who acquires a *lien,* or an equitable interest, in the collateral property in return for the funds lent. In effect the lien theory allows a defaulted borrower to retain possession, title, and all legal rights in the property until the lender perfects the lien against the collateral property, according to legal foreclosure procedures that recognize the borrower's redemption rights. This theory shows quite a shift in the priority of rights.

However, just as excessive power gave rise to abuses by lenders prior to the development of equity of redemption, lien theory, when coupled with the concept of statutory redemption, provides the opportunity for *borrowers* to become abusive. Whereas lenders previously were able to dispossess their borrowers arbitrarily, now defaulted borrowers are often able to remain in possession of their properties for long periods of time without making loan payments. Longer statutory redemption periods have resulted in endless problems for lenders trying to recover their collateral and minimize their losses within a reasonable time.

Therefore, some states have taken a modified position between the title and lien theories. This *intermediate* position allows a lender to take possession of collateral property in the event of a loan default, often without having to wait until foreclosure proceedings have resulted in a possessory judgment. But the lender does not receive title until after the expiration of statutory redemption periods prescribed by law.

General Requirements for a Finance Instrument

Regardless of the theory practiced in a particular state, all borrowers and lenders throughout the United States must observe the same general requirements to protect their rights when making a loan transaction. Real estate loans are contractual agreements that must contain certain basic elements to be valid. All terms of the loan transaction must be formalized in writing. They must include accurate descriptions of the interest and property being pledged as collateral and a complete statement detailing the loan repayment. The parties to the agreement must be legally competent; their consent must be indicated by their signatures, properly attested and affixed to the loan agreement, and a sufficient consideration must be paid.

The three basic instruments used to finance real estate—the note and deed of trust, the note and mortgage, and the contract for deed—all share the requirements listed above, but each has its own unique form and content.

THE NOTE AND DEED OF TRUST (TRUST DEED)

Trustor ①
Trustee ②
Beneficiary ③

A trust is described as a right of property, real or personal, being held by one party for the benefit of another. The parties to a trust include a **trustor,** who grants rights to a **trustee,** who holds the property in trust for a **beneficiary.** In all cases involving the establishment of a real estate trust, an instrument called a *trust deed* is executed by the trustor in order to transfer legal fee ownership, to be held for the beneficiary, in the name of the trustee.

When a trust deed is used for financing real estate it is called a *deed of trust*. The lender-beneficiary usually selects a trustee who, from the trustor-borrower, secures title to the collateral as well as the power to foreclose if necessary.

In title theory states, a deed of trust transfers the title of the collateral to the name of a third-party trustee, who retains this "ownership" position until the terms of the loan are satisfied. In lien and intermediate theory states, title remains with the borrower (trustor), and the trustee acquires only lien rights. If the loan goes into default, the trustee is empowered to foreclose on the collateral property. These foreclosure powers are described in Chapter 14.

Note Used with a Deed of Trust

NOTE w Deed of Trust is a Promisory NOTE

The **note** that accompanies a deed of trust includes the borrower's promise to pay the lender a designated sum under the terms and conditions specified. It also refers to the security of a specific deed of trust given to the trustee as collateral for the loan.

power of Sale
automatic action

In the event of a default under a note for a deed of trust, borrowers have assigned their defenses to the *automatic action* of the laws governing foreclosure of the debt instrument, known as the **power of sale.** This gives lenders the opportunity to secure more readily full legal title to the collateral, even when borrowers abandon their property and disappear. However, borrowers' rights are still protected by law. Lenders are required to give adequate notice to borrowers and allow them an appropriate period in which to redeem their property. This increased foreclosure power is the distinguishing feature between the deed of trust and the mortgage.

A note for a deed of trust must be signed by the borrowers and accepted by the trustees, acknowledging their role as holders of the deed of trust until the terms of the note are fulfilled. This note will not be acknowledged, and only one copy will be signed.

Deed of Trust — conveys property as collateral to secure a loan

An illustration of a deed of trust used as a financing instrument appears in Figure 7.1. In this form the borrower (trustor) conveys property as collateral to a trustee that will hold title on behalf of the lender (the beneficiary) until the terms of the loan are satisfied. When the loan is paid in full, the trustee will reconvey the property to the trustor, as directed by the **release clause.** If the loan goes into default, the trustee will foreclose on the collateral to secure full legal title and will sell the property to recover the balance of monies due to the lender. Please examine the 20 uniform covenants itemized in the form to understand more fully the legal relationships between the parties to this loan agreement.

NOTE AND MORTGAGE

Another real estate financing instrument is the note and mortgage. The *note* is the promise to pay a debt while the mortgage is the pledge of real estate as collateral to secure this promise. A *mortgage* instrument, although executed separately, invariably has a copy of the note attached to it or at least a reference to the note's conditions incorporated into the mortgage form. While a note by itself is legal evidence of a debt, a mortgage always needs a note in order to be a legally enforceable lien against the collateral.

The Note = Promise To Repay debt - MORTGAGE = pledge of real Estate as collateral

A note is a contract complete in itself. Its terms specify the amount of money borrowed and under which conditions the debt will be repaid. After being signed by a borrower, without any additional signatures or acknowledgments it becomes a legally enforceable and fully negotiable instrument of debt when in the possession of its bearer. If the terms of a note are met, the debt is discharged. If the terms of a note are broken, a lender may choose either to sue on the note or foreclose on the note's collateral if a mortgage has been arranged as security for the note.

UNSecured NOTE = Promise to repay debt w/out any collateral down

A note does not need to be tied to a mortgage. When a note is used as a debt instrument without any related collateral, it is described as an *unsecured note.* Unsecured notes are often used by banks and other lenders to extend short-term personal loans. However, a real estate loan, described as a *secured loan,* always includes a mortgage with a note, often called a *security.*

Secured NOTE = Real estate Loan

Figure 7.2 shows a typical note secured by a mortgage or deed of trust on real property. This basic format can be expanded to include any additional provisions needed. Even in its simplest form, the note is the fundamental document upon which a mortgage depends.

A note generally includes the following provisions:

Date Signed. The date of a note's origination is clearly delineated in the form. Accurate dates are vital to every legally enforceable contract because time is always of the essence in identifying the chronological order of priority rights.

FIGURE 7.1   Deed of Trust

——————————————————— **[Space Above This Line For Recording Data]** ———————————————————

DEED OF TRUST

THIS DEED OF TRUST ("Security Instrument") is made on .... ,
19 .... The trustor is ....
.... ("Borrower"), whose address is ....
.... The trustee is ....
.... ("Trustee"), whose address is ....
.... The beneficiary is
...., which is organized and existing
under the laws of .... , and whose address is ....
.... ("Lender").
Borrower owes Lender the principal sum of ....
.... Dollars (U.S. $ ....). This debt is evidenced by Borrower's note
dated the same date as this Security Instrument ("Note"), which provides for monthly payments, with the full debt, if not
paid earlier, due and payable on .... This Security Instrument
secures to Lender: (a) the repayment of the debt evidenced by the Note, with interest, and all renewals, extensions and
modifications of the Note; (b) the payment of all other sums, with interest, advanced under paragraph 7 to protect the security
of this Security Instrument; and (c) the performance of Borrower's covenants and agreements under this Security Instrument
and the Note. For this purpose, Borrower irrevocably grants and conveys to Trustee, in trust, with power of sale, the following
described property located in .... County, Arizona:

which has the address of .... , ...
  [Street]   [City]

Arizona .... ("Property Address");
       [Zip Code]

TOGETHER WITH all the improvements now or hereafter erected on the property, and all easements, appurtenances,
and fixtures now or hereafter a part of the property. All replacements and additions shall also be covered by this Security
Instrument. All of the foregoing is referred to in this Security Instrument as the "Property."

BORROWER COVENANTS that Borrower is lawfully seised of the estate hereby conveyed and has the right to grant
and convey the Property and that the Property is unencumbered, except for encumbrances of record. Borrower warrants
and will defend generally the title to the Property against all claims and demands, subject to any encumbrances of record.

ARIZONA—Single Family—**Fannie Mae/Freddie Mac UNIFORM INSTRUMENT**   **Form 3003**   9/90   *(page 1 of 6 pages*

FIGURE 7.1 Deed of Trust (continued)

THIS SECURITY INSTRUMENT combines uniform covenants for national use and non-uniform covenants with limited variations by jurisdiction to constitute a uniform security instrument covering real property.

UNIFORM COVENANTS. Borrower and Lender covenant and agree as follows:

1. Payment of Principal and Interest; Prepayment and Late Charges. Borrower shall promptly pay when due the principal of and interest on the debt evidenced by the Note and any prepayment and late charges due under the Note.

2. Funds for Taxes and Insurance. Subject to applicable law or to a written waiver by Lender, Borrower shall pay to Lender on the day monthly payments are due under the Note, until the Note is paid in full, a sum ("Funds") for: (a) yearly taxes and assessments which may attain priority over this Security Instrument as a lien on the Property; (b) yearly leasehold payments or ground rents on the Property, if any; (c) yearly hazard or property insurance premiums; (d) yearly flood insurance premiums, if any; (e) yearly mortgage insurance premiums, if any; and (f) any sums payable by Borrower to Lender, in accordance with the provisions of paragraph 8, in lieu of the payment of mortgage insurance premiums. These items are called "Escrow Items." Lender may, at any time, collect and hold Funds in an amount not to exceed the maximum amount a lender for a federally related mortgage loan may require for Borrower's escrow account under the federal Real Estate Settlement Procedures Act of 1974 as amended from time to time, 12 U.S.C. § 2601 *et seq.* ("RESPA"), unless another law that applies to the Funds sets a lesser amount. If so, Lender may, at any time, collect and hold Funds in an amount not to exceed the lesser amount. Lender may estimate the amount of Funds due on the basis of current data and reasonable estimates of expenditures of future Escrow Items or otherwise in accordance with applicable law.

The Funds shall be held in an institution whose deposits are insured by a federal agency, instrumentality, or entity (including Lender, if Lender is such an institution) or in any Federal Home Loan Bank. Lender shall apply the Funds to pay the Escrow Items. Lender may not charge Borrower for holding and applying the Funds, annually analyzing the escrow account, or verifying the Escrow Items, unless Lender pays Borrower interest on the Funds and applicable law permits Lender to make such a charge. However, Lender may require Borrower to pay a one-time charge for an independent real estate tax reporting service used by Lender in connection with this loan, unless applicable law provides otherwise. Unless an agreement is made or applicable law requires interest to be paid, Lender shall not be required to pay Borrower any interest or earnings on the Funds. Borrower and Lender may agree in writing, however, that interest shall be paid on the Funds. Lender shall give to Borrower, without charge, an annual accounting of the Funds, showing credits and debits to the Funds and the purpose for which each debit to the Funds was made. The Funds are pledged as additional security for all sums secured by this Security Instrument.

If the Funds held by Lender exceed the amounts permitted to be held by applicable law, Lender shall account to Borrower for the excess Funds in accordance with the requirements of applicable law. If the amount of the Funds held by Lender at any time is not sufficient to pay the Escrow Items when due, Lender may so notify Borrower in writing, and, in such case Borrower shall pay to Lender the amount necessary to make up the deficiency. Borrower shall make up the deficiency in no more than twelve monthly payments, at Lender's sole discretion.

Upon payment in full of all sums secured by this Security Instrument, Lender shall promptly refund to Borrower any Funds held by Lender. If, under paragraph 21, Lender shall acquire or sell the Property, Lender, prior to the acquisition or sale of the Property, shall apply any Funds held by Lender at the time of acquisition or sale as a credit against the sums secured by this Security Instrument.

3. Application of Payments. Unless applicable law provides otherwise, all payments received by Lender under paragraphs 1 and 2 shall be applied: first, to any prepayment charges due under the Note; second, to amounts payable under paragraph 2; third, to interest due; fourth, to principal due; and last, to any late charges due under the Note.

4. Charges; Liens. Borrower shall pay all taxes, assessments, charges, fines and impositions attributable to the Property which may attain priority over this Security Instrument, and leasehold payments or ground rents, if any. Borrower shall pay these obligations in the manner provided in paragraph 2, or if not paid in that manner, Borrower shall pay them on time directly to the person owed payment. Borrower shall promptly furnish to Lender all notices of amounts to be paid under this paragraph. If Borrower makes these payments directly, Borrower shall promptly furnish to Lender receipts evidencing the payments.

Borrower shall promptly discharge any lien which has priority over this Security Instrument unless Borrower: (a) agrees in writing to the payment of the obligation secured by the lien in a manner acceptable to Lender; (b) contests in good faith the lien by, or defends against enforcement of the lien in, legal proceedings which in the Lender's opinion operate to prevent the enforcement of the lien; or (c) secures from the holder of the lien an agreement satisfactory to Lender subordinating the lien to this Security Instrument. If Lender determines that any part of the Property is subject to a lien which may attain priority over this Security Instrument, Lender may give Borrower a notice identifying the lien. Borrower shall satisfy the lien or take one or more of the actions set forth above within 10 days of the giving of notice.

5. Hazard or Property Insurance. Borrower shall keep the improvements now existing or hereafter erected on the Property insured against loss by fire, hazards included within the term "extended coverage" and any other hazards, including floods or flooding, for which Lender requires insurance. This insurance shall be maintained in the amounts and for the periods that Lender requires. The insurance carrier providing the insurance shall be chosen by Borrower subject to Lender's approval which shall not be unreasonably withheld. If Borrower fails to maintain coverage described above, Lender may, at Lender's option, obtain coverage to protect Lender's rights in the Property in accordance with paragraph 7.

Form 3003   9/90   *(page 2 of 6 pages)*

FIGURE 7.1   Deed of Trust (continued)

All insurance policies and renewals shall be acceptable to Lender and shall include a standard mortgage clause. Lender shall have the right to hold the policies and renewals. If Lender requires, Borrower shall promptly give to Lender all receipts of paid premiums and renewal notices. In the event of loss, Borrower shall give prompt notice to the insurance carrier and Lender. Lender may make proof of loss if not made promptly by Borrower.

Unless Lender and Borrower otherwise agree in writing, insurance proceeds shall be applied to restoration or repair of the Property damaged, if the restoration or repair is economically feasible and Lender's security is not lessened. If the restoration or repair is not economically feasible or Lender's security would be lessened, the insurance proceeds shall be applied to the sums secured by this Security Instrument, whether or not then due, with any excess paid to Borrower. If Borrower abandons the Property, or does not answer within 30 days a notice from Lender that the insurance carrier has offered to settle a claim, then Lender may collect the insurance proceeds. Lender may use the proceeds to repair or restore the Property or to pay sums secured by this Security Instrument, whether or not then due. The 30-day period will begin when the notice is given.

Unless Lender and Borrower otherwise agree in writing, any application of proceeds to principal shall not extend or postpone the due date of the monthly payments referred to in paragraphs 1 and 2 or change the amount of the payments. If under paragraph 21 the Property is acquired by Lender, Borrower's right to any insurance policies and proceeds resulting from damage to the Property prior to the acquisition shall pass to Lender to the extent of the sums secured by this Security Instrument immediately prior to the acquisition.

6. Occupancy, Preservation, Maintenance and Protection of the Property; Borrower's Loan Application; Leaseholds.   Borrower shall occupy, establish, and use the Property as Borrower's principal residence within sixty days after the execution of this Security Instrument and shall continue to occupy the Property as Borrower's principal residence for at least one year after the date of occupancy, unless Lender otherwise agrees in writing, which consent shall not be unreasonably withheld, or unless extenuating circumstances exist which are beyond Borrower's control. Borrower shall not destroy, damage or impair the Property, allow the Property to deteriorate, or commit waste on the Property. Borrower shall be in default if any forfeiture action or proceeding, whether civil or criminal, is begun that in Lender's good faith judgment could result in forfeiture of the Property or otherwise materially impair the lien created by this Security Instrument or Lender's security interest. Borrower may cure such a default and reinstate, as provided in paragraph 18, by causing the action or proceeding to be dismissed with a ruling that, in Lender's good faith determination, precludes forfeiture of the Borrower's interest in the Property or other material impairment of the lien created by this Security Instrument or Lender's security interest. Borrower shall also be in default if Borrower, during the loan application process, gave materially false or inaccurate information or statements to Lender (or failed to provide Lender with any material information) in connection with the loan evidenced by the Note, including, but not limited to, representations concerning Borrower's occupancy of the Property as a principal residence. If this Security Instrument is on a leasehold, Borrower shall comply with all the provisions of the lease. If Borrower acquires fee title to the Property, the leasehold and the fee title shall not merge unless Lender agrees to the merger in writing.

7. Protection of Lender's Rights in the Property.   If Borrower fails to perform the covenants and agreements contained in this Security Instrument, or there is a legal proceeding that may significantly affect Lender's rights in the Property (such as a proceeding in bankruptcy, probate, for condemnation or forfeiture or to enforce laws or regulations), then Lender may do and pay for whatever is necessary to protect the value of the Property and Lender's rights in the Property. Lender's actions may include paying any sums secured by a lien which has priority over this Security Instrument, appearing in court, paying reasonable attorneys' fees and entering on the Property to make repairs. Although Lender may take action under this paragraph 7, Lender does not have to do so.

Any amounts disbursed by Lender under this paragraph 7 shall become additional debt of Borrower secured by this Security Instrument. Unless Borrower and Lender agree to other terms of payment, these amounts shall bear interest from the date of disbursement at the Note rate and shall be payable, with interest, upon notice from Lender to Borrower requesting payment.

8. Mortgage Insurance.   If Lender required mortgage insurance as a condition of making the loan secured by this Security Instrument, Borrower shall pay the premiums required to maintain the mortgage insurance in effect. If, for any reason, the mortgage insurance coverage required by Lender lapses or ceases to be in effect, Borrower shall pay the premiums required to obtain coverage substantially equivalent to the mortgage insurance previously in effect, at a cost substantially equivalent to the cost to Borrower of the mortgage insurance previously in effect, from an alternate mortgage insurer approved by Lender. If substantially equivalent mortgage insurance coverage is not available, Borrower shall pay to Lender each month a sum equal to one-twelfth of the yearly mortgage insurance premium being paid by Borrower when the insurance coverage lapsed or ceased to be in effect. Lender will accept, use and retain these payments as a loss reserve in lieu of mortgage insurance. Loss reserve payments may no longer be required, at the option of Lender, if mortgage insurance coverage (in the amount and for the period that Lender requires) provided by an insurer approved by Lender again becomes available and is obtained. Borrower shall pay the premiums required to maintain mortgage insurance in effect, or to provide a loss reserve, until the requirement for mortgage insurance ends in accordance with any written agreement between Borrower and Lender or applicable law.

Form 3003   9/90   *(page 3 of 6 pages)*

FIGURE 7.1   Deed of Trust (continued)

9. Inspection.   Lender or its agent may make reasonable entries upon and inspections of the Property. Lender shall give Borrower notice at the time of or prior to an inspection specifying reasonable cause for the inspection.

10. Condemnation.   The proceeds of any award or claim for damages, direct or consequential, in connection with any condemnation or other taking of any part of the Property, or for conveyance in lieu of condemnation, are hereby assigned and shall be paid to Lender.

In the event of a total taking of the Property, the proceeds shall be applied to the sums secured by this Security Instrument, whether or not then due, with any excess paid to Borrower. In the event of a partial taking of the Property in which the fair market value of the Property immediately before the taking is equal to or greater than the amount of the sums secured by this Security Instrument immediately before the taking, unless Borrower and Lender otherwise agree in writing, the sums secured by this Security Instrument shall be reduced by the amount of the proceeds multiplied by the following fraction: (a) the total amount of the sums secured immediately before the taking, divided by (b) the fair market value of the Property immediately before the taking. Any balance shall be paid to Borrower. In the event of a partial taking of the Property in which the fair market value of the Property immediately before the taking is less than the amount of the sums secured immediately before the taking, unless Borrower and Lender otherwise agree in writing or unless applicable law otherwise provides, the proceeds shall be applied to the sums secured by this Security Instrument whether or not the sums are then due.

If the Property is abandoned by Borrower, or if, after notice by Lender to Borrower that the condemnor offers to make an award or settle a claim for damages, Borrower fails to respond to Lender within 30 days after the date the notice is given, Lender is authorized to collect and apply the proceeds, at its option, either to restoration or repair of the Property or to the sums secured by this Security Instrument, whether or not then due.

Unless Lender and Borrower otherwise agree in writing, any application of proceeds to principal shall not extend or postpone the due date of the monthly payments referred to in paragraphs 1 and 2 or change the amount of such payments.

11. Borrower Not Released; Forbearance By Lender Not a Waiver.   Extension of the time for payment or modification of amortization of the sums secured by this Security Instrument granted by Lender to any successor in interest of Borrower shall not operate to release the liability of the original Borrower or Borrower's successors in interest. Lender shall not be required to commence proceedings against any successor in interest or refuse to extend time for payment or otherwise modify amortization of the sums secured by this Security Instrument by reason of any demand made by the original Borrower or Borrower's successors in interest. Any forbearance by Lender in exercising any right or remedy shall not be a waiver of or preclude the exercise of any right or remedy.

12. Successors and Assigns Bound; Joint and Several Liability; Co-signers.   The covenants and agreements of this Security Instrument shall bind and benefit the successors and assigns of Lender and Borrower, subject to the provisions of paragraph 17. Borrower's covenants and agreements shall be joint and several. Any Borrower who co-signs this Security Instrument but does not execute the Note: (a) is co-signing this Security Instrument only to mortgage, grant and convey that Borrower's interest in the Property under the terms of this Security Instrument; (b) is not personally obligated to pay the sums secured by this Security Instrument; and (c) agrees that Lender and any other Borrower may agree to extend, modify, forbear or make any accommodations with regard to the terms of this Security Instrument or the Note without that Borrower's consent.

13. Loan Charges.   If the loan secured by this Security Instrument is subject to a law which sets maximum loan charges, and that law is finally interpreted so that the interest or other loan charges collected or to be collected in connection with the loan exceed the permitted limits, then: (a) any such loan charge shall be reduced by the amount necessary to reduce the charge to the permitted limit; and (b) any sums already collected from Borrower which exceeded permitted limits will be refunded to Borrower. Lender may choose to make this refund by reducing the principal owed under the Note or by making a direct payment to Borrower. If a refund reduces principal, the reduction will be treated as a partial prepayment without any prepayment charge under the Note.

14. Notices.   Any notice to Borrower provided for in this Security Instrument shall be given by delivering it or by mailing it by first class mail unless applicable law requires use of another method. The notice shall be directed to the Property Address or any other address Borrower designates by notice to Lender. Any notice to Lender shall be given by first class mail to Lender's address stated herein or any other address Lender designates by notice to Borrower. Any notice provided for in this Security Instrument shall be deemed to have been given to Borrower or Lender when given as provided in this paragraph.

15. Governing Law; Severability.   This Security Instrument shall be governed by federal law and the law of the jurisdiction in which the Property is located. In the event that any provision or clause of this Security Instrument or the Note conflicts with applicable law, such conflict shall not affect other provisions of this Security Instrument or the Note which can be given effect without the conflicting provision. To this end the provisions of this Security Instrument and the Note are declared to be severable.

16. Borrower's Copy.   Borrower shall be given one conformed copy of the Note and of this Security Instrument.

17. Transfer of the Property or a Beneficial Interest in Borrower.   If all or any part of the Property or any interest in it is sold or transferred (or if a beneficial interest in Borrower is sold or transferred and Borrower is not a natural

FIGURE 7.1   Deed of Trust (continued)

person) without Lender's prior written consent, Lender may, at its option, require immediate payment in full of all sums secured by this Security Instrument. However, this option shall not be exercised by Lender if exercise is prohibited by federal law as of the date of this Security Instrument.

If Lender exercises this option, Lender shall give Borrower notice of acceleration. The notice shall provide a period of not less than 30 days from the date the notice is delivered or mailed within which Borrower must pay all sums secured by this Security Instrument. If Borrower fails to pay these sums prior to the expiration of this period, Lender may invoke any remedies permitted by this Security Instrument without further notice or demand on Borrower.

18. Borrower's Right to Reinstate. If Borrower meets certain conditions, Borrower shall have the right to have enforcement of this Security Instrument discontinued at any time prior to the earlier of: (a) 5 days (or such other period as applicable law may specify for reinstatement) before sale of the Property pursuant to any power of sale contained in this Security Instrument; or (b) entry of a judgment enforcing this Security Instrument. Those conditions are that Borrower: (a) pays Lender all sums which then would be due under this Security Instrument and the Note as if no acceleration had occurred; (b) cures any default of any other covenants or agreements; (c) pays all expenses incurred in enforcing this Security Instrument, including, but not limited to, reasonable attorneys' fees; and (d) takes such action as Lender may reasonably require to assure that the lien of this Security Instrument, Lender's rights in the Property and Borrower's obligation to pay the sums secured by this Security Instrument shall continue unchanged. Upon reinstatement by Borrower, this Security Instrument and the obligations secured hereby shall remain fully effective as if no acceleration had occurred. However, this right to reinstate shall not apply in the case of acceleration under paragraph 17.

19. Sale of Note; Change of Loan Servicer. The Note or a partial interest in the Note (together with this Security Instrument) may be sold one or more times without prior notice to Borrower. A sale may result in a change in the entity (known as the "Loan Servicer") that collects monthly payments due under the Note and this Security Instrument. There also may be one or more changes of the Loan Servicer unrelated to a sale of the Note. If there is a change of the Loan Servicer, Borrower will be given written notice of the change in accordance with paragraph 14 above and applicable law. The notice will state the name and address of the new Loan Servicer and the address to which payments should be made. The notice will also contain any other information required by applicable law.

20. Hazardous Substances. Borrower shall not cause or permit the presence, use, disposal, storage, or release of any Hazardous Substances on or in the Property. Borrower shall not do, nor allow anyone else to do, anything affecting the Property that is in violation of any Environmental Law. The preceding two sentences shall not apply to the presence, use, or storage on the Property of small quantities of Hazardous Substances that are generally recognized to be appropriate to normal residential uses and to maintenance of the Property.

Borrower shall promptly give Lender written notice of any investigation, claim, demand, lawsuit or other action by any governmental or regulatory agency or private party involving the Property and any Hazardous Substance or Environmental Law of which Borrower has actual knowledge. If Borrower learns, or is notified by any governmental or regulatory authority, that any removal or other remediation of any Hazardous Substance affecting the Property is necessary, Borrower shall promptly take all necessary remedial actions in accordance with Environmental Law.

As used in this paragraph 20, "Hazardous Substances" are those substances defined as toxic or hazardous substances by Environmental Law and the following substances: gasoline, kerosene, other flammable or toxic petroleum products, toxic pesticides and herbicides, volatile solvents, materials containing asbestos or formaldehyde, and radioactive materials. As used in this paragraph 20, "Environmental Law" means federal laws and laws of the jurisdiction where the Property is located that relate to health, safety or environmental protection.

NON-UNIFORM COVENANTS. Borrower and Lender further covenant and agree as follows:

21. Acceleration; Remedies. Lender shall give notice to Borrower prior to acceleration following Borrower's breach of any covenant or agreement in this Security Instrument (but not prior to acceleration under paragraph 17 unless applicable law provides otherwise). The notice shall specify: (a) the default; (b) the action required to cure the default; (c) a date, not less than 30 days from the date the notice is given to Borrower, by which the default must be cured; and (d) that failure to cure the default on or before the date specified in the notice may result in acceleration of the sums secured by this Security Instrument and sale of the Property. The notice shall further inform Borrower of the right to reinstate after acceleration and the right to bring a court action to assert the non-existence of a default or any other defense of Borrower to acceleration and sale. If the default is not cured on or before the date specified in the notice, Lender at its option may require immediate payment in full of all sums secured by this Security Instrument without further demand and may invoke the power of sale and any other remedies permitted by applicable law. Lender shall be entitled to collect all expenses incurred in pursuing the remedies provided in this paragraph 21, including, but not limited to, reasonable attorneys' fees and costs of title evidence.

If Lender invokes the power of sale, Lender shall give written notice to Trustee of the occurrence of an event of default and of Lender's election to cause the Property to be sold. Trustee shall record a notice of sale in each county in which any part of the Property is located and shall mail copies of the notice as prescribed by applicable law to Borrower and to the other persons prescribed by applicable law. After the time required by applicable law and after

Form 3003   9/90   *(page 5 of 6 pages)*

FIGURE 7.1   Deed of Trust (continued)

publication and posting of the notice of sale, Trustee, without demand on Borrower, shall sell the Property at public auction to the highest bidder for cash at the time and place designated in the notice of sale. Trustee may postpone sale of the Property by public announcement at the time and place of any previously scheduled sale. Lender or its designee may purchase the Property at any sale.

Trustee shall deliver to the purchaser Trustee's deed conveying the Property without any covenant or warranty, expressed or implied. The recitals in the Trustee's deed shall be prima facie evidence of the truth of the statements made therein. Trustee shall apply the proceeds of the sale in the following order: (a) to all expenses of the sale, including, but not limited to, reasonable Trustee's and attorneys' fees; (b) to all sums secured by this Security Instrument; and (c) any excess to the person or persons legally entitled to it or to the clerk of the superior court of the county in which the sale took place.

22.   Release. Upon payment of all sums secured by this Security Instrument, Lender shall release this Security Instrument without charge to Borrower. Borrower shall pay any recordation costs.

23.   Substitute Trustee. Lender may, for any reason or cause, from time to time remove Trustee and appoint a successor trustee to any Trustee appointed hereunder. Without conveyance of the Property, the successor trustee shall succeed to all the title, power and duties conferred upon Trustee herein and by applicable law.

24.   Time of Essence. Time is of the essence in each covenant of this Security Instrument.

25.   Mailing Addresses. Borrower's mailing address is the Property Address. Trustee's mailing address is.......
....

26.   Riders to this Security Instrument. If one or more riders are executed by Borrower and recorded together with this Security Instrument, the covenants and agreements of each such rider shall be incorporated into and shall amend and supplement the covenants and agreements of this Security Instrument as if the rider(s) were a part of this Security Instrument. [Check applicable box(es)]

☐ Adjustable Rate Rider   ☐ Condominium Rider   ☐ 1—4 Family Rider

☐ Graduated Payment Rider   ☐ Planned Unit Development Rider ☐ Biweekly Payment Rider

☐ Balloon Rider   ☐ Rate Improvement Rider   ☐ Second Home Rider

☐ Other(s) [specify]

BY SIGNING BELOW, Borrower accepts and agrees to the terms and covenants contained in this Security Instrument and in any rider(s) executed by Borrower and recorded with it.

Witnesses:

....(Seal)
                                                                                                       —Borrower

                                                          Social Security Number..

....(Seal)
                                                                                                       —Borrower

                                                          Social Security Number..

————————————————— [Space Below This Line For Acknowledgment] —————————————————

Form 3003   9/90   *(page 6 of 6 pages)*

FIGURE 7.2   Note Secured by Mortgage

NOTE

...., 19..........   ...., ...
                                                                                        [City]   [State]

....
[Property Address]

1. BORROWER'S PROMISE TO PAY

In return for a loan that I have received, I promise to pay U.S. $.. (this amount is called "principal"), plus interest, to the order of the Lender. The Lender is ....
.... I understand that the Lender may transfer this Note. The Lender or anyone who takes this Note by transfer and who is entitled to receive payments under this Note is called the "Note Holder."

2. INTEREST

Interest will be charged on unpaid principal until the full amount of principal has been paid. I will pay interest at a yearly rate of ....%.

The interest rate required by this Section 2 is the rate I will pay both before and after any default described in Section 6(B) of this Note.

3. PAYMENTS

(A) Time and Place of Payments

I will pay principal and interest by making payments every month.

I will make my monthly payments on the .... day of each month beginning on ...., 19......... I will make these payments every month until I have paid all of the principal and interest and any other charges described below that I may owe under this Note. My monthly payments will be applied to interest before principal. If, on ...., ..., I still owe amounts under this Note, I will pay those amounts in full on that date, which is called the "maturity date."

I will make my monthly payments at ....
.... or at a different place if required by the Note Holder.

(B) Amount of Monthly Payments

My monthly payment will be in the amount of U.S. $..

4. BORROWER'S RIGHT TO PREPAY

I have the right to make payments of principal at any time before they are due. A payment of principal only is known as a "prepayment." When I make a prepayment, I will tell the Note Holder in writing that I am doing so.

I may make a full prepayment or partial prepayments without paying any prepayment charge. The Note Holder will use all of my prepayments to reduce the amount of principal that I owe under this Note. If I make a partial prepayment, there will be no changes in the due date or in the amount of my monthly payment unless the Note Holder agrees in writing to those changes.

5. LOAN CHARGES

If a law, which applies to this loan and which sets maximum loan charges, is finally interpreted so that the interest or other loan charges collected or to be collected in connection with this loan exceed the permitted limits, then: (i) any such loan charge shall be reduced by the amount necessary to reduce the charge to the permitted limit; and (ii) any sums already collected from me which exceeded permitted limits will be refunded to me. The Note Holder may choose to make this refund by reducing the principal I owe under this Note or by making a direct payment to me. If a refund reduces principal, the reduction will be treated as a partial prepayment.

6. BORROWER'S FAILURE TO PAY AS REQUIRED

(A) Late Charge for Overdue Payments

If the Note Holder has not received the full amount of any monthly payment by the end of .... calendar days after the date it is due, I will pay a late charge to the Note Holder. The amount of the charge will be ....% of my overdue payment of principal and interest. I will pay this late charge promptly but only once on each late payment.

(B) Default

If I do not pay the full amount of each monthly payment on the date it is due, I will be in default.

(C) Notice of Default

If I am in default, the Note Holder may send me a written notice telling me that if I do not pay the overdue amount by a certain date, the Note Holder may require me to pay immediately the full amount of principal which has not been paid and all the interest that I owe on that amount. That date must be at least 30 days after the date on which the notice is delivered or mailed to me.

(D) No Waiver By Note Holder

Even if, at a time when I am in default, the Note Holder does not require me to pay immediately in full as described above, the Note Holder will still have the right to do so if I am in default at a later time.

(E) Payment of Note Holder's Costs and Expenses

If the Note Holder has required me to pay immediately in full as described above, the Note Holder will have the right to be paid back by me for all of its costs and expenses in enforcing this Note to the extent not prohibited by applicable law. Those expenses include, for example, reasonable attorneys' fees.

7. GIVING OF NOTICES

Unless applicable law requires a different method, any notice that must be given to me under this Note will be given by delivering it or by mailing it by first class mail to me at the Property Address above or at a different address if I give the Note Holder a notice of my different address.

Any notice that must be given to the Note Holder under this Note will be given by mailing it by first class mail to the Note Holder at the address stated in Section 3(A) above or at a different address if I am given a notice of that different address.

MULTISTATE FIXED RATE NOTE—Single Family—**FNMA/FHLMC UNIFORM INSTRUMENT**   Form 3200 12/83
(page 1 of 2 pages)

FIGURE 7.2 Note Secured by Mortgage (continued)

8. OBLIGATIONS OF PERSONS UNDER THIS NOTE

If more than one person signs this Note, each person is fully and personally obligated to keep all of the promises made in this Note, including the promise to pay the full amount owed. Any person who is a guarantor, surety or endorser of this Note is also obligated to do these things. Any person who takes over these obligations, including the obligations of a guarantor, surety or endorser of this Note, is also obligated to keep all of the promises made in this Note. The Note Holder may enforce its rights under this Note against each person individually or against all of us together. This means that any one of us may be required to pay all of the amounts owed under this Note.

9. WAIVERS

I and any other person who has obligations under this Note waive the rights of presentment and notice of dishonor. "Presentment" means the right to require the Note Holder to demand payment of amounts due. "Notice of dishonor" means the right to require the Note Holder to give notice to other persons that amounts due have not been paid.

10. UNIFORM SECURED NOTE

This Note is a uniform instrument with limited variations in some jurisdictions. In addition to the protections given to the Note Holder under this Note, a Mortgage, Deed of Trust or Security Deed (the "Security Instrument"), dated the same date as this Note, protects the Note Holder from possible losses which might result if I do not keep the promises which I make in this Note. That Security Instrument describes how and under what conditions I may be required to make immediate payment in full of all amounts I owe under this Note. Some of those conditions are described as follows:

Transfer of the Property or a Beneficial Interest in Borrower. If all or any part of the Property or any interest in it is sold or transferred (or if a beneficial interest in Borrower is sold or transferred and Borrower is not a natural person) without Lender's prior written consent, Lender may, at its option, require immediate payment in full of all sums secured by this Security Instrument. However, this option shall not be exercised by Lender if exercise is prohibited by federal law as of the date of this Security Instrument.

If Lender exercises this option, Lender shall give Borrower notice of acceleration. The notice shall provide a period of not less than 30 days from the date the notice is delivered or mailed within which Borrower must pay all sums secured by this Security Instrument. If Borrower fails to pay these sums prior to the expiration of this period, Lender may invoke any remedies permitted by this Security Instrument without further notice or demand on Borrower.

WITNESS THE HAND(S) AND SEAL(S) OF THE UNDERSIGNED

....(Seal)
-Borrower

....(Seal)
-Borrower

....(Seal)
-Borrower

[Sign Original Only]

Form 3200 12/83 *(page 2 of 2 pages)*

(handwritten margin note: Part of a Note)

Participants' Identities. The participants engaged in a loan contract are identified, and their relationship as borrower and lender is established. Some preprinted note forms identify the borrower as "the undersigned," and the lender's name is printed on the form.

Promise to Pay. The words *promise to pay* establish the precise legal obligation of the borrower. The fulfillment of the promise is the satisfaction of the obligation; a broken promise entitles the lender to seek legal remedies to recover any damages that might occur.

(handwritten note: amortization = systematic repayment program)

Payment Due Dates. The specific schedule of payments must be incorporated into the note. A systematic repayment program of principal and interest over the life of the loan is described as *amortization*. A plan can be designed for a number of time intervals, such as for monthly, quarterly, semiannual, or annual payments. Semiamortized notes call for periodic payments of principal and interest, with a large principal amount, called a *balloon payment*, due at the end of the loan term. Notes can also be designed to be paid at a monthly or annual rate of *interest only* with a single lump sum principal payment due at some future time. This form of finance is described as a *term loan*. In all cases, a note will specify when the payments will start, on what dates they will be due, and when they will stop.

Amount and Terms. The amount of the payments depends on the terms of a loan. If a term loan for $1,000 for one year at 8 percent interest per annum is designated, the note will stipulate a payment of $1,080, including principal and interest, to be due in full one year from the date of its inception.

The payments due on an amortized note will be based on the length of time involved and the agreed-upon interest rate. For example, a $65,000 note payable in monthly installments over a 30-year time span at 8 percent annual interest would require a $476.95 regular monthly payment to satisfy the obligation. This sum represents only the monthly principal and interest amounts due the lender. If hazard insurance premiums and property taxes are to be included in the monthly payment, these additional requirements must be described in the mortgage form. Only the scheduled amount of principal and interest owed to the lender is specified in the note.

The terms and conditions for the repayment of a loan can be as flexible and varied as a particular situation demands. However, the note is always the determining instrument in interpreting the intentions of the parties to a loan.

Reference to Security. After the terms of a loan are specified, a referral is made in the note that it is secured by a mortgage upon real property. This reference to a security is formalized when a copy of the note is attached to its mortgage, thereby firmly and legally establishing the security.

The mortgage is the liening document, the life of which depends on the note. The note is a freestanding contract *personally* obligating the borrower for the debt. A lender may sue for damages on the note instrument in the event the borrower defaults. The mortgage is the lender's final protection and may be foreclosed if a borrower cannot fulfill the obligation under the note. Thus, the note is the power instrument in this realty lending design.

Signatures and Endorsements. Although several copies of the note are prepared and distributed to the parties in the loan transaction, only one copy is signed. This signed copy is delivered to the lender, to be held until the debt is satisfied. This is important to a borrower because each signed note is a negotiable instrument in itself. Only *one note* should be signed in any loan transaction.

A note requires only the borrower's signature. The delivery of the signed note to the lender is adequate evidence of ownership. A note signed by a borrower is a negotiable instrument; a lender can assign it to another person by simply endorsing it on its back, much like a check. If a mortgage is involved, the process is more complicated, but the note itself is a viable, negotiable instrument. A transfer does not affect either terms or conditions of the original agreement, except that the place to which the borrower sends payments may change. When the loan is repaid, the lender marks "paid in full" across the face of the original note, signs under this comment, and returns the original to the borrower.

Cosigners. The lender who once made the statement that "there can never be too many signatures on a note" was referring to the fact that all signers on a note are individually and collectively responsible for its repayment. If a married couple is securing a loan, a lender will require both husband and wife to sign the note. Sometimes a lender may require the signatures of persons other than the borrower to provide additional guarantees that the obligation will be repaid. These additional signatures are usually the borrower's family or friends whose credit has been considered in qualifying the borrower for a loan. These cosigners share personal liability with the original maker of the note in the event of a default.

The number of signatures on a note does not have to conform with the number of persons who sign the accompanying mortgage. Because the property in question is being pledged as collateral to back up a specific note, only the property owners sign. Thus a note may have more or fewer signatures than its mortgage. In fact, the signatures on both instruments may be different, although this would be rare.

The Mortgage

A typical realty mortgage is shown in Figure 7.3. Mortgage provisions vary, depending on the policies of individual lenders and the circumstances in a particular transaction (as will be detailed in later chapters). Nevertheless, the components covered on the next pages are standard to most mortgage forms.

Recording Information. A mortgage is a lien on a specific property or properties to secure the fulfillment of a promise—usually a promise to repay a debt. The only way a lender has to notify the world that there is a lien on a specific property is to record the mortgage at the office of the recorder in the county where the property is located.

Without the recording of the mortgage lien, only the borrower and the lender would know of the transaction. Other parties having an interest in the property would not receive notice of the lien. Thus, for its protection, a lender will insist on recording the mortgage. Invariably this recording will take place *before* the proceeds of a loan are distributed. By holding back the disbursement of a loan until after recording, a lender or escrow agent has a last-minute opportunity to recheck the public records about the condition of the collateral property's title.

Most standard mortgage forms have a space at the top of the first page devoted to specific county recording information. Others leave a blank space elsewhere on the form to be filled in at the recorder's office. In any case, the appropriate information will be included in the space provided, and the lien is posted against the property described. This lien vests at the date and time impressed on the mortgage document by the recorder's clock stamp. The original document is usually copied on microfilm and returned to the appropriate person.

FIGURE 7.3 Realty Mortgage

When recorded mail to ________________________________

STATE OF ARIZONA } ss.
COUNTY OF PIMA }

I hereby certify that the within instrument was filed for record in Pima County, State of Arizona

Witness my hand and Official Seal.

ANNA SULLINGER,
County Recorder

By ________________________________
Deputy

No.

Book ____________ Page ________

Date:
Request of:

Fee:

Indexed	Paged	Blotted

Realty Mortgage

KNOW ALL MEN, That

[Borrowers' Names]

of Pima County, Arizona, hereinafter referred to as MORTGAGOR, in consideration of

[Loan Amount]

DOLLARS,

in hand paid by

[Lender's Name]

hereinafter referred to as MORTGAGEE, the receipt whereof is hereby acknowledged, does hereby grant, bargain, sell and convey to MORTGAGEE, and the successors, heirs and assigns of MORTGAGEE forever, the following real estate, lying and being in the County of Pima, State of Arizona, known and described as

Granting Clause

[Legal Description]

Together with: (1) All buildings and improvements now or hereafter placed thereon; (2) all rents, issues and profits thereof; (3) all classes of property now, or at any time hereafter, attached to or used in any way in connection with the use, operation or occupancy of the above described real property; (4) all property, rights and privileges now or hereafter owned by MORTGAGOR or now or hereafter appurtenant to said premises, which entitle MORTGAGOR or said premises to receive water or electrical power for use thereon. All of the foregoing shall be deemed to be, remain and form part of the realty and subject to the lien of this mortgage.

Habendum Clause

TO HAVE AND TO HOLD the same to MORTGAGEE, and the successors, heirs, executors, administrators or assigns of MORTGAGEE forever.

Covenant of Seisin

MORTGAGOR hereby covenants and warrants that MORTGAGOR is well and truly seized of a good and perfect title to the premises above conveyed in fee simple and has good right and lawful authority to convey the same, and that the title so conveyed is clear, free and unencumbered and that MORTGAGOR will forever warrant and defend the same to MORTGAGEE against all claims whatsoever.

This conveyance is intended as a mortgage to secure the payment of a promissory note given by the MORTGAGOR to the MORTGAGEE, a true copy of which note is hereto annexed and made a part hereof;

The Note

$__________ Arizona, ____________, 19____

For value received ______________________ Promise___ to pay to ______________________, or order, at ______________________ the sum of ______________________ DOLLARS, in installments of $__________ or more, monthly, payable on the __________ day of every month, beginning on the __________ day of __________, 19____, with interest on all unpaid principal from __________, 19____, until paid, at the rate of ______% per annum payable, monthly, the interest to be first deducted from the regular monthly installments, and the balance to be applied upon the principal.

Should default be made in the payment of any installment when due, then the whole sum of principal and interest shall become immediately due and payable at the option of the holder of this note, with interest from date of such default at eight per cent per annum until paid on the entire unpaid principal and accrued interest.

Should any installment due hereunder not be paid as it matures, the amount of such installment which has matured shall, at the option of the holder of this note, bear interest at eight per cent per annum from its maturity date until paid.

Principal and interest payable in lawful money of the United States of America.

Should suit be brought to recover on this note_____promise to pay as attorney's fees a reasonable amount additional on the amount found due hereunder.

The makers and endorsers hereof severally waive diligence, demand, presentment for payment and protest, and consent to the extension of time of payment of this note, without notice.

This note is secured by a mortgage upon real property.

____

Form 100-114 ________________________________

FIGURE 7.3   Realty Mortgage (continued)

PROVIDED, ALWAYS, and these presents are upon the express condition, that if MORTGAGOR shall: (1) Pay to MORTGAGEE the just and full sums due according to the terms and conditions of the promissory note hereinabove set forth; (2) pay to the proper officers before delinquency, all taxes and assessments, general or special, and all general or special assessments, charges, or taxes for irrigation water, power or appurtenant water stock, which shall be charged, levied or assessed upon said real estate; (3) pay when due all encumbrances, adverse claims, charges and liens on said property or any part thereof, which may have or acquire priority to or impair the security of this mortgage; and (4), insure and keep all improvements on said premises insured for the protection of MORTGAGEE in such manner, in such amounts and in such companies as MORTGAGEE may approve, and pay the premiums for said insurance, and keep the policies therefor, properly endorsed, on deposit with MORTGAGEE, it being understood and agreed that each insurance company concerned is hereby authorized and directed to make payment for such loss directly to MORT-GAGEE and that such loss proceeds shall, at MORTGAGEE'S option, be applied on said indebtedness, whether due or not, or to the restoration of said improvements; then these presents shall be null and void.

Acceleration Clause   {
In case of the non-payment of any sum of money, either principal, interest, taxes, assessments, dues or assessments for irrigation water or appurtenant water stock, power bills, adverse claims, encumbrances, charges or liens, or premiums of insurance, at the time or times herein provided for such payments, or upon the failure of MORTGAGOR to insure the buildings upon said premises and keep the policies assigned or made payable to MORTGAGEE, and deliver the said policies to MORT-GAGEE, all as provided by the conditions of these presents , or of the aforesaid promissory note, or in case of the failure of MORTGAGOR to keep or perform any other agreement, stipulation or condition, herein contained, then the whole principal sum of said note, at the option of MORTGAGEE, shall be deemed to have become due, and the same, with interest thereon at the rate contracted, shall thereupon be collectible in a suit at law or by foreclosure of this mortgage, in the same manner as if the whole of said principal sum had been made payable at the time when any such failure shall occur, as aforesaid.

MORTGAGOR further covenants and agrees, that in case of failure on the part of MORTGAGOR to pay any of said taxes, assessments, dues or assessments for irrigation water or appurtenant water stock, power bills, adverse claims, encumbrances, charges or liens, or premiums of insurance, as above provided, MORTGAGEE may pay the same, and the amount so paid, together with interest thereon at the rate of eight per cent per annum shall become a part of the debt secured by this mortgage and a lien on said premises immediately due and payable at the option of MORTGAGEE.

Maintenance Clause   {
MORTGAGOR also covenants and agrees with MORTGAGEE that MORTGAGOR will, during existence of this mortgage, neither permit nor commit waste on said premises; and, if the mortgaged premises are now or hereafter used as farm lands, will purchase and use thereon the amount of water necessary to preserve and protect any water rights to which said premises are or shall be entitled, and keep said premises in continuous cultivation and carefully irrigate the same; and will take the same care thereof that a prudent owner would take, and in any action to foreclose this mortgage a receiver shall, upon application of the plaintiff in such action and without notice to the defendants, be appointed by the Court to take charge of said property, to manage, carry on, protect, preserve and repair the same and receive and collect all the rents, issues and profits thereof, and apply the same to the payment of sums spent to protect, preserve and repair said property, the payment of taxes and other charges, including his own compensation, and to the payment of said note and interest, which may be due or become due during the pendency of the action until sale be finally made and deed made and delivered thereunder; and in case of such foreclosure MORTGAGOR will pay to MORT-GAGEE in addition to the taxable costs of the foreclosure suit, a reasonable amount as an attorney's fee, together with a reasonable fee for title search made in preparation and conduct of such suit, all of which shall be a lien on said premises and secured by this mortgage; and, in case of settlement after suit is brought but before trial, MORTGAGOR agrees to pay a reasonable attorney's fee, as well as all of the costs of such suit and the costs of the appointment of a receiver, if appointed and any sums expended by such receiver or MORTGAGEE in the management, carrying on, protection, preservation and repair of said property.

MORTGAGOR and MORTGAGEE further covenant and agree that this instrument shall be construed as covering and securing the indebtedness herein mentioned and any and all additional indebtedness, whether as future advancement or otherwise, together with any renewals or extensions of the said indebtedness herein secured or any advancements and any and all costs of collecting the same.

The covenants and agreements herein contained shall inure to the benefit of and be binding upon the heirs, executors, administrators, successors and assigns of the respective parties hereto.

DATED this............day of..............................., 19............

[Borrowers' Signatures]

....

....

....

....

Acknowledgment   {

STATE OF.............................. }

County of.............................. } ss.

This instrument was acknowledged before me this............day of.............................., 19........, by..

....

....

My commission will expire

....
Notary Public

Participants. The participants to a mortgage include a borrower-**mortgagor** and a lender-**mortgagee.** In exchange for a certain consideration, usually a sum of money, a mortgagor will pledge property as collateral to back up the promise to repay a mortgage. The proper names of both mortgagor and mortgagee must appear on the mortgage form.

Pledge. Any rights owned by a mortgagor in real estate may be pledged as collateral for a loan. Most mortgages include the pledge of a property's fee simple ownership, although leasehold, mineral, water, and other rights less-than-a-freehold interest can be pledged.

The portion of the mortgage that pledges the mortgagor's rights is called the *granting clause.* It includes the words *grant, bargain, sell and convey,* which are the same words that appear on the face of a deed that transfers the ownership of a property from a grantor to a grantee. These words of conveyance in the mortgage form actually transfer a quasi-legal, or equitable, form of ownership to the mortgagee, creating a lien that the mortgagee will either release when the loan is satisfied or perfect into a full legal fee if there is a default.

The equitable property interest that a mortgagee secures under the mortgage form becomes an asset that, according to the wording in the contract, inures to "the benefit of the mortgagee and successors, heirs, and assigns forever."

Property Description. All property pledged as collateral in a mortgage must be described accurately, without ambiguity, to prevent any future controversies. Securing the proper **legal description** is the responsibility of the person composing the loan documents. A description used in prior transactions is usually an adequate reference, and it can be copied onto the new forms. However, whenever a new subdivision is involved in a loan or some complication arises concerning a property description, a surveyor should be engaged to provide a precise legal description.

In addition to the real property described, most mortgage forms include the pledge of

> . . . all buildings and improvements now or hereafter placed thereon; all rents, issues, and profits thereof; all classes of property now, or at any time hereafter, attached to or used in any way in connection with the use, operation, or occupation of the above-described property; all property rights and privileges now or hereafter owned by a mortgagor. . . . All of the foregoing shall be deemed to be, remain, and form part of the realty and be subject to the lien of this mortgage.

Thus, the real property, anything that is permanently attached to it, and all of the mortgagor's rights in it are pledged as collateral for the loan.

Covenant of Seisin. The *covenant of seisin* is the clause stating that the mortgagors have title to the property described and that they have the authority to pledge the property as collateral. This covenant goes one step further by specifying that the mortgagors will warrant this title and guarantee that it is being pledged free and clear of any encumbrance not described in the mortgage document.

Although this clause is found in most standard mortgage forms, it is of little practical consequence because a mortgagor's warranty would be useless in the event of default. As a result, most mortgagees rely on a careful title examination and title insurance to protect against misrepresentation.

Note Attachment. It is not necessary to describe all terms and conditions of a note in the body of a mortgage. In fact, the parties to a loan often prefer not to reveal this information and merely indicate a reference to the note, using the phrase "this mortgage is given to secure the payment of a certain indebtedness evidenced by a note payable to the order of the mortgagee," or words to that effect.

However, some forms provide a space for the attachment of a true copy of the note. Whatever the case, the borrower agrees in the mortgage to pay the full sum due according to the terms of the note.

Property Taxes. In addition to being obligated to repay a mortgagee the just and full sum due, according to the terms and conditions of the promissory note, a mortgagor must pay all property taxes, assessments, adverse claims, charges, and liens that may jeopardize the priority position of the mortgagee. Any negligence on the part of a mortgagor to pay these claims technically puts a mortgage into default.

Depending on specific circumstances, mortgagees may protect their interests by including as a condition of the loan contract that the mortgagor pay a proportionate share of the annual taxes with each monthly payment of principal and interest. These tax payments would then be held in a special impound or escrow account to accumulate over the year and be paid to the tax collector, usually the county treasurer, when they are due. This procedure has eliminated many of the problems connected with mortgagors who simply were not conditioned to putting aside the funds necessary for annual property taxes. In most commercial loans and some residential loans, however, the mortgagors still retain control over these tax payments, and they are not impounded by a mortgagee.

A mortgagee will closely supervise the prompt payment of all current property taxes because a tax lien takes a priority position over any other liens, recorded or not.

Insurance. Just as mortgagees must protect themselves by supervising the prompt payment of property taxes, they must also specify in their mortgage contracts that hazard insurance is to be provided and paid for by the mortgagor in an amount and under terms adequate to protect the mortgagee's interest in the property. The insurance agency chosen by the mortgagor is subject to approval by the mortgagee.

Not only must adequate coverage be provided, the mortgagee must also be named as a coinsured party. The original policy must be deposited with the mortgagee and proportionate shares of the insurance premiums must be included together with the monthly payment of principal, interest, and taxes. These hazard insurance payments are deposited in the impound account, together with the property taxes collected, and the funds accumulated are used to pay the insurance premiums when they become due. In this manner, a mortgagee supervises the current status of the insurance coverage of the collateral.

If a loss occurs, the check for the insurance proceeds is issued either to the mortgagee only, or to the mortgagor and the mortgagee jointly, the latter having an opportunity to inspect the repairs prior to endorsing the check. In the former case the mortgagee usually retains the right to apply the proceeds to the amount of the indebtedness or make the necessary repairs. Thus, a mortgagee can protect the value of the collateral during the entire life of the loan.

Maintenance of the Collateral. As a further protection of the mortgagee's interests, a mortgagor is required by the terms of a mortgage to preserve the value of the premises by maintaining its physical condition. A mortgagor is charged "not to permit or commit waste on said premises" and "to preserve and repair said property."

Defeasance Clause and Acceleration. A mortgage usually includes a **defeasance clause.** It "defeats" foreclosure by stating that the mortgagor will regain full free and clear title upon the repayment of the debt. It has also become standard procedure to include an **acceleration clause,** which outlines the consequences of failure to pay on the part of the mortgagor. The acceleration clause usually states,

> In the event of nonpayment of any sum of money, either principal, interest, assessments . . . adverse claims, encumbrances, charges or liens, premiums of insurance when due or failure to maintain said premises or to keep or perform any other agreement, stipulation, or condition herein contained, then the whole principal sum of said note, at the option of the mortgagee, shall be deemed to have become due, and the same, with interest thereon at the rate contracted, shall thereupon be collectible in a suit at law *or* by foreclosure of this mortgage, as if the whole of said principal sum were payable at the time of any such failure.

This acceleration clause is at the heart of a mortgage in relation to a mortgagee's protection. Any of the neglects mentioned can result in a default of the contract's provisions and allow a mortgagee to accelerate the mortgage, granting the right to take the appropriate legal steps to recover the investment. A mortgagee can elect to sue on the note and pursue a mortgagor personally for any balance due or sue for foreclosure on the property pledged as collateral. In most jurisdictions, a mortgagee cannot pursue both actions at the same time. A default would invariably indicate some personal, usually economic, problem for a mortgagor. Thus, a default precludes seeking the first alternative, invariably resulting in a mortgagee's foreclosing against the collateral and with a subsequent suit against the mortgagor for any deficiency incurred as a result of not securing full redress from the sale of the collateral. In any event, in the *absence* of an acceleration clause, a mortgagee would have to sue *on each* payment as it became delinquent, not the entire debt. The full consequences of a default are examined in Chapter 14.

Signatures and Acknowledgment. Like the note, a mortgage must be signed by the mortgagors accepting the conditions of the contract. These signatures must also be dated and *acknowledged* by a notary public, attesting to their authenticity, because unacknowledged instruments are not accepted by a county recorder and are not admissible in a court as true evidence.

Release of Mortgage. When a mortgage loan is paid in full, it is removed from the records by recording a satisfaction of mortgage form, executed by the lender, indicating that the loan terms have been met.

CONTRACT FOR DEED (LAND CONTRACT) *Complete financing agreement between Buyer + Seller*

Alternately known as a *real estate contract,* a land contract, a *contract for sale,* an *agreement for deed,* an *installment sale,* and *articles of agreement,* a **contract for deed** has as many forms as it has synonyms. A contract for deed does not have an accompanying note; it is a single, complete financing and sales agreement executed between a buyer and a seller. A

IN A CONTRACT FOR DEED - Title does not convey until all terms are met.

contract for deed should not be considered a mortgage or deed of trust, even though the same basic conditions are incorporated into its form. These conditions include the pledge of specific property as collateral for the loan, the terms and conditions for the loan's repayment, the enumeration of the borrower's responsibilities, and a statement of the consequences of a default.

The contract for deed is an agreement drawn up between two parties, the buyer-borrower-**vendee** and the seller-lender-**vendor.** Under a contract for deed the *seller remains the legal fee owner* of the property, which is one major distinction between this form of financing instrument and the mortgage and deed of trust. Although the buyer agrees to pay the seller a specific price under certain terms and conditions, thereby gaining possession of the property, the *buyer does not receive full legal title* until the terms of the contract are met. This procedure provides the seller, who is financing the sale of the property, added protection in case of the buyer's default. The form in Figure 7.4 is an example of a contract for deed.

Because a contract for deed does not have a note accompanying it, all conditions of the sale are described in the contract form, including the purchase price and the terms of the loan. The contract specifies the buyer's responsibilities to pay the payments when due, as well as the taxes, special assessments, if any, and hazard insurance premiums. The contract also describes the deed that the seller will deliver to the buyer upon fulfillment of the contract or deposit with an escrow—if an escrow is used—to be held until the terms of the agreement have been met. The delivery and subsequent recording of this deed serve as proof of the satisfaction of the contract debt.

The contract directs the buyer to take possession of the subject property and maintain possession so long as the agreed-upon terms of the contract are met. In the event of a breach of contract, all payments made by the buyer are forfeited. The seller may then elect to bring an action against the buyer for specific performance of the agreement or may choose to use any other legal remedies granted in the contract for recovery of the property and any losses incurred.

A contract for deed is both a sale and financing agreement in one instrument; both the buyer and seller sign the document and have their signatures notarized in anticipation of recording.

The contract for deed goes one step further than the deed of trust. It places even more foreclosure power into the hands of the seller-lender in the event of a default. In fact, as shown in Chapter 14, a lender under a contract for deed may be able to recover property pledged as collateral in as little as 30 days, depending on specific circumstances. When compared to the much longer property recovery periods of up to two years specified in the mortgage form—and up to four months under the deed of trust—the short term provided by a contract for deed gives the seller-lender significant additional security in case of default.

Some states, such as Colorado and Florida, require the seller-lender to foreclose a contract for deed as if it were a mortgage or deed of trust. Most frequently the contract for deed form is used between individuals in the purchase and sale of real property when other means of financing are not readily available. Contracts for deeds are usually junior financing instruments, established between a buyer and seller, to close a particular sale when the buyer does not have sufficient cash or credit to secure a new senior mortgage or trust deed loan.

FIGURE 7.4   Contract for Deed

Real Estate Sale Contract

BETWEEN

_____

_____

AND

_____

_____

Perfection Legal Forms & Printing Co., Rockford, Ill.

Form 101-AR – REAL ESTATE SALE CONTRACT _____   Perfection Legal Forms & Printing   ..ckford, Ill.

_____agree___ to buy at

the price of_____ ($_____) Dollars

the following described real estate, in County of_____ and State of_____ :

and

agree   to sell said premises at said price, and to convey to buyer good title thereto by warranty deed, with release of dower and homestead rights, subject only to:

(1) Existing leases or tenancy expiring_____;
(2) Special taxes or assessments levied or confirmed after date of possession; (3) Easements for public utilities;
(4) General taxes for the year   and subsequent years; (5) Building lines and building and use restrictions of record; (6) Zoning and building laws or ordinances; (7) Party wall rights or agreements, if any; (8) Roads and highways, if any; (9) Drainage ditches, feeders and laterals

FIGURE 7.4 Contract for Deed (continued)

Rents, water taxes, insurance premiums and accrued mortgage interest are to be pro-rated as of date of possession of deed and existing leases and insurance policies, if any, shall thereupon be assigned and delivered to purchaser. Seller shall deliver possession on or before_____, 19____. General taxes for the year_____ are to be pro-rated from January 1, to date of possession. If the amount of such taxes is not then ascertainable, pro-rating shall be on the basis of the amount of the most recent available information.

Buyer has paid_____ _____($_____) Dollars earnest money to be applied on purchase price, and agrees to pay the balance of_____ _____($_____) Dollars, as follows:

with interest to begin_____, 19____, at the rate of_____% per annum, payable_____on the whole sum remaining from time to time unpaid, said payments to be applied first in payment of interest and balance to reduction of purchase price.

Within twenty days from date hereof, seller shall deliver to buyer or his agent as evidence of title covering date hereof, showing record title in seller (or grantor) one of the following: (1) Merchantable abstract, (2) Owner's Guarantee Policy of Title insurance in the amount of the purchase price or a customary preliminary report on title subject to the usual objections contained in such policies, but seller, on furnishing such report shall not be in default for failure to furnish policy until ten days after demand therefor by buyer, such policy or report on title to be conclusive evidence of good title subject only to the exceptions therein stated.

If abstract be furnished, buyer, within fifteen days after delivery thereof, shall deliver to seller a written statement of his objections to the title, if any, with the abstract, otherwise title shown by abstract shall be deemed good.

If evidence of title furnished discloses any defect in title except matters to which this sale is subject by the terms hereof seller shall have forty days, computed from delivery of objections in case of an abstract, and from delivery of evidence of title in any other case, in which to cure all defects, to which this sale is not subject. Seller, at his election, may cure all objections to title by delivery of guarantee policy covering such objections such as he might have furnished in the first instance. If such defects in title be not cured within such forty days buyer may terminate this contract or may at his election, take the title as it then is (with right to deduct from purchase price liens of definite or ascertainable amount) on giving seller notice of such election and tendering performance. If no such notice be given or tender made within ten days after notice to buyer of seller's inability to cure such defects, this contract then shall be null and void. If this contract be terminated except for buyer's default earnest money shall be returned.

If buyer defaults hereunder, then, at the option of seller, earnest money shall be forfeited as liquidated damages and this contract then shall be null and void.

Seller expressly warrants that no notice from any city, village or other governmental authority of any dwelling code violation concerning said premises has been received by the owner of said premises or the owner's agent.

All notices and demands herein required shall be in writing. The mailing of a notice by registered mail to seller at _____, or to buyer at _____shall be sufficient service thereof, on date of mailing.

Time is of the essence of this contract.

Seller agrees to pay a broker's commission to_____in the amount fixed in present schedule of commissions of the Real Estate Board applicable to this sale.

This contract and earnest money shall be held in escrow by_____ for the mutual benefit of parties hereto, and after consummation the canceled contract may be retained by the escrowee. Unless buyer be entitled to a refund of earnest money, it shall be applied first to payment of expenses incurred for seller, and second to payment of said commission, balance, to be paid to seller.

Dated at_____this_____day of_____A. D. 19____

_____   _____

_____   _____

Despite its seeming simplicity, the contract for deed form of financing real estate is relatively complicated. It must be recorded to protect the vendee's rights in the property. A collection escrow should be established to make sure the payments on the underlying loan or loans are made on time and that proper records are kept. Provisions must be made at the outset for delivery to the vendee of the deed when the contract is paid in full. This deed should be fully executed at the time of establishing the contract and deposited with the collection escrow. Because of these complexities (and others) in establishing a contract for deed, competent legal advice should be sought.

JUNIOR FINANCE INSTRUMENTS

When special problems or needs arise in the financing of real estate, junior financial instruments are often used as part of the solution. The three senior loan forms can also be used for **junior loans.** Generally, when a deed of trust, mortgage, or contract for deed is used as a second encumbrance, the loan involves a higher risk and the lender should be aware of this circumstance.

Under normal conditions, most real estate sales are finalized when a buyer secures a new first deed of trust or mortgage from a financial fiduciary to cover the major portion of a property's purchase price. The balance, if any, is usually paid in cash as a down payment. Frequently, however, a buyer who has insufficient cash for the entire amount of the required down payment will make an offer to purchase a property based on the condition that the seller carry back a portion of the sales price in the form of a junior encumbrance (called a **carryback loan).** A seller might be asked to accept a purchase-money second mortgage or deed of trust for the amount needed to complete the transaction.

Thrifts and commercial banks participate as junior financiers in an effort to enhance their earnings. Junior loans are being established at market interest rates and are eligible for sale to Fannie Mae when they meet its underwriting criteria. A junior loan is issued to a creditworthy customer when the total of the existing senior loan and the new loan does not exceed 80 percent of the value of the collateral. Currently private mortgage insurance companies are becoming involved in the junior loan market, raising loan-to-value ratios to 90 percent. Many lenders today are also offering combinations of first and second mortgages to avoid paying any mortgage insurance premium. Examples of these programs are an 80/10/10, 75/15/10, or even 80/15/5 with the first mortgage remaining at 80 percent or less, a second mortgage of 10 or 15 percent, and the remainder as down payment.

In addition, mortgage brokers, mortgage bankers, and various small loan companies operating on direct lines of credit from commercial banks also arrange junior loans. Some companies buy and sell these "second securities" on a regular basis. This latter activity has created a secondary market for instruments of junior finance.

In addition to financing the purchase of commercial and residential properties, junior financing often provides funds for land developers to pay for off-site improvements such as streets, sidewalks, sewers, and other utility installations. A lender advances the funds necessary for these improvements and accepts a lien on all of the property involved. Such a lien usually is in second position behind a developer's purchase-money loan, which has been given as part of the purchase price of the land in its raw form. Once the land is subdivided, improved, built on, and sold, the underlying first lien and the junior lien for improvements are replaced by individual conventional or guaranteed loans executed by the buyers of the buildings constructed on the developed land.

Junior financing is being used by owners who have accumulated measurable equity in their property. This equity, acquired through a paydown of the first mortgage principal balance, through an inflationary rise in a property's value or through both, is being pledged as collateral to secure funds over short-term periods of up to five years. When these **equity loans** come due, borrowers usually refinance the entire property to secure a new loan adequate to pay all liens in full.

Owners also pledge their equity to secure funds for home improvements. Improvement loans are somewhat safer than other types of junior financing because they are secured not only by the equity pledged but also by the enhanced value of the improved property. Therefore, improvement loans may have longer terms of repayment than other forms of junior finance—some for as long as 20 years.

Freddie Mac has a program for the purchase of secured Home Improvement Loans (HILs) and is currently purchasing up to 80 percent of a loan originator's portfolio of home improvement loans, allowing lenders to leverage into additional business.

There are also third mortgages and deeds of trust, but these are relatively rare and used only occasionally. An example of a third mortgage is a case in which a real estate broker accepts such an encumbrance for a commission behind an already existing first mortgage and a purchase-money second mortgage carried back by the seller.

Home equity loans face significant defaults when the economy slows. Particularly at risk are the high-yield loans amounting to more than 100 percent of the value of the collateral. Interest on these loans is well above standard rates. Because most of these loans are pooled into residential-backed mortgage securities, the risks are being spread to a wide group of investors. Added to the possibilities of increased loan deficiencies is the 2002 report that overall household borrowing is up 46 percent in the past five years according to the Federal Reserve.

Predatory lending is the practice of charging excessive interest rates and up-front fees on home loans. Such lending usually targets elderly and minority borrowers who have significant equity in their homes but lack the income necessary to repay the loans. The result can be the loss of the home. Protection against predatory lending exists under the Home Ownership and Equity Protection Act of 1994 (HOEPA).

The Federal Reserve Board has approved new regulations that became effective October 1, 2002, to strengthen Regulation Z. Home loans are covered if the annual interest rate exceeds the rate of Treasury securities of comparable maturity by more than eight percentage points or the fees and points paid by the borrower exceed $480 including the costs of credit insurance and other debt protection products paid at closing. The new rules also tighten the prohibition against extending credit without regard to the borrower's repayment ability.

Second Mortgage/Deed of Trust

As its name implies, a **second mortgage** or deed of trust is a lien on real property that is second, or junior, in position behind an existing first lien. Just as the senior loan requires the execution of a note specifying the terms and conditions of the promise to pay, the junior loan calls for such a promissory note. In addition, the junior loan form itself is exactly the same as the senior loan form, except that the junior instrument includes, typed boldly on its face, the word SECOND to identify its junior priority position. The property that is described as collateral for the junior loan is the same property that is pledged as collateral for the existing senior loan.

Because the second loan is in a subordinate position, the junior lienholder is in a relatively high-risk position. If the senior encumbrance is not paid according to its terms and conditions, the senior lienholder may foreclose on the collateral property and sell it to recover as much of the outstanding senior debt as possible. This foreclosure process could effectively eliminate the junior lienholder's position in the subject property without commensurate compensation. After costs, the proceeds from the sale would be allocated to the senior lienholder first and then to the junior lienholder or lienholders, according to their priority positions. If the property did not sell for a price sufficient to satisfy the senior lender, no funds would be left to distribute to the junior lienholder(s).

In the event of a default, a senior lender knowing of the existence of a junior lien gives the junior lender a chance to step in and make the delinquent payments. The junior lender then forecloses against the collateral property. But the primary lender, usually a financial fiduciary, must be protected and will pursue any legal means available to maintain the value of the investment.

Clauses. Certain provisions can be incorporated into a junior lending instrument to protect the position of the junior lienholder against that of the senior lender. A clause can be included that grants the junior lender the right to pay property taxes, insurance premiums, and similar charges for a borrower who is not making these payments. These charges can then be added to the total debt in anticipation of foreclosure. Another clause can require the borrower to pay into escrow the funds for taxes, insurance, and the first mortgage payments to offset any possible delinquencies. The junior lender can also reserve the right to cure any default on the first mortgage.

Some junior mortgages include a **lifting clause** _or subordination clause_ that allows a borrower to replace an existing first mortgage without disturbing the status of the junior mortgage. The amount of the new first mortgage cannot exceed the specific amount of the original first mortgage outstanding at the time the second mortgage was established. Finally, if a **cross-defaulting clause** is included in the junior mortgage provisions, a default on the first mortgage automatically triggers a default on the second mortgage.

Junior Loan Interest Rates. _→ Typically higher than Sr. Loans_ It appears that interest rates should be high on loans that are in a high-risk position, such as second and third real estate loans. In many instances this is correct. The high interest rates offset to some degree the possibility of losses due to defaults. Junior loans secured from mortgage brokers and bankers, fiduciary lenders, and small loan companies usually do carry relatively high interest rates. It is interesting to observe, though, that junior carryback loans issued by sellers intent on completing the sales of their properties often include interest rates that are _at_ or _below_ market rates.

This phenomenon stems from the different objectives of these various lenders. Those in the lending business seek to maximize their profits by charging as much as the law and the borrower will accept. Other persons are trying to sell their properties and, because of circumstances, are forced to carry back junior financing at low interest rates to actually complete a sale. Their motivation is the sale of the property, not the yield on the loan.

As a practical matter, there can never be an effective legal limitation on the amount of interest that can be charged on a loan. If the law stipulates a specific maximum interest rate, rates above which would constitute **usury,** a lender and borrower can circumvent the restriction by charging points or raising the principal amount to reach a desired *effective yield*. Thus, a charge of two points on an $80,000 loan will result in the borrower's receiving only $78,400 in actual proceeds. The effective interest rate on a ten-year loan will be raised about ¼ percent. The alternative is to add the $1,600 to the total loan amount owed to create the same effect. The imposition of usury limitations on real estate loans in this country is currently obsolete.

There is increasing interest on the part of private mortgage insurance companies to provide protection for junior lenders. Currently at least five companies are offering insurance on junior loans that meet their underwriting requirements. Some plans reach as high as 90 percent of a residential property's value and up to 80 percent of an investment property's value from a combination of senior and junior loans. In addition, Freddie Mac has established a market for all types of junior loans, joining Fannie Mae, which is already in the junior loan secondary market.

SPECIAL PROVISIONS IN MORTGAGE LENDING INSTRUMENTS

All three instruments for real estate financing may be enhanced and expanded by a multitude of provisions designed to serve the specific requirements of individual loans. Some of the provisions to be reviewed in this chapter have already become standard practice and are incorporated regularly into loan instruments—for example, prepayment privileges and/or penalties and due-on-sale clauses. Some special provisions are used only rarely and under unique circumstances, such as lock-in clauses, subordination, or release clauses.

The variety of mortgage terms and conditions is virtually inexhaustible, being a function of individual creativity applied to satisfy differing circumstances, so it is virtually impossible to cover every situation. However, those provisions explained in this chapter should establish the basis for a greater understanding of the modern financial concepts presented in Chapter 13.

Late Payment Penalty

Many real estate loans include a clause that imposes a penalty, called a *late charge,* on the borrower for any late payments. Although most lenders accept payments up to 10 days or 15 days after they are due without penalizing a borrower, later payments incur a penalty charge—usually a percentage of the total payment or a flat fee of some previously specified amount.

Prepayment Privilege

A prepayment privilege, or a **prepayment clause,** usually allows a borrower to repay the balance of a loan at any time without any restriction or penalty. Some loans include a provision permitting certain portions of the balance to be paid in specific years. For instance, a note might include a prepayment privilege of no more than 10 percent of the original principal amount to be paid in any one year. Other loans might stipulate a fixed sum of money that can be paid in addition to the regular payments in a single year.

Prepayment Penalties

Normally, a lender will not want a borrower to prematurely repay a high-yield loan. If a borrower with a high-interest loan seeks to refinance the property, the existing mortgage would be repaid in full and the lender will lose the opportunity for high earnings. As a result, controls are established on prepayments when the interest rates and the lenders' resultant earnings are high.

One form of control is the inclusion of a prepayment penalty clause in the loan contract. This penalty usually constitutes a certain percentage of the original face amount of the loan, a percentage of the outstanding balance of the loan, or some fractional penalty, such as three months' interest. For example, if a contract includes a prepayment penalty clause of 3 percent of the remaining loan amount, the owner of a property will be charged $1,500 to repay an existing $50,000 principal balance prior to its normal amortization.

A lender will usually enforce the prepayment penalty when an existing loan is replaced by a new loan at lower interest or by a loan secured from another lender. However, the penalty is often waived when the lender of record refinances the property with a new loan at a higher interest rate. Some states have abolished the prepayment penalty entirely. FHA, VA, and most loans purchased by Fannie Mae and Freddie Mac do not permit any prepayment penalties.

Lock-in Clause

The most drastic form of prepayment control is a *lock-in clause* whereby a borrower is actually forbidden to pay a mortgage loan in full before a specific date, sometimes for as long as ten years after its inception. It seems obvious that this lock-in clause would be imposed primarily on very high-yield mortgage loans in order to preserve a lender's earning position for a prescribed time period.

Often combinations of the prepayment privilege, prepayment penalty, and lock-in clause are included in a single loan. For example, no prepayment would be allowed at all for a specified period of time from the date of the loan's inception. Then proportionate amounts of the loan would become payable in advance according to an agreed-upon schedule, with some penalty imposed if the loan were repaid after the three years but before its regularly scheduled time.

Due-on-Sale Clause

Many financing arrangements include a **due-on-sale clause,** also known as a *call* clause or *right-to-sell* clause. This condition stipulates that a borrower "shall not sell, transfer, encumber, assign, convey, or in any other manner dispose of the collateral property or any part thereof, or turn over the management or operation of any business on the collateral property to any other person, firm, or corporation, without the express prior written consent of the lender." The due-on-sale clause further stipulates that if any of the foregoing events should occur *without* the lender's consent, the loan balance becomes immediately due in full, with the threat of foreclosure if it is not paid.

The due-on-sale clause is designed to protect a lender from default by any subsequent buyer of the property who assumes the original loan. Studies have shown that fewer foreclosures occur against original borrowers than against the second or third buyers who assume these loans. The due-on-sale clause was designed to require each new purchaser wanting to assume the loan to pass a credit examination. If a new buyer's credit is found unacceptable, a lender can exercise the due-on-sale power and call in the balance of the loan. In this manner a lender can avoid difficulties that might arise from a new buyer's inability to meet the loan payments.

In reviewing a new buyer's request for permission to assume a loan, lenders may insist on certain terms and conditions before approving such an assumption. Depending on the circumstances, a lender could require additional cash as a larger down payment, adjust the interest rate on the existing balance to reflect the current market rate more accurately, charge a fee for the assumption, or impose any or all of these conditions, as well as others.

These practices by lenders caused a great deal of active controversy regarding the legality of the due-on-sale clause. Various state supreme courts upheld its validity, while others denied its enforceability. Some state courts ruled differently in cases involving federally chartered lenders versus state-chartered lenders.

On June 28, 1982, in the California case of *Fidelity Federal Savings and Loan Association v. de la Cuesta*, the U.S. Supreme Court settled those controversies and ruled in favor of the ability of federally chartered banks and savings institutions to enforce the due-on-sale provisions. Thus, assumptions of conventional loans have to be cleared prior to closing. Lenders agree in most cases to negotiate new interest rates based on a compromise between the existing rate and the market rate. This *blended rate* has generally become the norm.

The Garn-St. Germain Act of 1982 limited the enforcement of the due-on-sale clause in special situations, such as divorce settlements and the passing of title by inheritance.

Assumption versus Subject To

In the absence of a due-on-sale clause, deeds of trust, mortgages, or contracts for deed are immediately assumable by buyers of the collateral property. A buyer may arrange with a seller to purchase a property, assume an existing encumbrance, and make any arrangements for financing the difference between the balance of the existing loan and the purchase price. This difference can be paid for either in cash or by some form of junior financing or both.

There are two ways for a buyer to arrange responsibility for an existing loan. The loan can be **assumed** or the property purchased **subject to** any existing encumbrances. If a loan is assumed, the buyer, along with the original borrower and any intervening buyers who have also assumed the loan, becomes *personally liable* to the lender for its full repayment. In the event of a default, the lender will foreclose, sell the collateral, and sue the original maker of the note and mortgage, as well as all subsequent persons who assumed it, for any deficiencies incurred.

On the other hand, a buyer may purchase a property with an existing encumbrance but stipulate the purchase is *subject to* the lien of the debt. This approach eliminates the buyer's contingent personal liability in the event of a deficiency judgment. Only the original borrower and any subsequent assumers are liable. Under the *subject to* format, a buyer may simply walk away from the property, forfeit any equity that has accumulated, and avoid any future responsibility in the transaction.

Knowledge of the difference between the two approaches can be extremely useful under certain circumstances. For instance, a seller in a low-down-payment transaction would insist the buyer assume the underlying mortgage to bind more tightly the responsibility for the mortgage payments. Conversely, a buyer making a substantial down payment would insist on the *subject to* approach to eliminate any contingent liability.

Whether the buyer assumes the loan or buys subject to the lien, the original maker of the note and mortgage remains primarily responsible to the lender until the loan is paid in full or a buyer goes through a process of full substitution.

Full substitution has the seller of a property end personal legal liability as the originator of a real estate loan other than by paying it in full. This technique is called **novation,** in which the original borrower, as seller, submits a request to the lender to be replaced with the new buyer as maker on the loan instrument. After the new buyer completes the qualifying process, including a credit analysis, and is accepted by the lender, the old borrower is completely released from liability. The transfer of obligation is completed by executing an amendment to the original loan contract. The new agreement is recorded to maintain the appropriate continuity of the property's title.

Subordination Clause — or Lifting Clause —

To **subordinate** means to place in a lower order, class, or rank. In real estate finance it involves placing an existing encumbrance or right in a lower-priority position to a new loan secured by the same collateral property.

Any real estate finance instrument can be designed to provide for its subordination to the rights of some future lien. For example, a loan created to finance the sale of vacant land to a developer could include a subordination clause granting the developer an opportunity to secure new financing to construct houses on a portion of the already encumbered land. Because the construction lender for the houses would insist on being in *first lien* position, the existing loan given to buy the land would have to be subordinated on those specific portions to be financed with construction mortgages. The land mortgage would then be in a *junior lien* position to the first mortgagee on those specific parcels on which houses were to be built. The wording used to establish this type of subordination could be "The mortgagee shall, upon written request from the mortgagor, subordinate the lien of this mortgage on the lot or lots specified in order of release, to the lien of a new construction loan or loans from a recognized lending institution." Subordination is also employed with land leases where the interests of a landlord are subordinated to a new mortgage secured by a tenant in order to develop a parcel of land (see Chapter 13).

Release Clause

When two or more properties are pledged as collateral for a loan, some provision for releasing a portion of the collateral as certain amounts of the loan are repaid is usually incorporated into the financing instrument. A comprehensive analysis of release clauses is included in Chapter 13.

Exculpatory Clause

When securing a new real estate loan, some borrowers require that their assets, other than the property being financed, be protected from attachment in the event of a future foreclosure. This limited personal liability can be established by the inclusion of an **exculpatory clause** in the loan contract. This clause stipulates that the borrower's liability under the loan is limited to the property designated in the legal description. In the event of a default, the lender is limited to the recovery of the collateral property only and cannot pursue any deficiency judgments against the borrower's remaining assets.

Nonrecourse Clause

Real estate loans are often sold in the financial market (see Chapter 4). When a **nonrecourse clause** is included in the sale's agreement, the seller of the security is not liable if the borrower defaults. The buyer of the security must take action to recover the unpaid balance of the loan from the borrower or foreclose on the collateral. However, if a real estate loan is sold *with recourse,* the seller of the security is obligated to reimburse the buyer if the borrower defaults.

Extensions and Modifications

Some loan instruments include provisions for extensions or modifications under special circumstances. Sometimes a lender will allow an extension of time for a financially troubled borrower to continue payments beyond a specific due date. Other lenders may make adjustments and modifications in loan contracts in order to meet particular problems arising after a loan has been in effect for some time. These modifications could include adjustments in payments, interest rates, due dates, or, in extreme cases, payment moratoriums.

Two major problems arise from an extension or modification of a real estate loan instrument. The first concerns the rights of an intervening lienor who may move into a priority position when an existing loan is recast. Lenders usually require a complete title examination prior to modifying their loans in order to meet such contingencies. The second problem is the possibility of negating the insurance or guarantee that a mortgage may have under its original form. In the event of any modifications to an insured loan, the guarantee may be lost.

Although a borrower may experience frequent difficulty in meeting payments, lenders are disinclined to make any permanent alteration in the terms of a loan, because of the problems mentioned above. Lenders prefer to waive either full or partial payments temporarily as the situation dictates. After the borrower has overcome temporary difficulties, these payments can be made up over the remaining term of the loan. Under some circumstances, such as a delinquent construction loan, the lender usually continues to carry the loan until the builder can sell the property to a qualified buyer. The delinquency is preferred to a modification and recasting of the loan, which might jeopardize lien priorities.

SUMMARY

A person can borrow money by pledging interests in real estate as collateral to guarantee the promise to repay. Usually a borrower's ownership interest in property is encumbered to a lender for this purpose. However, other property interests can also be pledged as collateral for a loan—interests such as leaseholds, life estates, and mineral, air, and water rights.

One instrument of real estate finance is the deed of trust, which pledges the subject property as collateral for a loan drawn in favor of a third-party trustee. A deed of trust includes a power of sale clause and if a default occurs, the trustee can sell the property to recover any losses in as little as four months.

Another real estate financing instrument is the note and mortgage. A note is a promise to pay, while a mortgage is the pledge of a specific parcel of real property as collateral to secure this promise. A note signed by a mortgagor is a negotiable instrument that specifies the terms and conditions for the repayment of a debt. A mortgage signed by both mortgagor and mortgagee establishes a lien on the collateral property as of the date it is recorded. When a mortgage debt is paid in full, the mortgagee marks the note "paid in full," signs it, and returns it to its maker, along with a satisfaction of mortgage form, which will clear the record of the mortgage lien.

A contract for deed is, at the same time, both a sales agreement and a financing instrument between the buyer-borrower-vendee and the seller-lender-vendor. The full terms of the sale, as well as the manner in which the loan will be repaid, are elaborated in this contract financing form. The buyer is granted possession and control of the property during the term of the payments under the conditions specified in the contract. When the terms of the contract are satisfied, the seller delivers a deed to the buyer, which transfers full legal title. The contract for deed form of real estate financing is used primarily when other financing means are not available.

When a prospective property buyer does not have enough cash to satisfy the down payment requirement, a second mortgage, second deed of trust, or junior contract for deed may be carried back by the seller to finance the difference. Owners often pledge their equity as collateral for loans for home improvements or personal needs. Junior instruments of finance are second in priority to an existing senior loan.

All three financing instruments may be expanded by a variety of provisions designed to serve the needs of individual borrowers and lenders. Real estate loans may include special provisions to allow for the prepayment of portions of the principal from time to time. Other loans impose prepayment penalties if the loan is paid prior to its regularly scheduled completion date. A lock-in clause prohibits any prepayment for certain specified time periods. Penalties imposed to inhibit prepayments are usually designed to preserve a lender's earnings position, and these penalties are generally included in high-interest rate loans.

Although some federally insured or guaranteed mortgages are assumable without the consent of their lenders, most conventional mortgages include a due-on-sale clause, which stipulates that a borrower cannot sell the collateral property or transfer it in any manner without the prior written consent of the lender. In the absence of a due-on-sale clause, property may be sold with the existing loan remaining in effect. The buyer has two ways in which to arrange responsibility for an existing loan. It can be "assumed," in which case the buyer along with the original borrower becomes personally liable for the loan. The buyer can also make the purchase "subject to" this encumbrance. The latter technique eliminates the buyer's personal liability on the loan, although the originator of the loan remains personally liable until the loan is paid in full. Infrequently, a seller requires a buyer to pursue a process of novation, which, upon its successful completion, substitutes the buyer for the seller on an existing loan contract.

To subordinate a finance instrument is to change its priority lien position in relation to subsequent loan instruments. Lending instruments may also be extended or modified to solve unforeseen financial problems. With the written agreement of all parties to a loan contract, a payment can be altered or waived for a certain time period.

CHAPTER 8

Conventional Loans

▼ KEY TERMS

adjustable-rate loan
Affordable Gold®
buydown
Community Home
  Buyer®

conforming loans
conventional loans
fixed-rate loans
loan-to-value (LTV) ratios

nonconforming loan
private mortgage
  insurance (PMI)
subprime loans

3 Types of Loans
1) conventional
2) Govt. Insured
_   by FHA_
3) Govt. Guaranteed
_   by VA_

There are three general types of real estate loans: conventional, government insured by the _FHA_ Federal Housing Administration (FHA), and government guaranteed by the Veterans _VA_ Administration (VA). The conventional loan has no insurance or guarantee by any agency of the federal government.

It is important to note that most of the real estate loans made today are **conventional loans.** Moreover most originators of conventional loans do not keep them for their own portfolios but sell them in the secondary market. They do keep the collection responsibilities and the commensurate fees. To sell these loans, the lenders adhere to the guidelines established by Fannie Mae and Freddie Mac, described in Chapter 4.

INTEREST RATES

The rate of interest is defined as the cost of borrowing money. It is the price that a borrower pays for the use of a lender's money. Conventional loans, as well as FHA and VA loans, are made at market rates.

Demand exceeds supply = interest rate ↑up

Interest rates result from the interplay of a complex variety of forces continually at work in the marketplace. Of primary importance is the relationship between the _supply of_ and the _demand for_ money. When demand exceeds supply, the cost of funds—the interest rate— goes up. The reverse is also true. Normally, when there is an increase in business activity, demand for funds increases, supplies of money decrease, and interest rates rise.

Fixed-Rate Loans

Conventional loans have traditionally been designed as **fixed-rate loans** in which the interest rate remains constant over the term of the loan (although other variable features can be included in the loan contract). Fixed-rate loans may be amortized over a specific number of years in equal monthly payments, including principal and interest. They also may be structured as term loans, requiring interest-only payments and a balloon payment at a specified future date. They can be designed as growing-equity mortgages (GEMs), where the borrower pays additional principal each month to accelerate its satisfaction. A fixed-rate loan may also be established under a graduated-payment mortgage (GPM) plan. The favorite fixed-rate loan has been the 30-year mortgage. The payment is predictable, and the opportunity always exists to pay the balance of the loan down or off, depending on the borrower's financial circumstances and the opportunity to refinance at a lower cost.

*F*OR EXAMPLE

30-Year Fixed-Rate Self-Amortizing Loan $100,000 @ 7%

Month	Fixed Payment	Interest	Principal	Balance
0				100,000.00
1	665.31	583.33	81.98	99,918.02
2	665.31	582.85	82.46	99,835.56
3	665.31	582.37	82.94	99,752.62
4	665.31	581.89	83.42	99,669.20
5	665.31	581.40	83.91	99,585.29

Etc., to 360

Fixed-rate loans for 15 years are becoming increasingly popular. Lenders like them because of their relatively short amortization time, and they market these loans on the basis of the borrower's being able to save significant amounts of interest, compared with the 30-year loan. Moreover, 15-year loans are usually offered at 25 to 50 basis points below market rates. (There are 100 basis points in 1 percent, so 25 basis points equal one-fourth of 1 percent, whereas 50 basis points equal one-half of 1 percent.) However, the monthly payment required on the 15-year loan is approximately 20 percent higher than the payment on the 30-year loan, which inhibits many borrowers.

*F*OR EXAMPLE

15-Year Fixed-Rate Self-Amortizing Loan $100,000 @ 7%

Month	Fixed Payment	Interest	Principal	Balance
0				100,000.00
1	898.83	583.33	315.50	99,684.50
2	898.83	581.49	317.34	99,367.16
3	898.83	579.41	319.42	99,047.74
4	898.83	577.77	321.06	98,726.68
5	898.83	575.90	322.93	98,403.75

Etc., to 180

Adjustable-Rate Mortgages (ARMs)

In a conventional **adjustable-rate loan** the borrower shares with the lender the risks of a fluctuating interest rate economy. The ARM allows the lender to make interest rate adjustments by referring to a national index readily available for the borrower's inspection.

ARMs vary in several respects. They vary in adjustment terms; Six-month, three-year, and five-year ARMs are typical. Some ARMs change twice in the first year and annually thereafter. Other ARMs do not change for three years but change annually thereafter.

ARMs also vary as to caps, the maximum interest rate or payments that can be charged. Some ARMs have no caps; others have annual and lifetime caps, annual caps only, lifetime caps only, or interest rate caps rather than payment caps—the latter providing the potential for negative amortization.

*F*OR EXAMPLE

Consider a loan where the payment is capped at an amount *less* than it would take to pay *only the interest amount* required under an annual index adjustment. The difference in interest owed would then have to be *added* to the outstanding principal balance, resulting in negative amortization.

ARMs vary as to indexes. There are many different indexes from which a lender can select:

- *Six-Month Treasury Bill Index.* This index is based on the results of the auction for 180-day T-bills, which is held every Monday. The index is the average yield as quoted on a bank discount basis. The auction results are available in Tuesday's *Wall Street Journal.*
- *Three-Year Treasury Index.* This is a composite or average of U.S. securities adjusted to a constant maturity of three years. This yield is published in the Federal Reserve statistical release with both weekly and monthly averages.
- *Five-Year Treasury Index.* The description is the same as for the three-year index, except the securities are adjusted to a constant maturity of five years.
- *Cost of Funds Index.* This index is compiled by the FHLB and is the average monthly costs of deposits and borrowing for thrifts in each bank district. This index, referred to as the *Monthly Median Cost of Funds,* is for all districts. However, some monthly or semiannual costs of funds indexes are linked to individual districts, as is the case with the 11th (San Francisco) District.
- *LIBOR.* The Lender Interbank Interest Rate.

ARMs vary in margin requirements. Two ARMs might be identical in all respects except margin, the percentage factor added to a future index to determine the rate and payment change. At the time of adjustment, the new rate is determined by adding a predetermined margin, usually 1.5 percent to 3 percent, to the current index. The rate adjustments may lead to an increase or decrease in payments, to ensure that the loan is paid in full within the original term.

Some ARMs are *convertible* and contain provisions that allow the borrower to convert to a fixed-rate loan at a future date.

*F**OR EXAMPLE***

Consider an ARM drawn at 7% interest for 30 years with an annual interest rate cap of 1% and a lifetime cap of 5%. It also includes a conversion privilege to a fixed-rate loan at 10% any time after five years. If the lender had adjusted the interest rate upwards at 1% per year for five years, to a 12% rate, it would behoove the borrower to exercise the conversion privilege at the first opportunity.

ARM programs allow the mortgage interest rate to be adjusted up or down periodically, every six months, three years, or five years, depending on the program that meets the needs of the borrower. ARM loans are usually amortized over a 30-year term, but 15-year plans are also available.

*F**OR EXAMPLE***

Consider a one-year ARM starting at 7.125% with 2% annual and 6% lifetime interest caps and a margin of 275 basis points (2.75%) tied to a three-year Treasury index, which is 4.55%.

- The rate cannot change by more than 2% at the annual adjustment.
- The rate can never be higher than 13.125% (7.125% + 6%).
- When it is time for a rate change, the lender will add 2.75% to the index 45 days prior to the rate change to determine the new rate. The rate will probably be rounded off to the nearest ⅛%. If this results in a rate change greater than 2%, the rate change will be limited to 2%.

A major advantage of an ARM to the borrower is greater affordability, because the interest rate, at least at the outset of the loan, is generally below the market interest rate. Under an ARM, there are usually no prepayment penalties and assumptions are normally allowed. However, jumbo ARMs, for more than $252,700, currently often include prepayment penalties. (See Chapter 13 for more information on the ARM.)

PRIVATE MORTGAGE INSURANCE (PMI)

Mortgage insurance is issued to protect the lender in case the borrower defaults on the loan payments. If a property is foreclosed, the insurance company either pays the lender in full and acquires the property or pays the lender in accordance with the terms of the insurance plan plus expenses, and the lender acquires the property.

Private mortgage insurance (PMI) is required on most conventional loans when the **loan-to-value (LTV) ratio** is in excess of 80 percent as stated in the Fannie Mae and Freddie Mac guidelines. Thus, the insurance covers the amount of the loan in excess of the 80 percent LTV ratio. In addition, some private mortgage insurance companies require first-time homebuyers to pursue a course of education on the responsibilities of home ownership prior to securing their loan. Private mortgage insurance programs can vary in the need for coverage and amount of coverage required. Rates can also vary depending on the private mortgage insurance carrier.

IN PRACTICE . . .

Jack Smart has decided that he likes the idea of an adjustable rate mortgage. The lower initial interest appeals to him because he is just starting his new job as a computer programmer at a fairly moderate salary, but he anticipates some large jumps in pay over the next five years. He and his loan officer, Bill Smith, are working out a table that would show the "worst case" scenario for the next five years on the ARM he is considering: $150,000 one-year ARM with an initial rate of 5.5%, 2/6 caps, based on a three-year T-bill index with a lender margin of 2.5%.

Regardless of changes in the note rate (index plus margin) the most the interest rate can increase is limited to 2% per year, and 11.5% for life of the loan.

Year 1	5.50%	$ 848
Year 2	7.50%	$1,042
Year 3	9.50%	$1,251
Year 4	11.50%	$1,471
Year 5	11.50%	$1,471

Although some borrowers may choose to pay part or all of the private mortgage insurance at closing, it is more common today for the annual renewal fee to be paid monthly and added to the PITI payment. The annual premium is calculated as a percentage of the loan amount (generally ranging from .65 percent to .90 percent depending on the amount of down payment) divided by 12 and added to the monthly mortgage PITI payment.

> $100,000 fixed rate, 30-year loan with 10 percent down (90 percent LTV)
> Premium: 0.75 percent of loan amount
> Calculation: $100,000 × 0.75 = $750 annual premium
> $750 ÷ by 12 = $62.50 added to PITI payment

There are also PMI payment plans in which the costs are financed. This is accomplished by adding the lump sum premium amount to the loan balance to be repaid over the life of the loan. There is also a plan where the lender pays the PMI, but the borrower pays a higher interest rate on the PMI portion of the loan. The advantage to the borrower is that all of the interest is deductible. The disadvantage is that the higher interest rate remains for the life of the loan.

PMI premiums continue until the lender releases the coverage, which depends not only on the increased equity position of the borrower, but on the payment history as well. Once the LTV ratio reaches 80 percent, the insurance company is no longer liable for any losses due to default by the borrower and the insurance premium payments should stop. Usually the borrower must initiate the release.

After years of controversy about the routine overpayment of private mortgage insurance premiums by uninformed borrowers, Congress passed the Home Owners Protection Act in 1998 to rectify the situation. The new law took effect on July 29, 1999, and applies only to residential mortgage loans secured by single-family, owner-occupied dwellings closed after July 29, 1999.

Under this law, PMI premiums must be terminated automatically when the LTV ratio is scheduled to reach 78 percent of the property's *original* value, not its current market value. Termination is required only if the loan payments are current. Borrowers may also request to have the PMI canceled when the LTV ratio reaches 80 percent, if their recent payment history is unblemished and there is no other debt on the property. If the borrower is current, under no circumstances can PMI be required beyond the midpoint of a loan's amortization period.

Fannie Mae and Freddie Mac have introduced some innovations in their requirements for private mortgage insurance. In January 1999 both agencies reduced the required insurance coverage on their 5 percent down loans from 30 percent to 25 percent and on their 10 percent down loans from 25 percent to 17 percent. The lower coverage results from their improved underwriting technology and special arrangements with private mortgage insurance companies.

In addition, both Fannie Mae and Freddie Mac have issued new guidelines insisting that mortgage lenders and servicers doing business with them automatically terminate PMI premiums on all *existing* loans that are halfway through their term. They have reiterated their long-standing policies to drop PMI once a homeowner reaches 20 percent equity, and they will calculate this figure by including the value of the home improvements and market appreciation. However, this approach is not automatic; the borrower must have a record of timely payments, formally request such an action, and will be charged a fee for a new appraisal.

A way for a borrower to totally avoid paying a PMI premium that has become popular in some areas is called an 80/10/10, an 80/15/5, or even an 80/20/0. In each case the first mortgage remains at 80 percent LTV, which requires no PMI. The second number represents a second mortgage which is held by the same lender but at a slightly higher rate and shorter term. The last number represents the down payment. The actual monthly payment is usually less than it would have been with a 95 percent or 97 percent LTV, and all of the interest is deductible.

PMI companies have expanded their coverages from basic residential insurance, which is presently the bulk of their business, into commercial and industrial mortgage and lease guarantee insurance. For example, the Mortgage Guaranty Insurance Corporation (MGIC) insures the top portion of loans on multifamily, commercial, and industrial properties. It owns a subsidiary company, the Commercial Leasehold Insurance Corporation (CLIC), which insures commercial tenants' lease payments and loans issued for leasehold improvements. These special policies are normally written for five years, and the insurance premiums can be either a percentage of the loan as a one-time charge or an agreed-upon annual premium. A renewal fee is charged at the end of the five-year term if the insurance is extended. Figure 8.1 lists the members of the Mortgage Insurance Companies of America.

PERMANENT/TEMPORARY (ESCROW) BUYDOWN PLAN

A **buydown** is money paid by someone (seller, builder, employer, buyer) to a lender in return for a lower interest rate and monthly payment. This buydown payment may lower the borrower's payments for the entire loan term (a permanent buydown) or for a lesser period of time, usually one year to three years (temporary or escrow buydown). (Also see Chapter 13.)

FIGURE 8.1   Members of the Mortgage Insurance Companies of America, 727 Fifteenth Street N.W., 12th floor, Washington, DC 20005, 202-393-5566.

GE Capital Mortgage
Insurance Co.
6601 Six Forks Road
Raleigh, NC 27615
1-800-334-9270
🖱 www.ge.com/capitalmortgage

Mortgage Guaranty Insurance Co.
250 East Kilbourn Avenue
Milwaukee, WI 53202
1-800-558-9900
🖱 www.mgic.com

PMI Mortgage Insurance Co.
3975 Fair Ridge Drive, Suite 450
Fairfax, VA 22033
🖱 www.pmi.com

Radian Guaranty
(merger of Amerin Guaranty and
   Commonwealth Mortgage Assurance Co.)
1601 Market Street
Philadelphia, PA 19103
1-800-523-1988
🖱 www.radianmi.com

Republic Mortgage
Insurance Co.
4964 University Parkway
Winston-Salem, NC 27106
1-800-999-7642
🖱 www.rmic.com

Triad Guaranty Insurance Co.
101 South Stratford Road,
   Suite 500
Winston-Salem, NC 27104
1-800-451-4872
🖱 www.tgic.com

United Guaranty Residential
Insurance Co.
230 North Elm Street
Greensboro, NC 27401
1-800-334-8966
🖱 www.ugcorp.com

*F*OR EXAMPLE

Assume a $100,000 loan for 30 years at 8% interest. TO PERMANENTLY buy down this interest rate to 7.75% would cost approximately 6 points, or 6% of the loan amount ($6,246).

$100,000 @ 8% for 30 years	$ 733.77 PI per month
$100,000 @ 7.75% 30 years	716.42 PI per month
Difference	17.35 per month x 360 months
Buydown Costs	$6,246.00

Depending on market conditions for a particular area, it might be possible to lower an interest rate from 8 percent to 7.75 percent by paying as little as one and one-half to two points, which would be much less than the calculated buydown cost.

*F*OR EXAMPLE

Assume a $100,000 loan for 30 years at 8%. To apply a TEMPORARY buy-down of 2-1-0 would cost $2,432.04, or approximately two and one-half points.

Payment	Rate	Reg. P&I	Effective Rate	P&I	Difference
1st year	8%	$733.77	6%	599.56	134.21
2nd year	8%	733.77	7%	665.31	68.46
3rd year	8%	733.77	8%	733.77	0.00
Etc.					

Buydown Cost 1st year	$134.21 × 12 =	$1,610.52
Buydown Cost 2nd year	$ 68.46 × 12 =	821.52
Total Buydown Costs		$2,432.04

BORROWER'S QUALIFICATIONS

The following Fannie Mae and Freddie Mac guidelines are generally used to qualify borrowers for conventional loans (It is important to know that loan underwriters have flexibility in applying these guidelines in specific cases and that the rules can be changed from time to time.) A conventional loan borrower worksheet is shown in Figure 8.2.

Rule 1.   Principal, interest, taxes, property insurance, private mortgage insurance, and any applicable condominium or homeowner association fees shall not exceed 28 percent of borrower's gross monthly income.

Rule 2.   All of the above plus monthly debts shall not exceed 36 percent of borrower's gross monthly income.

Rule 3.   Borrower must have good credit.

Rule 4.   Borrower must have stable employment.

*F*OR EXAMPLE 1:

(Refer to Figure 8.2, the Conventional Loan Borrower Qualification Worksheet.)

The borrowers have a combined gross monthly income of $5,000. The loan amount applied for is $100,000 at 7½% for 30 years payable at $699.22 per month principal and interest. The monthly property taxes are $300, insurance is $30, PMI premium is $62.50, and the neighborhood association fee is $20 per month. In addition, the borrowers have a monthly installment obligation of $100, a minimum revolving charge payment of $50, an auto loan payment of $175, child care expenses of $200 per month, and other monthly charges of $100. They have stable jobs and good credit. Do they qualify under rules number 1 and 2?

Combined Monthly Gross Income	$5,000.00
Housing Expenses:	
Principal and Interest	$699.22
Property Taxes	300.00
Hazard Insurance	30.00
PMI Premium	62.50
Association Fees	20.00
Total:	$1,111.72 ÷ 5,000 = 22.23% OK

(continued)

FIGURE 8.2   Conventional Loan Borrower Qualification Worksheet

Mortgage $ _____

Gross Monthly Income $ _____ (A)

Housing Expense
    Principal and Interest at 0% $ _____
    Property Taxes   _____
    Fire (Hazard) Insurance   _____
    Monthly PMI Premiums   _____
    Association Fees   _____
    Total $ _____ (B)

Debts
    Installment Obligations $ _____
    Revolving Charges (Minimum Payment)   _____
    Auto Loans   _____
    Child Support/Alimony Payable   _____
    Child Care Expenses   _____
    Other   _____
    Total Debts $ _____ (C)

(B/A) × 100 = _____ % Housing expense (B) should be less than 28% of gross monthly income (A)

[(B+C)/A)] × 100 = _____ % Housing expense (B) plus long-term debt (C) should be less than 36% of gross monthly income (A)

FOR EXAMPLE 1: (continued)

Debt Expenses:	
Installment Payments	100.00
Revolving Charges	50.00
Auto Loan	175.00
Child Care	200.00
Other	100.00
Total:	625.00
Plus Housing Expenses	1,111.72
Grand Total:	$1,736.72 ÷ 5,000 = 34.73% OK

FOR EXAMPLE 2:

A single parent's gross monthly income is $3,000. The loan amount applied for is $75,000 at 7½% for 30 years with a monthly principal and interest payment of $524.42. The property taxes are $200 per month, insurance is $20, and the PMI is $60. Installment obligations are $100 per month, the auto loan payment is $80, child care is $100, and other payments cost $100 per month. Does the borrower qualify under rules 1 and 2?

Monthly Gross Income	$3,000.00
Housing Expenses:	
Principal and Interest	$524.42
Property Taxes	200.00
Hazard Insurance	20.00
PMI Premium	60.00
Total:	$804.42 ÷ 3,000 = 26.81% OK

(continued)

*F*OR EXAMPLE 2: (continued)

Debt Expenses:	
Installment Payments	100.00
Auto Loan	80.00
Child Care	100.00
Other	100.00
Total:	380.00
Plus Housing Expenses	804.42
Grand Total:	$1,184.42 ÷ 3,000 = 39.48% Not OK

To qualify, this borrower will have to pay off the debt under "other."

SPECIAL CONVENTIONAL LOAN PROGRAMS

Following a trend to make home loans available to more people, even those with less than perfect credit histories and those with low down payments, lenders have developed new financing products to serve these emerging markets.

Community Home Buyer®

Fannie Mae first introduced **Community Home Buyer®** in its "affordable loan" products. With higher qualifying ratios of 33 percent for housing expense, and 38 percent for total debt ratio, many more people are able to qualify for a loan. Borrowers have to be within certain income limits based on median income figures for their particular geographic area and are required to attend a homebuyer education course. Another feature of this new loan product was in the treatment of the 5 percent down payment requirement. The borrower could now contribute 3 percent from their own funds; the remaining 2 percent could be in the form of a family member gift, housing assistance grant, or even a secured loan. More recently, both the Fannie Mae and Freddie Mac loans require only a 3 percent down payment.

Affordable Gold®

A Freddie Mac conventional loan program called **Affordable Gold®** is designed for home buyers with little or no debt. Purchasers are qualified with a total debt ratio of 38 percent. The program requires the borrower to fit within income limits and attend a homebuyer education class.

Both the Community Home Buyer® and the Affordable Gold® loan products allow for seller contributions to purchaser's closing costs up to 3 percent of the sales price with a 5 percent down payment, and up to 6 percent of the sales price with 10 percent down. Both products require PMI with less than 20 percent down.

The newest of the affordable loan products, Fannie Mae Flex '97 and Freddie Mac Alt '97 (as described in Chapter 4), have no restriction on the source of the 3 percent from the purchaser. They feature no income limits and lower PMI premiums (in some cases, none); however, they do require that the borrower have an excellent credit score.

Zero Down Payment Mortgage

The Bank of America introduced the "Neighborhood Advantage Zero Down Mortgage" to serve persons who have little cash for a down payment and low incomes but excellent credit histories. The bank researched this underserved market and found that many of their borrowers' credit quality is not necessarily related to their levels of income. The new mortgages are insured by the G.E. Capital Mortgage Insurance Corporation. The loans meet Fannie Mae and Freddie Mac **conforming loan** guidelines. Some closing costs are imposed but are about half of the cash requirements of other mortgages. These closing costs may be paid by gifts, a loan, a government grant, or by the seller.

Automatic Rate Reduction Loan

Some smaller mortgage loan companies are introducing a new product into the finance market, a real estate loan with an interest rate that can never go higher than the contract amount, but that refinances itself lower—with no closing fees to the borrower—whenever the market interest rates decline.

For example, in the East, clients of the Fairfax, Virginia-based Service Saver Finance Company, and in the West, clients of the San Diego-based City Line Mortgage Corporation can secure automatic rate reduction loans that impact when their existing loan interest rates are as little as ½ to ¾ of a percent higher than the going market rate. No credit checks, no appraisals, and no income verifications are required. The only criterion is that the borrowers must have made all payments on time during the prior 12 months and have maintained their creditworthiness and income levels that they had when they obtained the original loan.

Some of the major lenders such as Wells Fargo offer similar programs today as a result of the lenders' desire to keep their good loans on the books in the face of continuing refinancing pressures and be able to preserve their collection fees, which constitute a large part of their profit picture.

Subprime Loans

In the financial world, mortgage loans are designated as A, B, C, or D "paper." Ideally, all borrowers would be rated "A." There are cases, however, where the loan is considered to "B" quality—showing definite credit problems—"C" quality for borrowers with very marginal or poor credit, or even "D" quality, which indicates a very high risk on the loan. Lenders who provide loans or even specialize in the B, C, or D quality paper are called subprime lenders.

Subprime loans are made to persons with less-than-perfect credit ratings and usually carry higher interest rates and fees than the "prime" loans offered to applicants with no credit problems. In the current market, where prime loans are made at about 7 percent, subprime loans range from 8 percent to 12 percent.

Track Record Adjusted Mortgage

Dozens of lenders engaged in the "subprime" market, have developed a new loan that automatically reduces the interest rate after a period of time, often two years, of regular, on-time monthly mortgage payments. In addition, some borrowers may qualify for lower rates after completing a credit management counseling program and making timely payments for at least 12 months.

When subprime lenders offer their customers the opportunity to lower their interest rates, they hope to keep them on the books longer and to end up with lower numbers of defaults and foreclosures. Those who reestablish good credit will be less likely to refinance elsewhere knowing that they will be rewarded with a rate cut by their current lender.

Refinancing Existing Conventional Loans

With mortgage interest rates at relatively low levels for the past few years, many homeowners have considered refinancing their existing loans as a method for saving money by lowering their monthly payments. The amount of this saving may not be cost effective for everyone, however. The costs of refinancing are unregulated and vary dramatically among lenders. A new loan may require an application fee, title insurance, an appraisal, an attorney, and probably some discount charges in the form of points where one point equals one percent of the loan amount. Thus, it is important to determine the total costs before making a decision to refinance.

For example, assume a balance exists on a 30-year amortizing loan of $100,000 at 8 percent with a monthly payment of $733.77, including principal and interest. To refinance this amount with a new 30-year loan at 7 percent interest will require a monthly payment of $665.31, a savings of $68.46 per month. If the costs of securing this new financing total is $3,500, it will take about 51 months to recover the costs ($3,500 ÷ 68.46 = 51.12 months). It is generally accepted that a rule to use in analyzing the advisability of refinancing is that the costs of the new loan should be recovered over a two-year to three-year period. Thus, when the owner continues to occupy the property for a longer period of time, a savings will be achieved.

Some persons are better off not refinancing their home loans. Before making the decision, it is important to discuss a loan modification with the existing lender. Although some lenders may not be willing to modify their existing loan structures, many large mortgage companies have created customer retention programs to keep their best customers on the books. They may offer a lower interest rate with minimal transaction fees eliminating the need for refinancing.

Electronic Real Estate Loan Services

There are many sites on the World Wide Web offering real estate loans and related services. A borrower can arrange for a residential loan on the computer without the necessity for a face-to-face interview with the lender. It still requires the filing of a loan application and the probable submission of ancillary documents such as bank statements and annual income tax reports.

Applicants should be aware that the companies offering loans on the net are not regulated, and it is possible for some scam artists to offer loans for a fee and then disappear. It is also difficult for federal agencies to enforce their rules of disclosure under various settlement requirements. The following are some of the more popular web sites.

1. **Lending Tree (http://www.lendingtree.com)**
   This new company offers customized loan quotes within two days with no broker fees. The borrower needs to inform them of the loan requirements.
2. **Microsoft (http://homeadvisor.msn.com)**
   This company provides information for prospective homebuyers and features selected mortgage companies.
3. **Quicken Loans (http://quickenloans.quicken.com)**
   This company allows comparison shopping among its 15 lenders and provides for an application for a loan online.
4. **E-Loan (http://www.e-loan.com)**
   This company provides easy-to-use loan rate and term comparisons plus an e-mail update service on the mortgage.
5. **CyberLoan (http://www.cyberloan.com)**
   This company accepts online residential loan applications, prequalifies them, and sends them to more than 500 lending institutions nationwide. The system matches the financial information found in the loan application with a database detailing each lending institution's underwriting criteria and automatically routes the application to the most likely lender.
6. Other Lender Sites:
   Bank of America (http://www.bankofamerica.com)
   Citibank Mortgage (http://www.citibank.com)
   GMAC Mortgage Corp. (http://www.gmacmortgage.com)
   Wells Fargo Home Mortgage (http://www.wellsfargo.com/mortgage)

SUMMARY

There are three general types of real estate loans: government insured, government guaranteed, and conventional. In a conventional loan, there is no federal government insurance or guarantee.

Conventional loans are usually made at 75 percent to 80 percent of the property's value. Some loan-to-value (LTV) ratios are increased to as much as 97 percent with the addition of private mortgage insurance (PMI) to cover the portion above 80 percent.

Conventional loans traditionally have been fixed-rate loans, where the interest rate remains constant over the term of the loan. Adjustable-rate conventional loans (ARMs) are also available, where the lender has the right to adjust the interest rates periodically according to the terms of the loan.

Fannie Mae and Freddie Mac have an established set of loan guidelines to be followed by lenders who wish to sell their conventional loans to these participants in the secondary market. These guidelines include maximum loan amounts, acceptable LTV ratios, down payment requirements, buydown limitations, and minimum borrower financial capabilities in order to qualify for a loan. The guidelines also require that a borrower purchase PMI on any conventional loan with LTV greater than 80 percent. Such companies also insure commercial and industrial real estate loans and issue lease guarantee insurance.

Some new conventional loans now available include the Affordable Gold® loan designed for persons with little or no debt; the zero down loan available for persons with low income but good credit; the automatic reduction loan where the interest rate is reduced when the market rates drop below the contract rate; the track record adjusted loan where subprime loan interest rates are lowered when the borrower continues to make timely payments.

Opportunities to pursue real estate finance using the World Wide Web have increased dramatically in the past few years. There are numerous sites where anyone seeking to get a new mortgage can shop the market and make an application on line.

[handwritten: Know for: 9+10 Mon 2/28]

ORGANIZATION AND REQUIREMENTS

The FHA operates under the direction of the Department of Housing and Urban Development (HUD) from its headquarters in Washington, D.C., and its ten regional locations throughout the United States. Each region is divided into area offices located in almost every major city. Through these offices, the FHA closely supervises the issue of mortgage loans bearing its insurance.

Any lender participating in the FHA insurance program must grant long-term, self-amortizing loans at interest rates established in the marketplace. In the past, the maximum interest rate allowed on FHA loans was controlled by a rate ceiling set by HUD. With the exception of a few subsidized programs, all FHA-insured loans are now issued at market interest rates. The effect of this ruling is to allow government-insured mortgage rates to float in the market and permit them to be satisfactory to both borrower and lender. There is no limit on the number of points that may be paid by the borrower, although they must be reasonable. The FHA designates qualified *lenders* to underwrite loans directly without submitting applications to the FHA. These lenders participate in the direct endorsement program.

Every loan application is reviewed carefully to determine the borrower's financial credit and ability to make payments. In addition, a comprehensive written appraisal report is made on the condition and value of the property to be pledged as collateral for the loan. All property must meet certain minimum standards of acceptability. After qualifying the borrower and the property, the FHA issues a conditional commitment for mortgage insurance to the lender reflecting the value of the property. This commitment is valid for six months on existing property and for nine months on new construction.

Government housing officials recently established new rules for appraisers evaluating property for government insured loans. Since September 1999, appraisers have been required to pay more detailed attention to the physical defects of homes they examine. A seven-page "valuation condition" disclosure booklet must be completed to reveal any observable defects that do not meet minimum standards. This report is to be delivered to the borrower prior to the close of escrow. It must include the statement that "this review is not a physical inspection of the house and there is no guarantee that the property is free of any defects." The report also advises that the borrower may wish to have the house inspected by a professional inspector. The new disclosure form also requires appraisers to indicate whether they recommend inspections on the home's structural features, heating and cooling systems, plumbing, roofing, electrical, environmental factors, and pest control success. Under the FHA rules, any obvious property defects must be corrected before the mortgage closing.

Since August 1999, every FHA borrower has been required to receive and sign a form entitled, "For Your Protection: Get a Home Inspection."

PROGRAM SUMMARY

The FHA is designed as a program of mortgage insurance so it does *not* make direct loans to borrowers, except in very special circumstances involving the resale of properties acquired by the FHA as a result of foreclosure. Even under these circumstances, the FHA usually requires a buyer of a foreclosed property to secure financing elsewhere and pay the FHA cash for the property. In the event of a default and subsequent foreclosure, an insured lender will look to the FHA to recover the unpaid balance of the mortgage and any costs involved in the foreclosure action.

By designing a program of mortgage insurance funded by mortgage insurance premiums (MIPs), the FHA has reduced the down payment obstacle for cash-short buyers. The insurance program eliminates lenders' risks and preserves their fiduciary profiles by ensuring that FHA lenders will not lose any money on loans they make to eligible borrowers. This FHA insurance helps stabilize the mortgage market and develops an active national secondary market for FHA mortgage loans.

Existing Programs

Following are the major FHA programs under the National Housing Act:

Title I. Insures loans for home improvements, such as renovations and room additions.

Title II: Section 202. This is *not* an insurance program, but it authorizes direct loans from the federal government to private nonprofit sponsors to finance rental or cooperative housing for the elderly or handicapped.

Section 203(b) The largest FHA program, this program insures fixed interest rate loans for single-family owner-occupied homes.

Section 203(k) This program, which is becoming more popular, insures rehabilitation loans for existing homes and includes refinancing existing debt.

Section 203(v). Insures loans to eligible veterans.

Section 221(d)(2). Insures loans for low-income to moderate-income families.

Section 221(d)(3). This program, available for new construction and rehabilitation, insures up to 100 percent of loans for nonprofit sponsors to build multifamily rental housing for moderate-income families.

Section 221(d)(4). Insures up to 90 percent of loans for profit sponsors to build rental housing for moderate-income families.

Section 223(e). Insures loans for housing in declining neighborhoods where normal underwriting requirements cannot be met.

Section 223(f). Insures loans for purchase or refinancing of existing apartment buildings that are at least three years old.

Section 231. Insures loans to finance construction or rehabilitation of homes for the elderly or handicapped.

Section 234. Insures loans to finance construction or rehabilitation of apartment projects that are to be sold as individual condominium units.

Section 245. Insures graduated-payment loans.

Section 251. Insures adjustable-rate loans.

UNDERWRITING GUIDELINES

Like Fannie Mae and Freddie Mac, the FHA has its own set of guidelines to qualify eligible borrowers for acceptable loans. These requirements include all of the following elements.

FIGURE 9.1 2003 FHA Maximum Loan Limits

Type of Property	Standard	High Cost Area
Single-family	$154,896	$280,789
Duplex	198,288	359,397
Triplex	239,664	434,391
Four units	297,840	539,835

(All limits are 150 percent higher in Alaska, Guam, Hawaii, and the U.S. Virgin Islands.)

Maximum Loan Limitations

The FHA establishes maximum limitations on mortgages it will insure. These limitations vary by geographic area and are adjusted each October as a calculation of a percentage of the Fannie Mae and Freddie Mac conforming loan limits. Maximum FHA loan limits are set at 95 percent of the median house price for a metropolitan statistical area up to the limits shown in Figure 9.1.

The maximum loan amounts for your geographical area may be found on the Internet at www.hud.gov/mortprog.html, click on "Maximum Mortgage Limits."

Down Payment Requirements

In October 1998, the FHA greatly simplified its formula for calculating the down payment required on its insured loans. For properties of $50,000 or less, the down payment is 1.25 percent of the sales price. For properties more than $50,000, the down payment is 2.25 percent of the sales price.

FOR EXAMPLE

1.	$ 50,000	Sales Price
	×.0125	Factor
	625	Down Payment
	$ 49,375	Loan Amount
2.	$115,200	Sales Price
	×.0225	Factor
	2,592	Down Payment
	$112,608	Loan Amount

The purchaser must provide three percent of the sales price to be used for the down payment and/or closing costs. These funds may be the purchaser's own money, family member gifts, or grants from local, state, or nonprofit downpayment assistance programs such as the Nehemiah or AmeriDream programs. Both provide down payment assistance where a set fee is charged to the seller and then a percentage of the sales price is given to the buyer for the down payment. FHA accepts these funds as the equivalent of the borrower providing 3 percent of the sales price towards the transaction. For more information, check at www.nehemiah.org or www.ameridream.org. Under current FHA rules, the *seller* may contribute up to 6 percent of the sales price to be used for discount points, prepaids, and other allowable closing costs.

Borrowers' Income Qualifications

The FHA qualifies borrowers based on two ratios (the borrowers must qualify under *both ratios*):

1. The **housing ratio** of 29 percent. A borrower's total monthly housing expenses may not exceed 29 percent of the total gross monthly income. Included in these expenses are mortgage principal and interest, property taxes, home insurance premiums, mortgage insurance premiums, and homeowners or condominium association fees if applicable.

   The housing ratio may be raised if the borrowers have certain compensating factors, such as:

   - low long-term debt;
   - a large down payment;
   - minimal credit use;
   - excellent job history;
   - excellent payment history for amounts equal to or higher than new loan payment; or
   - additional income potential.

2. The **total obligations ratio** of 41 percent. A borrower's total monthly obligations may not exceed 41 percent of the total monthly gross income. Included in these obligations are monthly housing expenses plus monthly debt payments. Debts that will be paid in full within 10 months generally are not included. Alimony and child support payments are deducted from monthly gross income before calculating the qualifying ratio.

---

*F*OR *EXAMPLE*

Assume that borrowers want to qualify for a $100,000 FHA-insured home loan at 7% interest for 30 years. The principal and interest payments are $665 per month. Property taxes are $200 per month, the hazard insurance premium is $20 per month, and the MIP is $57 per month. The borrowers pay $400 per month on other debt.

$ 665	Principal and Interest
200	Property Taxes
20	Hazard Insurance Premiums
+ 57	MIP
942	Housing Costs ÷ 0.29 = $3,248 Ratio 1
+ 400	Other Debts
$1,342	Total Obligations ÷ 0.41 = $3,273 Ratio 2

To qualify for this loan, the borrowers would need to earn at least $3,273 in combined gross monthly income.

The FHA is now able to utilize Freddie Mac's Loan Prospector® automated underwriting program to qualify prospective borrowers electronically.

Mortgage Insurance Premium (MIP)

When the FHA issues an insurance **commitment** to a lender, it promises to repay the balance of the loan in full if the borrower defaults. This guaranty is funded by imposing a **mortgage insurance premium (MIP)** that must be paid by the borrower when obtaining an FHA-insured loan. It can be paid in cash or financed even if the loan plus the MIP exceeds the maximum loan limit.

The current FHA MIP is an upfront fee of 1.50 percent of the loan amount. In addition, the borrower must pay an annual renewal premium of 0.5 percent for a 30-year loan or 0.25 percent for a 15-year loan, payable monthly to be included in the regular payment. Thus with a $100,000 FHA-insured 30-year loan the borrower would pay a $1,500 MIP at closing or financed ($100,000 × 0.015 = $1,500), plus $41.66 per month ($100,000 × 0.005 = $500 ÷ 12 = $41.66).

The 0.5 percent annual MIP applies to all types of FHA loans. There are currently no upfront MIPs on condominiums. Borrowers may be entitled to a refund of a portion of the upfront MIP if the loan is paid in full prior to its amortization date. See Figure 9.2 for a comparison of a Fannie Mae 97 and an FHA loan on a home priced at $150,000.

[handwritten annotations: "½%", "know for test"]

IN PRACTICE . . .

Loan officer Hilda Martin is still working with John and Mary Brown whose combined monthly gross income totals $4,000. They have found a 20-year-old three-bedroom house with a large yard in an older neighborhood just 15 miles from downtown where they both work. They love the house, but the sales price of $120,000 seems to be out of their range. Hilda has suggested they look into an FHA loan. Today they are meeting to go over the FHA guidelines.

1. The maximum loan amount for their geographic area is $143,000: No problem.
2. The minimum down payment is 2.25%, but the purchaser must provide 3% of the sales price towards the down payment and/or closing: The Browns will put the full 3% into the down payment and ask the seller to contribute up to 6% towards their closing costs. If the seller is not willing to contribute this much, the Browns will ask their parents for a gift for the down payment, using their own $5,000 for closing costs.
3. Qualifying ratios of 29/41: $4,000 × 29% = $1,160; $4,000 × 41% = $1,640.

Deducting the $550 monthly debt from $1,640 = $1,090 for PITI. $1,090 minus $272 (25% for TI) = $817. $817 divided by $7.34 (rate factor for 8%) = $111,380 able to be borrowed.

If they could pay off some of the credit card debt, reducing the monthly obligation from $550 to $480, they would stay within the guidelines and be able to use $1,160 for PITI ($1,640 – $480 = $1,160).

$1,160 minus $290 (25% for TI) = $870. $870 divided by 7.34 (rate factor for 8%) = $118,530 able to be borrowed.

4. FHA mortgage insurance of 1.5% upfront added to the mortgage amount, 0.5% monthly: Final calculations for the Browns' "dream house":

Sales price:	$120,000.00
Down payment:	– 3,600.00
Loan amount	116,400.00
Plus 1.5% upfront MIP ($1,746)	118,146.00
Monthly PI:	$867.19
Est. TI & PMI (25%):	+ 216.79
Total PITI payment:	$1,083.98
$1,083.98 ÷ 4,000 = 27%	
Plus long-term debt:	480.00
$1,563.98 ÷ 4,000 = 39%	

FIGURE 9.2   Comparison of Fannie 97 and FHA Programs with $150,000 Purchase Price

	Fannie 97	FHA
Down Payment	3% or $4,500 (borrower's own funds	3% or $4,500 (borrower's own funds OR gift)
Loan Amount	$145,500	$145,500
Ratios	33/38	29/41
Seller Contribution Allowed	3%	6%
Insurance	PMI	MIP
	Approximately 0.8% of loan amount ÷ 12 for monthly payment = $97	1) 1.50% of loan amount added to loan amount financed over life of loan. $2,182.50 = 16.02 per month. 2) Plus 0.5% paid monthly $727.50 = $60.63 per month
Homebuyer Education	Homebuyer education required	No homebuyer education
PI	$1,067.63	$1,067.63
TI	266.91	266.91
Subtotal	1,334.54	1,334.54
Insurance	(PMI) 97.00	(MIP) upfront 16.02 monthly 60.63
Total Monthly Payment	**$1,431.54**	**$1,411.19**

Second Mortgages/Buydowns

The FHA will allow a second mortgage to be acquired on the collateral property. There are certain conditions, however:

- The total of the first and second mortgages must not exceed the allowable maximum LTV ratio.
- The borrower must qualify to make both payments.
- There can be no balloon payment on the second mortgage if it matures before five years.
- The payments on the second mortgage must not vary to any large degree.
- The second mortgage must not contain a prepayment penalty.

The FHA allows mortgage buydowns when the borrower or seller can make an advance cash payment to lower the interest rate for a period of time. This effectively reduces the corresponding monthly payments. The FHA also allows the borrower the advantage to qualify for the loan at the *bought-down* interest rate, not the contract interest rate.

Assumptions

FHA loans originated prior to December 1989 are generally assumable without qualifying but the original borrower retains some responsibility in the event of a default. For FHA loans originated after December, 1989, all sellers were released from liability under an assumption. Buyers have to qualify under the current 29%, 41% rule and must occupy the property. The FHA currently prohibits the assumption of loans by investors.

OTHER FREQUENTLY USED FHA LOANS

The FHA also provides special insurance programs for qualified veterans, graduated payment plans, adjustable rate mortgage plans, and home improvement loans.

Section 203(v): Veteran FHA Loan

A special category of FHA-insured home loans is available to eligible veterans who have either already used their VA entitlement or may wish to save their entitlement for some future use. Honorably discharged veterans who have secured a certificate of eligibility issued by the Department of Veterans Affairs (VA) can apply for an FHA loan.

Most veterans prefer to use the more liberal terms provided by their GI benefits from the VA, shown in Chapter 10. However, the availability of this special FHA program does expand a veteran's borrowing opportunities at reduced down payments, and it may be used more than once by a veteran. Moreover, this program does not affect a borrower's normal VA entitlement, and it may be used by a qualified veteran who has no VA entitlement.

Section 245(a): Graduated-Payment Mortgage (GPM)

The FHA has a **graduated-payment mortgage (GPM)** program known as the FHA 245(a) graduated-payment mortgage. This program is designed to provide younger, first-time homebuyers with initially low monthly payments. The payments increase at varying rates per year, depending on the plan. At the end of each plan's period, the borrower begins making the higher regular payments, which continue for the remainder of the life of the loan. Because payments in the early years are less than the interest accruing, the outstanding principal balance increases during the period. This is known as **negative amortization**, but it is expected that borrowers will be able to make higher payments as their earnings increase over time.

The FHA GPM loans are available only on owner-occupied single-family dwellings. The loan limits are the same as for the FHA 203(b) program. Assumptions are permitted, and borrowers may convert to a fixed-rate FHA loan at any time. The FHA 245(a) program may be used for new and existing properties.

FHA 251, One-Year Adjustable-Rate Mortgage (ARM)

The FHA ARMs are available to owner-occupants of one-family to four-family dwelling units. The maximum mortgage amounts are the same as for 203(b) and are written for

30-year terms. Adjustments have a 1 percent per year interest rate cap with a 5 percent lifetime cap. Negative amortization is not allowed. (See Chapter 8.)

The FHA ARMs are fully assumable and buydowns are permitted. When qualifying at the buydown rate of interest, it is possible for the borrower to receive a larger loan amount.

FHA 203(k), Rehabilitation Loan

This program provides insurance for loans based on the purchase price plus the costs for rehabilitation of the property. The **rehabilitation loan FHA 203(k)** includes the following special features:

1. Rehab costs must be at least $5,000.
2. The borrower pays only taxes and insurance during the first six months.
3. The rehab funds are paid to the borrower in draws.
4. The rehab costs and installation time must be approved by the lender before the loan can be granted.
5. The loan is made at 97 percent LTV with 3 percent down.
6. The FHA 203(k) program is not available to investors.

Complete information on the FHA 203(k) program can be found on www.hud.gov.

DIRECT ENDORSEMENT AND COINSURANCE

To simplify the FHA insurance procedures, in 1983 HUD introduced two major programs. Lenders can secure FHA single-family and multifamily mortgage insurance through direct endorsement and coinsurance.

Under the **direct endorsement program,** applications for many of FHA's single-family mortgage insurance programs can be underwritten by an approved lender that certifies the mortgage complies with applicable FHA requirements. The lender performs all appraisal duties and analyzes the borrower's credit. Direct endorsement leaves FHA with the risk of loss from default but gives it control through its ability to remove the lender from the program. Direct endorsement has become increasingly popular with lenders. The majority of all FHA mortgage insurance applications are now being processed under its format. Lenders who avoided FHA insurance because of the delays and red tape now use direct endorsement as an alternative to private insurance.

Under **coinsurance,** an approved lender both processes and underwrites qualified mortgages. The coinsuring lender shares losses with the FHA in the event of a default.

ADVANTAGES OF THE FHA MORTGAGE

There are several advantages to using the FHA mortgage. These include the following:

- *The loan-to-value (LTV) ratio is high.* In many cases an FHA mortgage may be obtained with as little as 1.25 percent down payment.

- *Many different types of loans are available.* The FHA has loan structures to meet a variety of borrowers' needs. There are fixed-rate or adjustable-rate loans amortized by level or graduated monthly payments. The FHA also insures loans for low-income housing, subsidized interest loans, and mobile home purchases.
- *There is no due-on-sale clause.* The original terms of the loan can remain the same and cannot be changed because of a sale. Most FHA loans are fully assumable with qualification.
- *There is no prepayment penalty.* The absence of a prepayment penalty allows the borrower to increase the monthly payment or prepay the loan. For loans made prior to August 2, 1985, 30 days' written notice is required to pay a loan in full prior to its amortization time. For loans made after August 2, 1985, prepayments may be made, but only on the monthly due date.

FHA CONTRIBUTIONS TO REAL ESTATE FINANCE

Every financier recognizes the significance of the FHA's major contributions to the stabilization of the real estate mortgage market. These contributions are summarized below:

- *The FHA instituted new standards for qualifying borrowers.* Credit applications and borrower creditability criteria were standardized, so all lenders who issue FHA-insured loans use the same basic language and tools.
- *The FHA instituted new standards for appraising property.* Minimum construction standards have been established that must be met before a property can qualify for an FHA-insured loan. These standards apply to both new and used buildings, and they are measured by an FHA appraisal of the potential collateral.
- *The long-term amortized loan was devised.* Prior to the FHA's long-term amortization design, in which a borrower has from 15 years to 30 years to repay a loan in equal monthly payments, mortgage loans had to be *paid in full* or *refinanced* approximately every five years. This created hardships for both borrowers and sellers, and contributed to the many foreclosures during the depression years. Currently the FHA monthly payments include an amount for principal, interest, property taxes, hazard insurance, and, if required, property improvement assessments and FHA mortgage insurance premiums.
- *The FHA lending standards and amortization design provided the foundation for a national market in mortgage securities.* By developing reliability and safety in mortgage loan investments that had never existed before 1934, the FHA enabled financial investors from all over the United States to trade in these securities.

SUMMARY

The Federal Housing Administration (FHA) was established during the crisis of the depression under the provisions of the National Housing Act of 1934 and is under the jurisdiction of the Department of Housing and Urban Development (HUD). The FHA instituted new standards for qualifying borrowers and appraising property. The FHA designed the long-term self-amortizing loan, enabling borrowers to secure affordable monthly payments. Its actions were indispensable in reversing the dismal economy of the 1930s.

Under FHA insurance, borrowers enjoy low down payments, a variety of loan arrangements, no due-on-sale clauses, fully assumable loans and no prepayment penalties. Upfront insurance premiums are required that total 1.50 percent of the loan amount. In addition, the FHA collects monthly payments for annual renewal premiums on all newly issued loans. These premiums constitute the reserves from which the FHA pays the lenders for defaulted loans.

The FHA provides insurance for loans on single-family dwellings, one-family to four-family apartment units, medical clinics, and hospitals. The FHA also provides special subsidized programs to pay interest or rent for low-income to moderate-income families. It has limitations on the size of their loans, depending on the area in the country in which the property is located.

The FHA also requires borrowers to qualify for loan payments. Borrowers' monthly housing payments cannot exceed 29 percent of their total monthly gross income, or the monthly housing payments plus other regular monthly obligations cannot exceed 41 percent of their total gross monthly income.

A special FHA program is the graduated-payment mortgage (GPM) under Section 245(a). This program allows first-time homebuyers an opportunity to qualify under less-than-interest-only payments (negative amortization) in anticipation of their increased earnings over time. The payments rise gradually to match the increasing financial capabilities of the borrowers. An alternative to the GPM is the FHA 251, a one-year ARM.

The FHA provides eligible veterans an opportunity to use the FHA/VA 203(v) program as an alternative to their regular VA entitlement. The FHA also offers a 203(k) rehabilitation loan program to help borrowers secure funds to repair their newly purchased homes.

Past criticisms of the time-consuming FHA loan process have been diminished by the efficient direct endorsement and coinsurance programs. Now loan originators can issue loans directly, eliminating unnecessary red tape.

TABLE 10.1   VA Loan Guarantee Periods

December 28, 1945	$ 4,000
July 12, 1950	7,500
May 7, 1968	12,500
December 31, 1974	17,500
October 1, 1978	25,000
March 1, 1988	36,000
December 20, 1989	46,000
October 13, 1995	50,750
January 1, 2002	60,000

that amount. This allows the maximum amount of a no down payment VA loan to reach $240,000 (four times $60,000).

Title III has been expanded to include guarantees for loans on condominiums, cooperatives, and mobile homes. A program for refinancing existing VA loans also is available. Complete copies of the various VA pamphlets on veteran's benefits including home mortgage loans can be downloaded and printed from www.va.gov.

PROGRAM APPLICATION

In general, the VA is concerned with guaranteeing loans made by institutional lenders, such as commercial banks, thrift organizations, life insurance companies, and mortgage bankers and brokers. It tries to eliminate any risks taken by these lenders when they make loans on real estate to eligible veterans. If a veteran cannot continue to meet the required payments, the lender is compensated by the VA for any losses incurred in the foreclosure and subsequent sale of the property, up to the limit of the guarantee.

The operations of the VA real estate loan guarantee program are managed by 55 regional offices located in major communities throughout the country. The program is not designed to be used indiscriminately. Each loan application is reviewed carefully to determine the veteran's eligibility, credit history, and ability to pay. The value of the property is firmly established by an appraisal, and assurances are secured that the veteran will occupy the premises as the major residence. Poor risks are denied loans and are referred to other programs. The VA guarantees about 200,000 loans per year.

Several veterans, related or not, may purchase one-family to four-family homes as partners, as long as they intend to occupy the property. A veteran and a nonveteran who are not married may purchase a home together as coborrowers, although the VA will not guarantee the nonveteran's portion of the loan. However, the VA does qualify common-law marriages without reduction of the loan guarantee for the nonveteran, as long as proper documentation has been supplied.

Eligibility/Entitlement

A veteran's eligibility or **entitlement** to participate in the program is derived from the following active-duty criteria:

- More than 90 days of continuous active duty; or discharge because of a service-connected disability; or separation under other than dishonorable conditions during any of the following wartime periods:

World War II	September 16, 1940, to July 25, 1947
Korean Conflict	June 27, 1950, to January 31, 1955
Vietnam War	August 5, 1964, to May 7, 1975
Persian Gulf War	August 2, 1990, to the present

- More than 180 days of continuous active duty for other than training purposes; or discharge because of a service-connected disability; or separation under other than dishonorable conditions during the following peacetime periods:

Post-World War II	July 26, 1947, to June 26, 1950
Post-Korean Conflict	February 1, 1955, to August 4, 1964
Post-Vietnam War	May 8, 1975, to September 6, 1980 (enlisted), October 16, 1981 (officer)

- For enlisted personnel, two years of continuous active duty or separation under other than dishonorable conditions during the peacetime period from 1980 to the present. For officers, two years of continuous active duty or separation other than dishonorable discharge during the peacetime period from 1981 to the present.
- At least six years of continuous active duty as a reservist in the Army, Navy, Air Force, Marine Corps, or Coast Guard or as a member of the Army or Air National Guard (in effect until September, 2009).

Unremarried spouses of veterans may be eligible for VA loans if the veteran died of a service-connected injury or illness while in service. Unremarried spouses of veterans who are listed as missing in action may also be eligible for VA home loans.

Certificate of Eligibility

One of the most important documents needed for a loan application by a veteran is a **certificate of eligibility.** To receive this certificate, the veteran must secure forms to determine eligibility as well as an available loan guarantee entitlement. These forms must be accompanied by evidence of military service. At present, veterans receive their certificate of eligibility with their discharge from service.

There is no time limit on the entitlement, and it remains in effect until completely used up. This loan guarantee must be used in the United States, its territories, and its protectorates. A certificate may be requested on VA Form 26-1880 and submitted along with the DD Form 214 (Certificate of Release or Discharge) through the local VA office. Detailed information is available on www.va.gov. After using the VA guarantee for a real estate loan, the veteran may gain the restoration of eligibility when the loan is paid in full and the property has been conveyed to another owner. (There is a one-time exemption of the conveyance requirement.)

TABLE 10.2   VA Schedule of Guarantees

Loan Amount	Guarantee Amount
Up to $45,000	50%
$45,001 to $56,250	$22,500
$56,251 to $239,999	The Lesser of $36,000 or 40% of Loan
$240,000 or more	The Lesser of $60,000 or 25% of Loan

Schedule of Guarantees

The VA home loan program is designed to provide eligible veterans up to 100 percent financing for home purchases. However, unlike the FHA programs, which insure the total amount of the balance of a loan, the VA program guarantees only the *top portion* of a loan's balance according to the schedule listed in Table 10.2. A lender can look to the VA for reimbursement of only a portion of a defaulted loan balance. But, the top portion of a loan is exactly what lenders need to have guaranteed, because that is where the greatest risk lies in the event of a default.

Using the information listed in Table 10.2, a qualified veteran can utilize the VA guarantee as a down payment and secure a 100 percent loan on an eligible property. A rule-of-thumb approach reveals that a veteran may obtain a 100 percent loan at four times the remaining eligibility.

*F*OR EXAMPLE

A veteran, qualified to make the payments, can purchase a home for $240,000 with a $60,000 loan guarantee by the VA and make no down payment. If the veteran were to default on this loan at the very beginning without making any payments, the VA would send a check for $60,000 to the lender. To recover the balance owed, the lender would have to sell the property for $180,000 ($240,000 – $60,000 = $180,000). This amount represents 75% of the property's value ($180,000 ÷ $240,000 = 0.75) and most likely could be secured even in a down market.

There is no limit on the amount of a loan eligible for a VA guarantee. The limitation applies only to the amount of the guarantee that can be issued.

For EXAMPLE

A qualified veteran purchases a home for $100,000 and secures a $36,000 loan guarantee from the VA. The veteran defaults on the loan five years later, when the balance has been reduced to $95,000. The VA issues a check to the lender for $36,000 and the lender sells the foreclosed property for $59,000 to recover its investment ($95,000 − $36,000 = $59,000). This represents just 62% of the property's depreciated value ($59,000 ÷ $95,000 = 0.62).

Partial Entitlement

Veterans who have used their benefits in the past may be eligible for another VA loan if they have any remaining entitlement. With a **partial entitlement,** a veteran may pay cash down to the maximum loan amount and still benefit accordingly.

To determine any remaining entitlement, examine Table 10.1 and subtract the amount used previously from the amount currently in effect. This is the amount available for the guarantee. Finally, to determine the maximum VA loan allowed under a partial entitlement, take 75 percent of the appraised value and add the remaining entitlement amount.

For EXAMPLE (See Table 10.1)

Consider a veteran who purchased a house in 1989 using the entitlement of $46,000. In 1999, the veteran decided to purchase a new house but wanted to keep the original residence for an income property. With the new house appraised for $150,000, a new VA loan of $117,250 was acquired using the following process:

Maximum 1999 entitlement	$ 50,750
1989 entitlement	− 46,000
Remaining entitlement	4,750
75 percent of $150,000	+112,500
	$117,250

To complete the transaction, the veteran paid $32,750 as a cash down payment.

Certificate of Reasonable Value (CRV)

The VA requires a certified real estate appraiser to submit a formal estimate of the value of the property to be financed. The appraiser issues a **certificate of reasonable value (CRV),** stating the amount of the appraisal. This CRV is valid for 6 months for existing properties and 12 months for new construction. It may not be extended.

If a sale is made subject to a CRV and the appraisal comes in at *less* than the sale price, the following may occur:

- The buyer can make up the difference in cash.
- The seller can accept the lower amount as the sale price.
- The buyer and seller can compromise.
- The transaction can be canceled.

In any case, the seller is not allowed to carry back a second mortgage for the difference between the sale price and the appraised value.

In the purchase of a home in excess of the maximum guaranteed VA loan amount with no money down, the veteran is required to pay 25 percent of the difference as a down payment as long as the property meets the CRV. Any time the veteran purchases *over* the CRV, the difference is required to be paid in cash. The VA reserves the right to approve the source of the cash. This is to insure that the veteran is not borrowing an additional amount that would adversely affect the total debt ratio.

ex. 260,000
240 000 may
20,000 × 25% = 5000

Interest

In the past, the VA specified the interest rate the lender could charge the veteran. Now, however, the VA allows the borrower the opportunity to shop the marketplace and negotiate the best rate available. Thus, all types of mortgage loans are competitive as to interest rates, leveling the financing market.

Income Qualifying Requirements

The VA utilizes only one ratio to analyze a borrower's ability to qualify for the loan payment. This ratio is 41 percent of the borrower's gross monthly income and includes principal, interest, taxes, insurance, utilities, maintenance, repairs, and other monthly obligations. The VA publishes information pertinent to maintenance, repair, and utility estimates for various regions in the United States. This information is based on a property's square footage and age, and whether the property has a pool, air-conditioning, or evaporative cooling. For example, one regional office allocates $76 per month for maintenance and repairs to a house more than three years old, consisting of 1,600 square feet, including a pool and air-conditioning. Furthermore, it allocates $214 per month for the utilities at this property.

FOR EXAMPLE

A veteran applies for a VA loan of $100,000 at 7% interest for 30 years. The monthly principal and interest payment is $665. Other monthly costs include $70 for taxes, $15 for insurance, $214 for utilities, $76 for maintenance, and $200 for other obligations. The veteran's total gross monthly income will have to be at least $3,024 or $36,288 per year to qualify for this loan.

(continued)

FOR EXAMPLE (continued)

Principal and Interest	$ 665
Property Taxes	70
Hazard Insurance	15
Utilities	214
Maintenance	76
Other Payments	200
Total Obligations	$ 1,240
VA Income Ratio	÷ 0.41
Gross Monthly Income Required	$ 3,024
	x 12
Gross Annual Income Required	$36,288

Residual Income Test. The VA has a second test to qualify potential borrowers. Called **residual qualifying,** the VA publishes tables of monthly income amounts defined by family size and the region in which it lives. This table is reproduced in Table 10.3.

FOR EXAMPLE

As shown in Table 10.3 below, for a family of three in the West to qualify for a $100,000 loan at 7% for 30 years, the borrower would have to earn a minimum of $990 per month. The principal and interest required on this loan is $665 per month.

TABLE 10.3   Table of Residual Income by Region, Effective January 1, 2003

Family Size	Northeast	Midwest	South	West
(for loan amounts of $79,999 and below)				
1	$ 390	$ 382	$ 382	$ 425
2	654	641	641	713
3	788	772	772	859
4	888	868	868	967
5	921	902	902	1,004
(Add $75 for each additional person up to a family of 7.)				
(for loan amounts of 80,000 and above)				
1	$ 450	$ 441	$ 441	$ 491
2	755	738	738	823
3	909	889	889	990
4	1,025	1,003	1,003	1,117
5	1,062	1,039	1,039	1,158
(Add $80 for each additional person up to a family of 7.)				

SOURCE: Veterans Administration, Phoenix, Arizona, Regional Office.

Closing Costs

Closing costs may *not* be included in VA loans. All costs are paid in cash at closing but may be paid by the seller. Closing costs charged to the veteran may not be in excess of those allowed under VA regulations. They include the following:

Loan Origination Fee	1 percent
Loan Discount Fee (points) (VA eliminated 1 percent ceiling)	Market price
Appraisal Fee	$250
Credit Report	$55
Lender's Title Insurance	Market price
Recording Fee	$20

A seller may pay up to an additional 4 percent on top of paying all points, closing costs, etc., in order to pay off the purchaser's debts, or to pay the funding fee to allow easier loan qualification. In addition, the veteran is responsible for prorations of interest and taxes and the initial deposits for the impound account. Following is a list of VA loan closing items and who can pay them:

Appraisal	Veteran or Seller
Origination Fee	Veteran or Seller
Discount Points	Veteran or Seller
Funding Fee	Veteran or Seller
Prepaid Interest	Veteran or Seller
1st Year's Hazard Insurance	Veteran or Seller
Tax/Insurance Reserves	Veteran or Seller
Title Insurance	Veteran or Seller
Recording Fees	Veteran or Seller
Survey	Veteran or Seller
Settlement or Closing Fee	Veteran or seller
Pest Inspection	Seller Only
Repairs	Seller Only
Underwriting Fee	Seller Only
Document Prep. Fee	Seller Only
Tax Service Fee	Seller Only
Stamps on Deed	Seller Only

Funding Fee

The VA charges a **funding fee,** which may be paid in cash or *included in the loan amount,* even in excess of the CRV. However, the addition of the funding fee to the original loan amount may not exceed the maximum allowable loan. The funding fee is required on all VA loans except from veterans receiving compensation for service-connected disabilities, from veterans receiving retirement pay in lieu of disability compensation, from spouses of veterans who died in service or died from service-connected disabilities, and in some transactions in which a large down payment is made. (See Table 10.4.)

TABLE 10.4   Schedule of Funding Fees For VA Loans

Category	First Time Use	National Guard/ Reservist	Subsequent Use
0% to 5% Down	2.00%	2.75%	3.00%
5.1% to 9.9% Down	1.50%	2.25%	1.50%
10% or More Down	1.25%	2.00%	1.25%
Assumptions	0.50%		
Refinancing	0.50%		

*F*OR EXAMPLE

The funding fee charged on a $100,000 VA loan where the veteran makes no down payment is $2,000:

$$\begin{array}{r} \$\ 100,000 \\ \times\ \ 0.020 \\ \hline \$2,000.00 \end{array}$$

*F*OR EXAMPLE

The funding fee charged on a $100,000 VA loan where the veteran makes a 10% down payment is $1,250:

$$\begin{array}{r} \$\ 100,000 \\ \times\ \ 0.0125 \\ \hline \$\ \ \ \ \ 1,250 \end{array}$$

*F*OR EXAMPLE

The funding fee charged on a $100,000 VA loan secured for refinancing is $500:

$$\begin{array}{r} \$\ 100,000 \\ \times\ \ 0.005 \\ \hline \$\ \ \ \ \ \ 500 \end{array}$$

Second Mortgages

The VA will allow second mortgages to be placed on the collateral property under the following conditions:

- The second mortgage document must be approved by the VA legal department prior to loan closing.
- The total of the first and second mortgage liens may not exceed the value of the property.
- The interest rate on the second mortgage may not exceed the interest rate on the first.
- The second mortgage may not have a prepayment penalty or a balloon payment.
- The second mortgage must be amortized for at least five years.

Buydowns

Buydowns are allowed only on VA loans issued with level payments. A buydown is an amount of money paid in advance, accepted by the lender, to reduce the interest rate on the loan. The buydown fee may be paid by the seller, the buyer, or family members. The borrower must qualify at the first year's payment rate. (See Chapter 13.)

Assumptions

Prior to March 1988, VA loans were fully assumable without prior lender approval of the buyer's credit. For VA loans made after this date, the buyer's credit must be approved by the lender prior to the assumption of an existing loan. Any unauthorized assumption may trigger a technical default and the loan balance can be called in full. In any approved assumption, the loan interest rate will not be changed.

IN PRACTICE . . .

Sally Green's real estate office is located very close to a military base, and she is currently working with four clients who are all interested in obtaining VA loans to purchase new houses. Sally is trying to determine their eligibility status. Mark Brown served for one year between March 1985 and March 1986 and has been told that only 180 days are required. Sam Jones served for 90 days during Desert Storm. Michael Green served for eight years in the National Guard. John Smith used his VA eligibility in 1978. Sally finds that Mark will not be eligible because two years of active service are required after 1980 (except for the Gulf War period). Sam and Michael should have full eligibility.

John Smith may have a partial entitlement. The entitlement in 1978 was $25,000. Today it is $60,000, which would leave him a $35,000 partial entitlement. The banks will generally lend four times that amount for a no-money-down loan. If John wants to purchase a house costing $150,000 the bank will lend 75% of the appraised value, plus the partial entitlement ($150,000 × 0.75 + $35,000 = $147,500). John will only have to make a down payment of $2,500 ($150,000 − $147,500 = $2,500).

John may be pleasantly surprised to find that he has his full entitlement back! By checking with his regional VA office, he finds that the house that he purchased in 1978 and sold in 1984, letting the purchaser assume his loan, has been subsequently sold with all new conventional financing. John will have regained his entitlement at the current amount of $60,000. He can now obtain a VA loan for up to $240,000 as long as he meets all qualifying standards. One small catch—he will have to pay a 3% Funding Fee this time unless he is receiving disability payments from the VA.

Release of Liability/Novation

ON TEST!⁶

The original makers of a VA loan remain liable until it is paid in full or the veteran receives a **release of liability** or a **substitution of entitlement** from a cooperating buyer. The release of liability relieves the veteran-seller of the responsibility for repayment and any deficiencies resulting from a default on the loan. It does not, however, reinstate the full entitlement as does the substitution of entitlement.

Know Novation for test

Although it is unusual for a veteran to have more than one VA loan in effect at any one time, it is not unusual for a veteran to secure a complete release from the liability of a previous VA loan and a restoration of eligibility for a new maximum guarantee. General requirements for restoration of entitlement by the VA call for the veteran to sell the property and repay the debt in full. A recent change allows for a one-time only provision for restoration of entitlement with repayment of the debt without having to dispose of the property. In addition, a veteran can qualify to ask the VA for a substitution of entitlement if the home is sold to another qualified veteran willing to assume the loan.

In cases in which a veteran's loan is assumed by a purchaser who is not a veteran, the VA will not allow the seller-veteran to regain maximum entitlement. The purchaser, however, can agree to assume the veteran's liability to reimburse the VA in case of default, and the buyer and seller can then petition the VA to release the veteran from all obligations. This full substitution technique is called **novation.** If the new buyers meet the credit requirements of the old lender, the VA may accept them in lieu of the veteran and release the veteran's liability on the loan. Note, however, that release of a veteran's liability does not restore eligibility for the maximum guarantee amount. It will not be restored until the loan is finally paid off by the purchaser.

VA GRADUATED-PAYMENT MORTGAGE (GPM)

Under the VA Graduated-Payment Mortgage plan, the monthly payment is scheduled to increase annually by a fixed percentage for a stated period, usually five years. After this period expires, the monthly payment levels off and remains the same for the balance of the loan period.

The reduction of the initial monthly payments is accomplished by deferring a portion of the interest due on the loan each month and adding that amount of unpaid interest to the loan balance. This causes the balance to increase during this period, an effect known as *negative amortization.*

SUMMARY

The Serviceman's Readjustment Act, the GI Bill of Rights, was passed by Congress in 1944, shortly before the end of World War II. Among other benefits, it guarantees lenders making real estate loans to eligible veterans that the Department of Veterans Affairs (VA) will pay if the borrower defaults.

To be eligible for the loan guarantee, a veteran must have served more than 90 days of continuous active duty in wartime, or more than 180 days in peacetime. In addition, reservists and National Guard members are included, as are unremarried spouses of

FIGURE 11.1   The Loan Approval Process

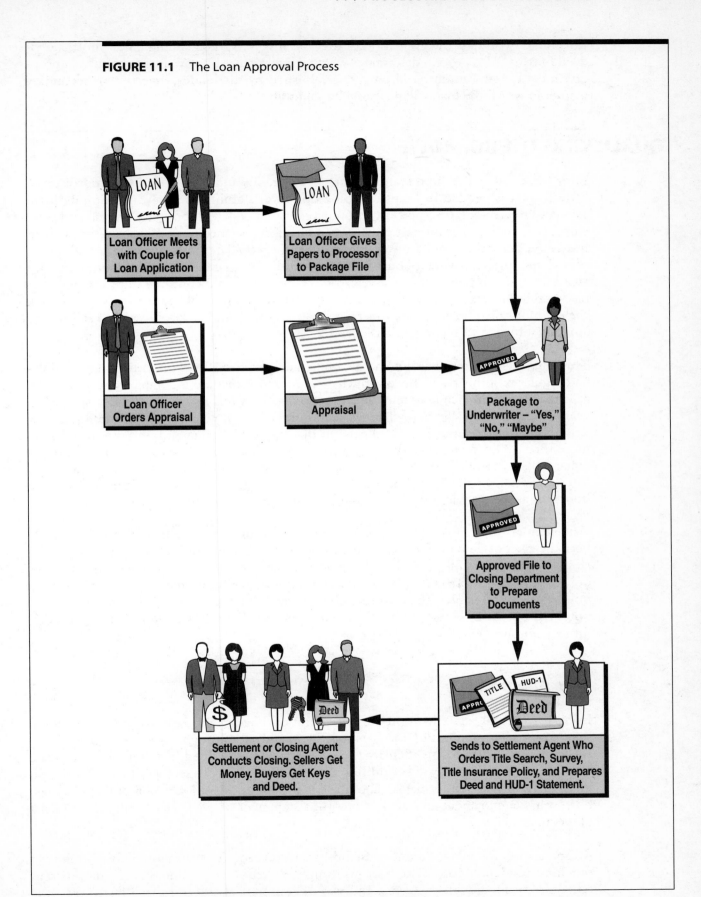

Loan underwriting is the evaluation of the risks involved when issuing a new mortgage or deed of trust. This process determines whether a particular borrower and the subject property meet the minimum requirements established by the lender, investor, or secondary market in which the loan will probably be sold.

QUALIFYING THE BORROWER

Prior to the advent of high loan-to-value (LTV) ratios and long-term loan amortization, little emphasis needed to be placed on a borrower's ability to repay a real estate loan. Loans were created at 50 percent to 60 percent of a collateral property's value and were based on a payment of interest only for certain short specified periods, usually one year to five years. The entire principal was due in full at the stop date. If the principal could not be paid in full, partial payment could be made and the balance of the loan amount recast for an additional five years. This five-year rollover pattern could continue until the debt was paid in full. However, if a borrower did not meet the payment obligations promptly and in the amount called for in the contract, the collateral was quickly foreclosed and sold for an amount sufficient to recompense the lender.

This repayment pattern has not changed much despite the 30-year amortization schedules and regular monthly payments of principal *and* interest that are the framework of our current real estate financing system. The average age of a real estate loan is still only seven years to eight years. What *has* changed, and quite dramatically, are the LTV ratios. Today lenders are able to lend up to 100 percent of a property's value and, in some cases, even more than 100 percent. As a result of increasing the loan amounts close to or exceeding a collateral's total value, the lenders' emphasis has shifted from relying on the successful foreclosure sale of the collateral to protect the investment to looking to the credit of the borrower as the primary protection along with mortgage insurance and guarantees.

While lenders under insured or guaranteed programs of real estate finance do not directly bear the risks of default, they still must follow the guidelines of their guaranteeing agencies. They must carefully screen loan applicants to derive some reasonable estimate of not only the *ability* of borrowers to pay but also their *attitudes* about meeting their contractual obligations responsibly. Thus, a great effort is made to check and evaluate thoroughly a potential borrower's past credit history and current financial status in order to predict future economic stability.

Loan Application

Every formal real estate loan processing operation begins with a borrower completing a standardized loan application form (Figure 11.2) and submitting it to a prospective lender. All loan application forms identify the property to be pledged, the borrower, and the amount of money requested. Additional facts about the prospective borrower are also included, along with information about the loan sought. Most loan applications show the borrower's employment and income record, a statement of assets and liabilities, and a list of credit references.

An application for a commercial or an industrial loan requires even more information than one for a residential loan. The borrower might be requested to supply such data as rent schedules or tenants' lease terms. In cases of commercial and industrial borrowers, the application form will usually outline every phase of the borrower's present business, such as management, sales, production, purchasing, research and development, personnel, plant, and equipment, and include financial statements and audits of the total operations of each phase. A Dun & Bradstreet *credit report* might be required. These financial statements would go back about ten years to give perspective to the general market profile of the borrower corporation and show the pattern of asset-liability ratios over a sufficient length of time. From these past profit and loss statements, the lender should be able to determine the corporation's profitability, the effectiveness of its management, and the prospects for future corporate growth.

All loan applications are designed to reveal a borrower's financial ability to meet the basic obligations of the loan agreement. The form in Figure 11.2 is an example of a typical residential loan application. This and similar forms are used by lenders to obtain pertinent information from an applicant requesting a real estate loan. The bulk of the application is devoted to securing personal information from the borrower about family size and ages of dependent children, sources of income, employment history, and a comprehensive financial statement. In addition, the property is identified by its legal description.

Financial Statement. Most **financial statements** follow a standard format that lists all assets in a column on the left and all liabilities in a column on the right. This enables a lender to assess the current financial status of an applicant quickly and efficiently.

Assets consist of all things of value, encumbered or not, owned by the applicant—and cash heads the list. Cash consists of money in hand, on deposit in checking and savings accounts, and the cash given as a deposit on the property being purchased. Lenders place great weight on a borrower's cash position as a reflection of liquidity and money management habits. A strong cash balance develops a sense of confidence in a borrower's ability to maintain payments and meet other obligations, even in the event of temporary setbacks.

Next in the financial statement asset column are listed all monies invested in stocks and bonds, notes or accounts receivable, personal business ventures, and other real estate. The value of the applicant's automobiles, surrender value of life insurance policies, other personal property, and any other assets is enumerated. All dollar amounts assigned to these items must reflect their realistic current market value, not their purchase price or some imagined value.

When more than one bond, stock, or parcel of real estate is owned, additional spaces are provided for their itemization in an appropriate schedule on the application form. Should the applicant need more space than is provided, additional pages will be affixed to this inventory to fulfill these important requirements.

Liabilities consist of all monetary obligations of the borrower-applicant. Heading the list of liabilities are any notes payable because these are considered a priority claim against cash assets. Next in order of importance are all installment accounts, such as charge accounts and automobile payments. Other accounts payable, such as medical bills or insurance premiums, follow the list of installment accounts. Remaining long-term liabilities are then enumerated: alimony and child support payments, any encumbrances on the real estate listed as assets, accrued and unpaid real estate property and/or income taxes, security obligations on personal property such as furniture, loans on the life insurance policies listed as assets, and any other debts for which the applicant is responsible.

FIGURE 11.2 Uniform Residential Loan Application

Uniform Residential Loan Application

This application is designed to be completed by the applicant(s) with the lender's assistance. Applicants should complete this form as "Borrower" or "Co-Borrower", as applicable. Co-Borrower information must also be provided (and the appropriate box checked) when [ ] the income or assets of a person other than the "Borrower" (including the Borrower's spouse will be used as a basis for loan qualification or [ ] the income or assets of the Borrower's spouse will not be used as a basis for loan qualification, but his or her liabilities must be considered because the Borrower resides in a community property state, the security property is located in a community property state, or the Borrower is relying on other property located in a community property state as a basis for repayment of the loan.

Mortgage Applied for:	[ ] V.A. [X] Conventional [ ] FHA [ ] FmHA [ ] Other:		Agency Case Number		Lender Case Number

| Amount $ 108,000 | Interest Rate 8 % | No. of Months 360 | Amortization Type | [X] Fixed Rate [ ] GPM | [ ] Other (explain): [ ] ARM (type): |

Subject Property Address (street, city, state, ZIP)
1097 Timber Crossing   St. Joseph Missouri   No. of Units 1

Legal Description of Subject Property (attach description if necessary)
Lot 3 Block G of the Harris Billups Estate Plat Book 8 p.37   Year Built 1983

Purpose of Loan [X] Purchase [ ] Construction [ ] Other (explain): [ ] Refinance [ ] Construction-Permanent   Property will be: [x] Primary Residence [ ] Secondary Residence [ ] Investment

Complete this line if construction or construction-permanent loan.

Year Lot Acquired	Original Cost $	Amount Existing Liens $	(a) Present Value of Lot $	(b) Cost of Improvements $	Total (a + b) $

Complete this line if this is a refinance loan.

Year Acquired	Original Cost $	Amount Existing Liens $	Purpose of Refinance	Describe Improvements [ ] made [ ] to be made Cost: $

Title will be held in what Name(s) | **Manner in which Title will be held** | **Estate will be held in:** [ ] Fee Simple [ ] Leasehold (show expiration date)

Source of Down Payment, Settlement Charges and/or Subordinate Financing (explain)

Borrower's Name (include Jr. or Sr. if applicable)
Frank L. Barr

Co-Borrower's Name (include Jr. or Sr. if applicable)
Elizabeth M. Barr

Social Security Number 000-00-000	Home Phone (incl. area code) 791-954-0723	Age 32	Yrs. School 16	Social Security Number 000-00-000	Home Phone (incl. area code) 791-954-0723	Age 31	Yrs. School 16

[X] Married [ ] Separated [ ] Unmarried (include single, divorced, widowed) Dependents (not listed by Co-Borrower) no. 0 ages | [X] Married [ ] Separated [ ] Unmarried (include single, divorced, widowed) Dependents (not listed by Borrower) no. 0 ages

Present Address (street, city, state, ZIP) [ ] Own [X] Rent 4 No. Yrs.
103 Wilson Street
St. Joseph Missouri

Present Address (street, city, state, ZIP) [ ] Own [X] Rent 4 No. Yrs.
103 Wilson Street
St. Joseph Missouri

If residing at present address for less than two years, complete the following:

Former Address (street, city, state, ZIP) [ ] Own [ ] Rent No. Yrs. | **Former Address** (street, city, state, ZIP) [ ] Own [ ] Rent No. Yrs.

Former Address (street, city, state, ZIP) [ ] Own [ ] Rent No. Yrs. | **Former Address** (street, city, state, ZIP) [ ] Own [ ] Rent No. Yrs.

Name & Address of Employer [ ] Self Employed ABC Corp. 444 A Street St. Joseph Missouri	Yrs. on this job 5 Yrs. employed in this line of work/profession 8	Name & Address of Employer [ ] Self Employed Intense Corp. 1301 Walker Drive St. Joseph Missouri	Yrs. on this job 4 Yrs. employed in this line of work/profession 7

| Position/Title/Type of Business Manager, Human Resources | Business Phone (incl. area code) 791-838-2591 | Position/Title/Type of Business Consultant, Advertising | Business Phone (incl. area code) 791-847-3965 |

If employed in current position for less than two years or if currently employed in more than one position, complete the following:

Name & Address of Employer [ ] Self Employed	Dates (from - to) Monthly Income $	Name & Address of Employer [ ] Self Employed	Dates (from - to) Monthly Income $
Position/Title/Type of Business	Business Phone (incl. area code)	Position/Title/Type of Business	Business Phone (incl. area code)
Name & Address of Employer [ ] Self Employed	Dates (from - to) Monthly Income $	Name & Address of Employer [ ] Self Employed	Dates (from - to) Monthly Income $
Position/Title/Type of Business	Business Phone (incl. area code)	Position/Title/Type of Business	Business Phone (incl. area code)

Freddie Mac Form 65 10/92   Fannie Mae Form 1003 10/92

FIGURE 11.2   Uniform Residential Loan Application (continued)

V. MONTHLY INCOME AND COMBINED HOUSING EXPENSE INFORMATION

Gross Monthly Income	Borrower	Co-Borrower	Total	Combined Monthly Housing Expense	Present	Proposed
Base Empl. Income*	$ 3,100	$ 2,500	$ 5,600	Rent	$ 600	
Overtime	200	325	525	First Mortgage (P&I)		$ 793
Bonuses				Other Financing (P&I)		
Commissions				Hazard Insurance		50
Dividends/Interest				Real Estate Taxes		90
Net Rental Income				Mortgage Insurance		45
Other (before completing, see the notice in "describe other income" below)				Homeowner Assn. Dues		0
				Other:		
Total	$ 3,300	$ 2,825	$ 6,125	Total	$ 600	$ 978

* Self Employed Borrower(s) may be required to provide additional documentation such as tax returns and financial statements.

B/C	Describe Other Income Notice: Alimony, child support, or separate maintenance income need not be revealed if the Borrower (B) or Co-Borrower (C) does not choose to have it considered for repaying this loan.	Monthly Amount
		$

VI. ASSETS AND LIABILITIES

This Statement and any applicable supporting schedules may be completed jointly by both married and unmarried Co-Borrowers if their assets and liabilities are sufficiently joined so that the Statement can be meaningfully and fairly presented on a combined basis; otherwise separate Statements and Schedules are required. If the Co-Borrower section was completed about a spouse, this Statement and supporting schedules must be completed about that spouse also.

Completed [XX] Jointly   [ ] Not Jointly

ASSETS	Cash or Market Value	Liabilities and Pledged Assets. List the creditor's name, address and account number for all outstanding debts, including automobile loans, revolving charge accounts, real estate loans, alimony, child support, stock pledges, etc. Use continuation sheet, if necessary. Indicate by (*) those liabilities which will be satisfied upon sale of real estate owned or upon refinancing of the subject property.		
Description		LIABILITIES	Monthly Pmt. & Mos. Left to Pay	Unpaid Balance
Cash deposit toward purchase held by:	$	Name and address of Company	$ Pmt./Mos.	$
R.E. Broker	4,000	Hardy Credit	$120/11	1,200
List checking and savings accounts below		3423 S. 3rd Street		
Name and address of Bank, S&L, or Credit Union		San Jose CA		
First Bank - Checking				
123 Elm Street				
St. Joseph Missouri		Acct. no.		
		Name and address of Company	$ Pmt./Mos.	$
Acct. no. 222222	$ 3,300			
Name and address of Bank, S&L, or Credit Union		Proposed Loan	978/360	108,000
First Bank - Savings				
123 Elm Street				
St. Joseph Missouri		Acct. no.		
Acct. no. 27328	$ 21,800	Name and address of Company	$ Pmt./Mos.	$
Name and address of Bank, S&L, or Credit Union				
		Acct. no.		
		Name and address of Company	$ Pmt./Mos.	$
Acct. no.	$			
Name and address of Bank, S&L, or Credit Union				
		Acct. no.		
		Name and address of Company	$ Pmt./Mos.	$
Acct. no. 35358	$			
Stocks & Bonds (Company name/number & description)	$			
Olde Discount	18,300	Acct. no.		
		Name and address of Company	$ Pmt./Mos.	$
Life insurance net cash value	$			
Face amount: $				
Subtotal Liquid Assets	$ 47,400			
Real estate owned (enter market value from schedule of real estate owned)	$ 20,000	Acct. no.		
Vested interest in retirement fund	$	Name and address of Company	$ Pmt./Mos.	$
Net worth of business(es) owned (attach financial statement)	$			
Automobiles owned (make and year)	$			
Ford '92	4,000	Acct. no.		
Nissan '97	11,000	Alimony/Child Support/Separate Maintenance Payments Owed to:	$	
Other Assets (itemize)	$	Job Related Expense (child care, union dues, etc.)	$	
		Total Monthly Payments	$ 1,098	
Total Assets a.	$ 82,400	Net Worth (a minus b) $ -26,800	Total Liabilities b.	$ 109,200

Freddie Mac Form 65 10/92   Page 2 of 4   Fannie Mae Form 1003 10/92

FIGURE 11.2 Uniform Residential Loan Application (continued)

VI. ASSETS AND LIABILITIES (cont.)

Schedule of Real Estate Owned (If additional properties are owned, use continuation sheet.)

Property Address (enter S if sold, PS if pending sale or R if rental being held for income)	Type of Property	Present Market Value	Amount of Mortgages & Liens	Gross Rental Income	Mortgage Payments	Insurance, Maintenance, Taxes & Misc.	Net Rental Income
Lot 7, Becker Drive	land	$ 20,000	$ 0	$ 0	$ 0	$ 0	$ 0
Totals		$	$	$	$	$	$

List any additional names under which credit has previously been received and indicate appropriate creditor name(s) and account number(s):

Alternate Name	Creditor Name	Account Number

VII. DETAILS OF TRANSACTION

a. Purchase price	$ 120,000
b. Alterations, improvements, repairs	0
c. Land (if acquired separately)	0
d. Refinance (incl. debts to be paid off)	0
e. Estimated prepaid items	1,200
f. Estimated closing costs	5,000
g. PMI, MIP, Funding Fee	
h. Discount (if Borrower will pay)	
i. Total Costs (add items a through h)	126,200
j. Subordinate financing	
k. Borrower's closing costs paid by Seller	
l. Other Credits (explain)	
m. Loan amount (exclude PMI, MIP, Funding Fee financed)	108,000
n. PMI, MIP, Funding Fee financed	
o. Loan amount (add m & n)	108,000
p. Cash from/to Borrower (subtract j, k, l & o from i)	18,200

VIII. DECLARATIONS

If you answer "Yes" to any questions a through i, please use continuation sheet for explanation.

	Borrower Yes	Borrower No	Co-Borrower Yes	Co-Borrower No
a. Are there any outstanding judgments against you?		X		X
b. Have you been declared bankrupt within the past 7 years?		X		X
c. Have you had property foreclosed upon or given title or deed in lieu thereof in the last 7 years?		X		X
d. Are you a party to a lawsuit?		X		X
e. Have you directly or indirectly been obligated on any loan which resulted in foreclosure, transfer of title in lieu of foreclosure, or judgment? (This would include such loans as home mortgage loans, SBA loans, home improvement loans, manufactured (mobile) home loans, any mortgage, financial obligation, bond, or loan guarantee. If "Yes," provide details, including date, name and address of Lender, FHA or V.A. case number, if any, and reasons for the action.)		X		X
f. Are you presently delinquent or in default on any Federal debt or any other loan, mortgage, financial obligation, bond, or loan guarantee? If "Yes," give details as described in the preceding question.		X		X
g. Are you obligated to pay alimony, child support, or separate maintenance?		X		X
h. Is any part of the down payment borrowed?		X		X
i. Are you a co-maker or endorser on a note?		X		X
j. Are you a U.S. citizen?	X		X	
k. Are you a permanent resident alien?		X		X
l. Do you intend to occupy the property as your primary residence? If "Yes," complete question m below.	X		X	
m. Have you had an ownership interest in a property in the last three years?	X		X	
(1) What type of property did you own—principal residence (PR), second home (SH), or investment property (IP)?	IP		IP	
(2) How did you hold title to the home—solely by yourself (S), jointly with your spouse (SP), or jointly with another person (O)?	SP		SP	

IX. ACKNOWLEDGMENT AND AGREEMENT

The undersigned specifically acknowledge(s) and agree(s) that: (1) the loan requested by this application will be secured by a first mortgage or deed of trust on the property described herein; (2) the property will not be used for any illegal or prohibited purpose or use; (3) all statements made in this application are made for the purpose of obtaining the loan indicated herein; (4) occupation of the property will be as indicated above; (5) verification or reverification of any information contained in the application may be made at any time by the Lender, its agents, successors and assigns, either directly or through a credit reporting agency, from any source named in this application, and the original copy of this application will be retained by the Lender, even if the loan is not approved; (6) the Lender, its agents, successors and assigns will rely on the information contained in the application and I/we have a continuing obligation to amend and/or supplement the information provided in this application if any of the material facts which I/we have represented herein should change prior to closing; (7) in the event my/our payments on the loan indicated in this application become delinquent, the Lender, its agents, successors and assigns, may, in addition to all their other rights and remedies, report my/our name(s) and account information to a credit reporting agency; (8) ownership of the loan may be transferred to successor or assign of the Lender without notice to me and/or the administration of the loan account may be transferred to an agent, successor or assign of the Lender with prior notice to me; (9) the Lender, its agents, successors and assigns make no representations or warranties, express or implied, to the Borrower(s) regarding the property, the condition of the property, or the value of the property.
Certification: I/We certify that the information provided in this application is true and correct as of the date set forth opposite my/our signature(s) on this application and acknowledge my/our understanding that any intentional or negligent misrepresentation(s) of the information contained in this application may result in civil liability and/or criminal penalties including, but not limited to, fine or imprisonment or both under the provisions of Title 18, United States Code, Section 1001, et seq. and liability for monetary damages to the Lender, its agents, successors and assigns, insurers and any other person who may suffer any loss due to reliance upon any misrepresentation which I/we have made on this application.

Borrower's Signature	Date	Co-Borrower's Signature	Date
X		X	

X. INFORMATION FOR GOVERNMENT MONITORING PURPOSES

The following information is requested by the Federal Government for certain types of loans related to a dwelling, in order to monitor the Lender's compliance with equal credit opportunity, fair housing and home mortgage disclosure laws. You are not required to furnish this information, but are encouraged to do so. The law provides that a Lender may neither discriminate on the basis of this information, nor on whether you choose to furnish it. However, if you choose not to furnish it, under Federal regulations this Lender is required to note race and sex on the basis of visual observation or surname. If you do not wish to furnish the above information, please check the box below. (Lender must review the above material to assure that the disclosures satisfy all requirements to which the Lender is subject under applicable state law for the particular type of loan applied for.)

BORROWER

	I do not wish to furnish this information
Race/National Origin:	☐ American Indian or Alaskan Native ☐ Asian or Pacific Islander ☐ White, not of Hispanic Origin ☒ Black, not of Hispanic origin ☐ Hispanic
	Other (specify) _____
Sex:	☐ Female ☒ Male

CO-BORROWER

	I do not wish to furnish this information
Race/National Origin:	☐ American Indian or Alaskan Native ☐ Asian or Pacific Islander ☐ White, not of Hispanic Origin ☒ Black, not of Hispanic origin ☐ Hispanic
	Other (specify) _____
Sex:	☒ Female ☐ Male

To be Completed by Interviewer

This application was taken by:
☒ face-to-face interview
☐ by mail
☐ by telephone

Interviewer's Name (print or type)	Name and Address of Interviewer's Employer
Bob Interviewer	First Savings Bank St. Joseph Missouri
Interviewer's Signature ___ Date ___	
Interviewer's Phone Number (incl. area code) 954-761-0264	

Freddie Mac Form 65 10/92   Page 3 of 4   Fannie Mae Form 1003 10/92

It is hoped that the total of the assets will exceed the total of the liabilities, with the difference being an applicant's **net worth.** The amount of net worth is added to the total liabilities in order to balance both sides of the financial statement. A two-to-one current ratio indicates that the applicant has twice as many current assets as current liabilities and is a good credit risk. If total liabilities exceed an applicant's total assets, a loan would probably be denied at this point and the file closed. Assuming an applicant has a positive net worth, a series of related actions begin.

Data Verification

As discussed in Chapter 4 under Fannie Mae's electronic underwriting system (Desktop Underwriter®) and Freddie Mac's Loan Prospector®, much of the data involved in analyzing a potential loan is available from firms like Experian, Equifax, or Transunion Corporations. Some larger lenders, such as Wells Fargo, now use their own automated underwriting systems, programmed to meet Fannie Mae's and Freddie Mac's approval.

The loan officer charged with processing the loan verifies the information included in the application by actually checking with the various references given, the banks where deposits are held, and the applicant's employer. Some lenders will accept alternate documentation, pay stubs, bank statements, etc., to speed up processing.

Deposits. The borrower is obliged to sign deposit verification forms that authorize the bank to reveal to the lender the current balances in the borrower's accounts. Without a verification form, such confidential information could not be released by the bank under the Federal Right to Privacy Act. A typical form for verification of deposit is reproduced in Figure 11.3.

A deposit verification permission form must be signed by the borrower for each bank account to enable the loan processor to ascertain all the current balances. The knowledge that the loan processor can verify account amounts is usually enough incentive for the borrower to be truthful in reporting financial information. When the deposit balances are verified, the appropriate entries are made in the applicant's file.

Employment. Likewise, an applicant is required to sign an employment verification form similar to that illustrated in Figure 11.4. It authorizes the employer to reveal confidential information concerning the applicant's job status. Not only are an applicant's wages and length of employment verified, but the employer is requested to offer an opinion of the applicant's job attitude and give a prognosis for continued employment and prospects for advancement.

Credit Report. Simultaneously with the gathering of financial and employment information, a loan processor sends a formal request for a borrower's **credit report** to a local company offering this service. Within a few days if the applicant is a local resident, or longer if out-of-town credit must be checked, the credit search company sends the loan officer a confidential report on its findings. A sample credit report is reproduced in Figure 11.5.

The credit report is an itemization of the status of current accounts. In addition, it indicates the quality and dates of the payments made and their regularity, delinquency, or any outstanding balances. This payment history is the most important part of the entire report. Credit managers and loan officers frequently state that a person's future attitude is in most

FIGURE 11.3 Request for Verification of Deposit

FannieMae

Request for Verification of Deposit

Privacy Act Notice: This information is to be used by the agency collecting it or its assignees in determining whether you qualify as a prospective mortgagor under its program. It will not be disclosed outside the agency except as required and permitted by law. You do not have to provide this information, but if you do not your application for approval as a prospective mortgagor or borrower may be delayed or rejected. The information requested in this form is authorized by Title 38, USC, Chapter 37 (If VA); by 12 USC, Section 1701 et.seq. (If HUD/FHA); by 42 USC, Section 1452b (If HUD/CPD); and Title 42 USC, 1471 et.seq. or 7 USC, 1921 et.seq. (If USDA/FmHA).

Instructions: Lender — Complete Items 1 through 8. Have applicant(s) complete Item 9. Forward directly to depository named in Item 1.
Depository — Please complete Items 10 through 18 and return DIRECTLY to lender named in Item 2.
The form is to be transmitted directly to the lender and is not to be transmitted through the applicant(s) or any other party.

Part I — Request

1. To (Name and address of depository)	2. From (Name and address of lender)

I certify that this verification has been sent directly to the bank or depository and has not passed through the hands of the applicant or any other party.

3. Signature of lender	4. Title	5. Date	6. Lender's No. (Optional)

7. Information To Be Verified

Type of Account	Account in Name of	Account Number	Balance
			$
			$
			$

To Depository: I/We have applied for a mortgage loan and stated in my financial statement that the balance on deposit with you is as shown above. You are authorized to verify this information and to supply the lender identified above with the information requested in Items 10 through 13. Your response is solely a matter of courtesy for which no responsibility is attached to your institution or any of your officers.

8. Name and Address of Applicant(s)	9. Signature of Applicant(s)

To Be Completed by Depository
Part II — Verification of Depository

10. Deposit Accounts of Applicant(s)

Type of Account	Account Number	Current Balance	Average Balance For Previous Two Months	Date Opened
		$	$	
		$	$	
		$	$	

11. Loans Outstanding To Applicant(s)

Loan Number	Date of Loan	Original Amount	Current Balance	Installments (Monthly/Quarterly)		Secured By	Number of Late Payments
		$	$	$	per		
		$	$	$	per		
		$	$	$	per		

12. Please include any additional information which may be of assistance in determination of credit worthiness. (Please include information on loans paid-in-full in Item 11 above.)

13. If the name(s) on the account(s) differ from those listed in Item 7, please supply the name(s) on the account(s) as reflected by your records.

Part III — Authorized Signature - Federal statutes provide severe penalties for any fraud, intentional misrepresentation, or criminal connivance or conspiracy purposed to influence the issuance of any guaranty or insurance by the VA Secretary, the U.S.D.A., FmHA/FHA Commissioner, or the HUD/CPD Assistant Secretary.

14. Signature of Depository Representative	15. Title (Please print or type)	16. Date
17. Please print or type name signed in item 14	18. Phone No.	

Fannie Mae
Form 1006   July 96

FIGURE 11.4   Request for Verification of Employment

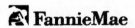

Request for Verification of Employment

Privacy Act Notice: This information is to be used by the agency collecting it or its assignees in determining whether you qualify as a prospective mortgagor under its program. It will not be disclosed outside the agency except as required and permitted by law. You do not have to provide this information, but if you do not your application for approval as a prospective mortgagor or borrower may be delayed or rejected. The information requested in this form is authorized by Title 38, USC, Chapter 37 (if VA); by 12 USC, Section 1701 et. seq. (if HUD/FHA); by 42 USC, Section 1452b (if HUD/CPD); and Title 42 USC, 1471 et. seq., or 7 USC, 1921 et. seq. (if USDA/FmHA).

Instructions: Lender — Complete items 1 through 7. Have applicant complete item 8. Forward directly to employer named in item 1.
Employer — Please complete either Part II or Part III as applicable. Complete Part IV and return directly to lender named in item 2.
The form is to be transmitted directly to the lender and is not to be transmitted through the applicant or any other party.

Part I — Request

1. To (Name and address of employer)	2. From (Name and address of lender)

I certify that this verification has been sent directly to the employer and has not passed through the hands of the applicant or any other interested party.

3. Signature of Lender	4. Title	5. Date	6. Lender's Number (Optional)

I have applied for a mortgage loan and stated that I am now or was formerly employed by you. My signature below authorizes verification of this information.

7. Name and Address of Applicant (include employee or badge number)	8. Signature of Applicant

Part II — Verification of Present Employment

9. Applicant's Date of Employment	10. Present Position	11. Probability of Continued Employment

12A. Current Gross Base Pay (Enter Amount and Check Period)

☐ Annual ☐ Hourly
☐ Monthly ☐ Other (Specify)
$ _____ ☐ Weekly

12B. Gross Earnings

Type	Year To Date	Past Year 19___	Past Year 19___
Base Pay	Thru _____ 19___ $	$	$
Overtime	$	$	$
Commissions	$	$	$
Bonus	$	$	$
Total	$	$	$

13. For Military Personnel Only

Pay Grade

Type	Monthly Amount
Base Pay	$
Rations	$
Flight or Hazard	$
Clothing	$
Quarters	$
Pro Pay	$
Overseas or Combat	$
Variable Housing Allowance	$

14. If Overtime or Bonus is Applicable, Is Its Continuance Likely?

Overtime	☐ Yes	☐ No
Bonus	☐ Yes	☐ No

15. If paid hourly — average hours per week

16. Date of applicant's next pay increase

17. Projected amount of next pay increase

18. Date of applicant's last pay increase

19. Amount of last pay increase

20. Remarks (If employee was off work for any length of time, please indicate time period and reason)

Part III — Verification of Previous Employment

21. Date Hired	23. Salary/Wage at Termination Per (Year) (Month) (Week)
22. Date Terminated	Base _____ Overtime _____ Commissions _____ Bonus _____
24. Reason for Leaving	25. Position Held

Part IV — Authorized Signature - Federal statutes provide severe penalties for any fraud, intentional misrepresentation, or criminal connivance or conspiracy purposed to influence the issuance of any guaranty or insurance by the VA Secretary, the U.S.D.A., FmHA/FHA Commissioner, or the HUD/CPD Assistant Secretary.

26. Signature of Employer	27. Title (Please print or type)	28. Date
29. Print or type name signed in Item 26	30. Phone No.	

Fannie Mae
Form 1005   July 96

FIGURE 11.5   Credit Report Form

National Credit
STANDARD FACTUAL DATA REPORT

CREDIT PROFILE

CONFIDENTIAL REPORT

Type of Report:

Acct. Number: 100   Requested by: ABC MORTGAGE CO.   VA ☐   FHA ☐
Date of Report: 11/16/98   Date Ordered: 11/16/98   FNMA ☒
Name (& Spouse): CONSUMER, JOHN A.   SALLY
Present Address: 123 SECOND STREET
CHICAGO IL 60649   This Report Contains:
Property Address: 345 THIRD STREET   ☒ Joint Information   ☐ Individual Information
CHICAGO IL 60637

Sources: _____

PERSONAL

	PERSONAL	☒ Rents ☐ Buying ☐ Owns (free & Clear)
1. Length of time at address shown above:	1. 6 YEARS	
2. Former address (if less than 2 years at present address):	2. --	
3. Social Security Number(s):	3. 123-45-6789	Spouse: 345-67-8901
4. Approximate age of subject:	4. 37	Spouse: 33
5. Marital status – dependents (Exclude subject & spouse):	5. MARRIED	Dependents: -1-

EMPLOYMENT

	EMPLOYMENT	☒ Verified ☐ Not Verified
6. Name of employer:	6. XYZ CORPORATON	Since: 1988
7. Position held – length of present employment:	7. MANAGER	
8. Employment verified by:	8. HUMAN RESOURCES	
9. Approximate income from employment:	9. 3300/MONTH	
10. Former employment (if less than 2 years above):	10. --	☐ Verified ☒ Not Verified

CO. APP. EMP.

	CO. APP. EMP.	☐ Verified ☒ Not Verified
11. Name of co-applicant's employer:	11. SELF EMPLOYED	
12. Position held – length of present employment:	12. REAL ESTATE AGENT	Since: 10/88
13. Employment verified by:	13. SEE FINANCIAL STATEMENT	
14. Approximate income from employment:	14. 3500/MONTH	
15. Former employment (if less than 2 years above):	15. --	☐ Verified ☒ Not Verified

CERTIFICATION

1. National Credit certifies that (a) X public records have been checked for judgments, garnishments, bankruptcies, chattels, liens and other legal actions involving the subject; or, (b) equivalent information has been obtained through a qualified public records reporting service.

2. National Credit certifies that the subject's credit record in the payment of bills and other obligations has been checked; (a) __ through credit extended by the designated credit grantors under the classes and trades identified in the contract for the community in which the subject resides; or, (b) X through accumulated credit records of such credit grantors of community in which the subject resides, with the results indicated below.

This report is provided to assist in the decision to grant credit. It is based upon information from credit grantors in good faith. The accuracy of the same, however is in no way guaranteed. The information is strictly confidential. Neither National Credit nor any of its employees shall be held responsible for violation of these conditions and by your acceptance of this report you specifically agree to the same.

CREDIT HISTORY

Credit Grantor	Date Opened	Date Reported	High Credit	Terms	Balance Owing	Amount Past Due	Date Last Past Due	Paying Record	Footnote Number
CITIBANK	9/87	11/98	6000.	FLEXIBLE	4110.	-0-	---	SATIS	-
B OF A M/C	2/85	11/98	1200.	FLEXIBLE	556.	-0-	---	SATIS	-
FINANCE AMERICA	3/84	11/98	1000.	84X119	247.	-0-	---	SATIS	-
1ST CHGO. VISA	12/82	11/98	600.	FLEXIBLE	125.	-0-	---	SATIS	-
SEARS	9/88	11/98	1000.	FLEXIBLE	34.	-0-	---	SATIS	-
PENNEYS	9/87	11/98	300.	FLEXIBLE	56.	-0-	---	SATIS	1
WARDS	10/89	11/98	300.	FLEXIBLE	220.	-0-	---	SATIS	1
CARSON PIRIE SCOTT	8/88	11/98	1000.	FLEXIBLE	113.	-0-	4/90	CURRENT	-
MARSHALL FIELD'S	11/88	11/98	1500.	FLEXIBLE	4110.	-0-	---	PDSATIS	-
CHEMICAL BANK	3/90	11/98	1500.	36MONTHS	-0-	-0-	---	SATIS	-
ROBINSON'S	6/91	11/98	500.	FLEXIBLE	-0-	-0-	---	SATIS	-
NORDSTROM	9/89	11/98	1000.	FLEXIBLE	-0-	-0-	---	SATIS	-
SAKS 5TH AVE.	4/89	11/98	400.	FLEXIBLE	-0-	-0-	---	SATIS	-

INQUIRES   3/5/98 AMERICAN EXPRESS-APPLICATION FOR CREDIT CARD.
2/25/98 AMOCO APPLICATION FOR CREDIT CARD.

PUBLIC RECORDS: JUDGMENT FILED 2/84 IN CHICAGO MUNICIPAL COURT, CASE #123456 FOR $450., FILED BY A&B COMPANY WAS SATISFIED 1/86.

FOOTNOTES:

1. ACCOUNT HELD IN THE NAME OF SALLY CONSUMER.

ADDITIONAL INCOME: (STATED) APPLICANT CLAIMS $500./MONTH OVERTIME.

REPORT FOR:	ABC MORTGAGE COMPANY			
PREPARED BY:	NATIONAL CREDIT	P.O. BOX 678	CHICAGO ILLINOIS	60657 (312)555-8916
		City	State	Zip Code

cases a reflection of past behavior in meeting financial obligations. Research tends to reinforce these opinions, indicating that slow and erratic payers generally retain those attitudes when securing new loans, and prompt and steady payers are also consistent in meeting their future obligations.

When a credit report is returned revealing a series of erratic and delinquent payments, the loan is usually denied at this point and the file closed. If there are only one or two unusual entries in a group of otherwise satisfactory transactions, the applicant is asked to explain these variations, noted in writing to be kept for future reference.

As with many standardized procedures, credit reporting has become computerized, dramatically shortening the time needed for completing a check. However, in exchange for time efficiency, these bureaus risk sacrificing the borrower's confidentiality. Credit reports should be used only by the persons or institutions requesting the information and only for the purposes stated.

As a result of increased seller financing, credit bureaus are receiving more requests from agents and sellers to check the credit of potential purchasers. Most credit agencies insist on seeing a buyer's written permission before issuing any information in order to protect the buyer's confidentiality. After the deposit and employment verifications are returned with acceptable information and a favorable credit report is obtained, the lending officer makes a thorough credit evaluation of the data collected.

Credit Evaluation

Not only is the quantity of an applicant's income evaluated for loan qualification, its quality is evaluated as well. The lender is looking for income that is stable, regular, and recurring. Thus, income from all sources is added together to find an acceptable total on which to apply the qualifying ratios.

In a normal transaction, the wages and earnings of the coborrowers are considered. In the event a cosigner is involved, this person's income is included as well. Extra income is considered if it is received regularly and for a period of at least three years; thus, bonuses and overtime pay can be included if they fit this criterion. Pensions, interest, and dividends are treated as regular income, although it is recognized that interest and dividends do fluctuate over time and may cease if the investment is cashed out.

A second or part-time job is accepted as part of the regular monthly income if it can be shown that the job has existed for approximately two years and there is good reason to believe it will continue. Child support can also be included in the determination of monthly income, but only if it is the result of a court order or has a proven track record. Also, under ECOA, government entitlement funds must be considered. Self-employed borrowers, including commissioned wage earners, need at least two years of established income to qualify for a mortgage loan.

Divorced buyers are required to submit a copy of their decree to inform lenders which party is responsible for liabilities, how the assets are divided, and whether there are support and/or alimony obligations. For alimony to be considered as income, most lenders require a one-year history of payment receipts and reasonable assurance that payments will continue for at least three years from the date of the loan application.

On the other hand, alimony or child support payments are considered a debt of the borrower responsible for these, and must be included in the financial analysis.

In addition to the total quantity of income, a loan analyst pays careful attention to its quality. An applicant's employer is asked for an opinion of job stability and possible advancement. Length of time on the job no longer carries the heavy clout it once did. Applicants whose employment records show frequent shifts in job situations that result in upward mobility each time are given full consideration. Lenders will, however, be wary of an applicant who drifts from one job classification to another and cannot seem to become established in any specific type of work.

Loan Qualifying Income Ratios. When analyzing the borrower's ability to make the required loan payments, loan underwriters currently apply the following pairs of income ratios:

Loan Type	Housing Ratio	Total Debt Ratio
Conventional loans	28 percent	36 percent
Conventional affordable loans	33 percent	38 percent
FHA loans	29 percent	41 percent
VA loans	–	41 percent

The 28 percent and 29 percent ratios refer to the total of principal, interest, taxes, insurance, and homeowner's association fees as a percentage of acceptable gross monthly income. The 36 percent and 41 percent ratios refer to the total of the mortgage payment *plus* other monthly installment obligations such as car or furniture payments, as a percentage of acceptable gross monthly income. In this latter category, some flexibility exists, such as eliminating a car payment that will end in six months or less.

FOR EXAMPLE

Consider a conventional loan of $82,000 at 8% interest for 30 years. The property taxes are $1,800 per year and the hazard insurance premium is $240. The homeowner's association fee is $180 for the year. The borrowers have car payments of $200 per month with two years left to pay.

Conventional Loan

$82,000 @ 8 percent/30 Years' Principal and Interest	$ 601.70
Property Taxes	150.00
Hazard Insurance	20.00
Homeowner's Association Fee	15.00
Monthly Payment	786.70
Conventional Housing Expense Ratio	÷ 0.28
Required Gross Monthly Income	$2,809.64
Monthly Payment	786.70
Car Payment	200.00
Total Monthly Payment	986.70
Conventional Total Debt Ratio	÷ 0.36
Required Gross Monthly Income	$2,740.83

Because the required income to satisfy the total debt ratio is less than that required by the housing expense ratio, the $2,809.64 would apply. The income required to meet the housing expense ratio must be met. The total debt ratio only affects the required monthly income if the amount is higher.

(continued)

FOR EXAMPLE (continued)

FHA Loan

Monthly Payment	786.70
FHA Housing Expense Ratio	÷ 0.29
Required Monthly Income	$2,712.75
Total Monthly Payment	986.70
FHA/VA Total Debt Ratio	÷ 0.41
Required Monthly Income	$2,406.68

From the above analysis, to qualify for the conventional loan, the borrowers would need to show a combined gross monthly income of $2,809.64. To qualify for an FHA loan, $2,712.75 monthly income would be required. As VA loans use one ratio of 41%, they would only have to show a combined gross monthly income of $2,406.68, assuming the residual income requirement is adequate.

After reviewing all the information provided in the application and making the appropriate ratio analyses of the income and expense data, the loan officer collects all pertinent papers and sends the package to the company underwriters for a final determination. If a special report of unusual circumstances is warranted, it is included. During the borrower's qualification process, an appraiser is evaluating the collateral, and this appraisal report is included in the submission.

QUALIFYING THE COLLATERAL

Despite the current trend toward emphasizing a borrower's financial ability as the basic loan-granting criterion, real estate lenders and guarantors are practical and fully understand that life is filled with unpredictable, uncontrollable events. Death is an ever-present specter that can abruptly eliminate a family's breadwinner. Negative economic activities in a particular geographical area can exert devastating financial impacts. Applicants can be left unemployed as a result of local plant shutdowns; mistakes in personal decisions can result in bankruptcies and divorces, often damaging or destroying credit in the process. To hedge these risks and others, real estate lenders look to the value of the collateral as the final assurance for recovery of their investments in a default situation. Therefore, an accurate estimate of the value of this collateral becomes another pivotal point in the lending process.

Definition of Value

Value is defined as the ability of an object to satisfy, directly or indirectly, the needs or desires of human beings. As such, it is called by economists **value in use**. When the value of an object is measured in terms of its power to purchase other objects, it is called **value in exchange**.

From these definitions it is apparent that value is a function of use and demand. As such, it is *subjective* by its very nature. A seller may have an entirely different idea of the value of a property than a potential buyer. A condemning agency would probably offer a different

IN PRACTICE . . .

Jim and Mary Smith recently made an offer on a little Cape Cod style house near Jim's office. Their offer of $140,000 was accepted with a $7,000 down payment and a 95% LTV mortgage loan of $133,000. Never having purchased a home before, Jim and Mary thought that was all they needed to start packing for the move to their new home. Over the past few weeks they have learned a lot about the pitfalls that can happen between the time of a contract acceptance and a successful closing!

First, in qualifying for their loan, they were surprised to learn that they have accumulated too much credit card debt. The lender is requiring that they pay off the outstanding balances and close out three of their credit cards.

They never realized that the property itself had to "qualify." When the appraisal came in at $138,000 the lender was no longer willing to give them a mortgage loan of $133,000! As Jim and Mary do not have the extra cash to make up the difference, they were greatly relieved when the seller eventually agreed to reduce the sales price to $138,000, leaving the down payment at $7,000 with a $131,000 loan.

With settlement only four days away, the Smiths thought they were all set when an unexpected call came from their agent telling them that the title search had come up with a "cloud on the title." It seems that there is an outstanding mechanic's lien for $3,500 still recorded on the property! Fortunately, the sellers have cancelled checks showing that the contractor who replaced their roof three years ago was in fact paid in full although there had been lengthy arguments about the quality of the work, which had delayed payment.

Finally, 30 days from acceptance of their offer, Jim and Mary are scheduled for settlement tomorrow morning at 10:00 A.M. with borrowers, collateral, and title all satisfactorily qualified!

---

opinion of a property's value than its owner. Tax assessors and property owners disagree about a particular property's value, as do many other persons under varying circumstances. However, an appraiser must make an objective estimate of value based on supply and demand in the marketplace.

There can be only one market value for a specific real property at any given point in time. **Market value** is defined as the price a property would most likely bring if it were exposed for sale in the open market for a reasonable period of time. Implicit in this definition is that both buyer and seller are well informed and under no undue pressure to influence the decision of either party.

In terms of market value, it is important to note the fine distinctions that exist among cost, price, and value. Cost, a measure of past expenses, may not reflect current market value, especially if a building is fairly old. Price, on the other hand, is a present measure but one that may be affected by some unusual circumstances of a specific transaction. Unique financing terms or a temporarily active local housing market in which potential buyers briefly exceed available properties may cause prices to rise above actual market values. Therefore, each parcel of property pledged for collateral must be inspected and appraised carefully to estimate its fair market value, because this amount will be employed as the basis for determining the mortgage loan amount. Depending on the type of loan to be issued and its concurrent LTV ratio, either the amount of the formal appraisal made as part of the loan process or the purchase price, *whichever is less,* will determine the amount of the loan.

Staff or Fee Appraisers

Financial fiduciaries actively engaged in making real estate loans maintain a staff of experienced appraisers whose duties include estimating and verifying property values. Lenders who are less active in the real estate market as well as the FHA and the VA often hire professional fee appraisers. Sometimes, when very large loans are made, more than one opinion is sought and both staff and fee appraisers participate in an appraisal project.

An **appraisal** is the estimate of a property's value at a specific point in time. It must be reported in writing, in accordance with the Uniform Standards of Professional Appraisal Practice (USPAP), using the Uniform Residential Appraisal Report (see Figure 11.6), by competent individuals whose professional performance is adequately supervised.

Furthermore, to qualify, an appraiser must be state licensed and/or certified by passing an examination consistent with and equivalent to the Uniform State Certification Examination endorsed by the Appraiser Qualification Board of the Appraisal Foundation.

For loans to be issued by federally regulated banks and thrifts, appraisal documents must be provided by licensed and/or certified appraisers. Usually, standards used to certify are more stringent than those used to license. To assist in the development of these professional traits there are a number of appraisers' associations. The American Institute of Real Estate Appraisers and the Society of Real Estate Appraisers have joined together under The Appraisal Institute. Other appraisal organizations include the American Society of Appraisers, the National Association of Independent Fee Appraisers, and the National Association of Review Appraisers. Some of these groups maintain active education programs and award achievement designations for completing a number of formal courses and for serving a number of years as an appraiser. For example, The Appraisal Institute offers the MAI (Member, Appraisal Institute), the SRA (Senior Residential Appraiser), the SREA (Senior Real Estate Appraiser), and the SRPA (Senior Real Property Appraiser) designations.

The methods of appraisal are predominantly mathematical. Nevertheless, an appraiser relies on personal interpretive skills to a great degree. Appraising is, therefore, a science that is artfully interpreted.

The Appraisal Process

In most appraisals the appraiser comprehensively examines the property and provides a detailed description of its attributes and shortcomings. Based on the ability of accessing data on the Internet pertinent to appraising a specific property, sometimes an appraiser performs a **drive-by appraisal** of the property when more detail is not required. Drive-by appraising involves the appraiser literally driving by the property for a quick inspection for an opinion of its outward appearance. If it appears to be well-kept and in good condition, it is assumed that the interior is also well maintained and the appraisal will be made on the square footage and location. If, on the other hand, the property looks worn and not well-kept, the drive-by appraiser's report would reveal this information and include a recommendation for a more comprehensive examination or even a denial of the loan.

The appraisal process generally includes defining the appraisal problem, determining the purpose for the appraisal, examining the neighborhood and property being appraised, collecting the pertinent data, applying the appropriate approaches to estimate value, reconciling these value estimates, and preparing the appraisal report.

FIGURE 11.6 Uniform Residential Appraisal Report

File No. 96-100 Page # 1

Summary Appraisal Report
Property Description

UNIFORM RESIDENTIAL APPRAISAL REPORT   File No. 96-100

| Property Address | 1097 Timbers Crossing | City St. Joseph | State MO | Zip Code 94334 |

Legal Description Lot 3, Block G, Harris Billups Estate, Plat Book 8, P. 37 County Buchanan

Assessor's Parcel No. 9223-03-0471   Tax Year 1994   R.E. Taxes $ 1,207.10 Special Assessments $ N/A

Borrower Barr, Frank & Elizabeth   Current Owner Stewart   Occupant [X] Owner ☐ Tenant ☐ Vacant

Property rights appraised [X] Fee Simple ☐ Leasehold   Project Type ☐ PUD ☐ Condominium (HUD/VA only) HOA $ N/A /Mo.

Neighborhood or Project Name Harris Billups Estate   Map Reference _____ Census Tract _____

Sale Price $ 120,000 Date of Sale _____   Description and $ amount of loan charges/concessions to be paid by seller None

Lender/Client Barber Savings Association   Address 4390 N. Main St., St. Joseph MO 94330

Appraiser Michelle Tipton   Address 2125 S. Main St., St. Joseph MO 94330

Location	[X] Urban	☐ Suburban	☐ Rural	Predominant occupancy	Single family housing		Present land use %		Land use change

Location [X] Urban ☐ Suburban ☐ Rural
Built up [X] Over 75% ☐ 25-75% ☐ Under 25%
Growth rate ☐ Rapid [X] Stable ☐ Slow
Property values ☐ Increasing [X] Stable ☐ Declining
Demand/supply ☐ Shortage [X] In balance ☐ Over supply
Marketing time ☐ Under 3 mos. [X] 3-6 mos. ☐ Over 6 mos.

Predominant occupancy: [X] Owner ☐ Tenant [X] Vacant (0-5%) ☐ Vac.(over 5%)

Single family housing PRICE $(000) / AGE (yrs): 70 Low 00 / 155 High 50 / Predominant 120 20

Present land use %: One family 85 / 2-4 family 5 / Multi-family 5 / Commercial 5

Land use change: [X] Not likely ☐ Likely ☐ In process   To: _____

Note: Race and the racial composition of the neighborhood are not appraisal factors.

Neighborhood boundaries and characteristics: Area of mostly single family homes located north of Oak Park Blvd., west of Highway 60, South of Floral Road and east of Dixie Drive.

Factors that affect the marketability of the properties in the neighborhood (proximity to employment and amenities, employment stability, appeal to market, etc.): The subject is located close to neighborhood shopping, parks, public schools and employment centers. The subject's neighborhood exhibits the typical appeal and condition for the area. The presence of 5% commercial utilization is limited to the main thoroughfares and does not adversely affect the subject's value or marketability.

Market conditions in the subject neighborhood (including support for the above conclusions related to the trend of property values, demand/supply, and marketing time -- such as data on competitive properties for sale in the neighborhood, description of the prevalence of sales and financing concessions, etc.): Mortgage money is readily available in the St. Joseph market. Any loan discounts, interest buydowns or concessions do not adversely affect the subject. The subject is located in a family oriented neighborhood whose supply and demand appear to be in balance.

Project Information for PUDs   (If applicable) - - Is the developer/builder in control of the Home Owners' Association (HOA)? ☐ Yes ☐ No
Approximate total number of units in the subject project _____   Approximate total number of units for sale in the subject project _____
Describe common elements and recreational facilities: N/A

Dimensions 80 x 120 (Subject to survey)		Topography	Typical Level

Dimensions 80 x 120 (Subject to survey)
Site area 9600   Corner Lot ☐ Yes [X] No
Specific zoning classification and description Residential (RM-25)
Zoning compliance [X] Legal ☐ Legal nonconforming (Grandfathered use) ☐ Illegal ☐ No zoning
Highest & best use as improved: [X] Present use ☐ Other use (explain)

Topography Typical Level
Size Typical
Shape Rectangular
Drainage Apparently Adequate
View Residential
Landscaping Adequate/ Typical
Driveway Surface Asphalt
Apparent easements None observed
FEMA Special Flood Hazard Area ☐ Yes [X] No
FEMA Zone _____ Map Date _____
FEMA Map No. _____

Utilities	Public	Other	Off-site Improvements	Type	Public	Private
Electricity	[X]		Street	Asphalt	[X]	
Gas			Curb/gutter	None		
Water	[X]		Sidewalk	None		
Sanitary sewer	[X]		Street lights		[X]	
Storm sewer			Alley	None		

Comments (apparent adverse easements, encroachments, special assessments, slide areas, illegal or legal nonconforming zoning use, etc.): No apparent adverse easements, encroachments or conditions observed.

GENERAL DESCRIPTION		EXTERIOR DESCRIPTION		FOUNDATION		BASEMENT		INSULATION	
No. of Units	1	Foundation	Concrete	Slab	Yes	Area Sq. Ft.	N/A	Roof	☐
No. of Stories	1	Exterior Walls	CBS	Crawl Space	No	% Finished		Ceiling	☐
Type (Det./Att.)	Detached	Roof Surface	Shingle	Basement	No	Ceiling		Walls	☐
Design (Style)	Ranch	Gutters & Dwnspts.	Typical	Sump Pump	N/A	Walls		Floor	☐
Existing/Proposed	Yes/No	Window Type	Awning	Dampness	N/A	Floor		None	☐
Age (Yrs.)	15	Storm/Screens	No/Yes	Settlement	N/A	Outside Entry		Unknown	[X]
Effective Age (Yrs.)	14 - 17	Manufactured House	No	Infestation	N/A				

ROOMS	Foyer	Living	Dining	Kitchen	Den	Family Rm.	Rec. Rm.	Bedrooms	# Baths	Laundry	Other	Area Sq. Ft.
Basement												N/A
Level 1		X	X	X		X		3	2	X		1950
Level 2												

Finished area above grade contains: 7 Rooms; 3 Bedroom(s); 2 Bath(s); 1,950 Square Feet of Gross Living Area

INTERIOR	Materials/Condition	HEATING		KITCHEN EQUIP.		ATTIC		AMENITIES		CAR STORAGE:	2
Floors	Carpet/Vinyl/*	Type	Centrl	Refrigerator	[X]	None	[X]	Fireplace(s) #		None	☐
Walls	Plaster/Avg	Fuel	Electr	Range/Oven	[X]	Stairs	☐	Patio	Concrete [X]	Garage	# of cars
Trim/Finish	Wood/Average	Condition	Avg	Disposal	☐	Drop Stair	☐	Deck	☐	Attached	☐
Bath Floor	Vinyl/Average	COOLING		Dishwasher	☐	Scuttle	[X]	Porch	Open [X]	Detached	☐
Bath Wainscot	Ceramic/Avg	Central	X	Fan/Hood	☐	Floor	☐	Fence	☐	Built-in	☐
Doors	Wood/Average	Other		Microwave	☐	Heated	☐	Pool	☐	Carport	2
* Average		Condition	Avg	Washer/Dryer	[X]	Finished	☐			Driveway	Single

Additional features (special energy efficient items, etc.): Typical, ceiling fans (4).

Condition of the improvements, depreciation (physical, functional, and external), repairs needed, quality of construction, remodeling/additions, etc.: The subject shows average condition on the interior and exterior and exhibits the typical appeal for the area. No functional or external obsolescence observed.

Adverse environmental conditions (such as, but not limited to, hazardous wastes, toxic substances, etc.) present in the improvements, on the site, or in the immediate vicinity of the subject property.: No apparent adverse environmental conditions were observed.

Freddie Mac Form 70 6/93   PAGE 1 OF 2   Fannie Mae Form 1004 6/93

FIGURE 11.6   Uniform Residential Appraisal Report (continued)

File No. 96-100 Page # 2

UNIFORM RESIDENTIAL APPRAISAL REPORT

File No. 96-100

Valuation Section

ESTIMATED SITE VALUE	32,000	= $	32,000

ESTIMATED REPRODUCTION COST-NEW-OF IMPROVEMENTS:

Dwelling 1,950 Sq. Ft. @$ 58.00	= $	113,100
N/A Sq. Ft. @$	=	
Appliances/Patio/Porch	=	2,500
Garage/Carport 430 Sq. Ft. @$ 11.00	=	4,730
Total Estimated Cost New	= $	120,330
Less Physical Functional External		
Depreciation 30,083	= $	30,083
Depreciated Value of Improvements	= $	90,247
"As-Is" Value of Site Improvements drive. landscp.	= $	2,200
INDICATED VALUE BY COST APPROACH	= $	124,447

Comments on Cost Approach (such as, source of cost estimate, site value, square foot calculation and for HUD, VA and FmHA, the estimated remaining economic life of the property): Cost estimates derived from Marshall Valuation Services publications.

The subject's land to building ratio is typical for the area and does not adversely affect the subject value or marketability. Est. remaining economic life: 40-45 years

ITEM	SUBJECT	COMPARABLE NO. 1	COMPARABLE NO. 2	COMPARABLE NO. 3
Address	1097 Timbers Crossin St. Joseph	1255 NE 34 Street	1297 NE 34 Street	1539 NE 38 Street
Proximity to Subject		1 Block Southwest	1 Block South	5 Blocks Northeast
Sales Price	$ 120,000	$ 119,000	$ 126,500	$ 121,000
Price/Gross Living Area	$ 61.54	$ 63.47	$ 65.89	$ 61.58
Data and/or Verification Source	Inspection	MLS	MLS	MLS

VALUE ADJUSTMENTS	DESCRIPTION	DESCRIPTION	+(−)$ Adjust	DESCRIPTION	+(−)$ Adjust	DESCRIPTION	+(−)$ Adjust
Sales or Financing Concessions		VA	−1,000	Conventional		Conventional	
Date of Sale/Time		8/96		9/96		7/96	
Location	Average	Average		Average		Average	
Leasehold/Fee Simple	Fee Simple	Fee Simple		Fee Simple		Fee Simple	
Site	9600	Corner/Avg		Corner/Avg		Inside/Avg	
View	Residential	Commercial	+2,000	Residential		Residential	
Design and Appeal	Ranch	Ranch/Avg		Ranch/Avg		Ranch/Avg	
Quality of Construction	CBS	CBS		CBS		CBS	
Age	15	16		14		16	
Condition	Average	Average		Average		Average	
Above Grade Room Count	Total 7 Bdrms 3 Baths 2	Total 7 Bdrms 3 Baths 2		Total 7 Bdrms 3 Baths 2		Total 7 Bdrms 3 Baths 2	
Gross Living Area	1,950 Sq. Ft.	1,875 Sq. Ft.	+1,125	1,920 Sq. Ft.		1,965 Sq. Ft.	
Basement & Finished Rooms Below Grade	N/A	None		None		None	
Functional Utility	Average	Average		Average		Average	
Heating/Cooling	Central	Central		Central		Central	
Energy Efficient Items	Typical	Typical		Typical		Typical	
Garage/Carport		Carport (2)		Garage (2)	−5,000	Carport (2)	
Porch, Patio, Deck, Fireplace(s), etc.	Porch Patio	Porch Patio		Porch Patio		Porch Patio	
Fence, Pool, etc.	Average	Average		Fence	−1,000	Average	
Net Adj. (total)		[X] + [ ] − $	2,125	[ ] + [X] − $	6,000	[X] + [ ] − $	0
Adjusted Sales Price of Comparable		$	121,125	$	120,500	$	121,000

Comments on Sales Comparison (Including the subject property's compatibility to the neighborhood, etc.): All comparables utilized are of similar single family homes located in the same neighborhood as the subject with a range from $120,500 to $121,125. A time adjustment could not be supported by the market.

ITEM	SUBJECT	COMPARABLE NO. 1	COMPARABLE NO. 2	COMPARABLE NO. 3
Date, Price and Data Source, for prior sales within year of appraisal	N/A	N/A	N/A	N/A

Analysis of any current agreement of sale, option, or listing of subject property and analysis of any prior sales of subject and comparables within one year of the date of appraisal: The subject was not listed for sale on the open market.

INDICATED VALUE BY SALES COMPARISON APPROACH	$	121,000
INDICATED VALUE BY INCOME APPROACH (If Applicable) Estimated Market Rent $ 1275 /Mo. x Gross Rent Multiplier 95	= $	121,125

This appraisal is made [X] "as is" [ ] subject to the repairs, alterations, inspections or conditions listed below [ ] subject to completion per plans & specifications.
Conditions of Appraisal: No personal property was included in the estimate of value.

Final Reconciliation: Weight was given to all three approaches, with the most weight given to the market data approach as it best reflects the action of the buyers and sellers.

The purpose of this appraisal is to estimate the market value of the real property that is the subject of this report, based on the above conditions and the certification, contingent and limiting conditions, and market value definition that are stated in the attached Freddie Mac Form 439/FNMA form 1004B (Revised 6/93).
I (WE) ESTIMATE THE MARKET VALUE, AS DEFINED, OF THE REAL PROPERTY THAT IS THE SUBJECT OF THIS REPORT, AS OF September 4, 1996 (WHICH IS THE DATE OF INSPECTION AND THE EFFECTIVE DATE OF THIS REPORT) TO BE $ 121,000

APPRAISER: Michelle Tipton	SUPERVISORY APPRAISER (ONLY IF REQUIRED):
Signature	Signature [ ] Did [ ] Did Not Inspect Property
Name Michelle Tipton	Name
Date Report Signed September 4, 1996	Date Report Signed
State Certification # St.Cert.Res.REA RD 010092 State MO	State Certification # State
Or State License # State MO	Or State License # State

Freddie Mac Form 70 6/93 — PAGE 2 OF 2 — Fannie Mae Form 1004 6-93

The single most important skill in appraising is the collection of data pertinent to the problem. The appraiser estimates value primarily by carefully examining the subject property and comparing it with properties with like features (comps). The appraiser must not only seek to find properties similar to the subject property in age, size, physical condition, location, and zoning, but must gather recent relevant data about these comparable properties to help estimate the value. The estimate of value will be based on the appraiser's opinion of the subject property's probable worth as a result of skillfully interpreting the data acquired from the most appropriate appraisal approach.

Three basic approaches are used to arrive at an estimate of a property's value. These three techniques—the direct sales comparison approach, the cost approach, and the income approach—will be described in general terms here. Any student seeking a more in-depth analysis of these approaches should consult *Fundamentals of Real Estate Appraisal.**

Direct Sales Comparison Approach

The **direct sales comparison approach**, formerly known as the market data approach, to estimating a property's value is based on a comparison of the subject property with similar properties in the same locale that have sold recently. An appraiser searches the records of the county recorder's office and the various multiple-listing services and maintains a comprehensive and current filing system. Thus, the appraiser is usually able to discover the sales prices and terms involved in recent transfers of properties similar to the property being appraised. In addition to these sources of information, an appraiser can usually review the lender's files and find many comparables to use in estimating the subject property's value.

The proficiency of an appraiser is never more clearly tested than in the direct sales comparison approach. Training and experience must be employed artfully to interpret, evaluate, and reconcile the data collected from comparable sales into a dollar amount that represents the subject property's value. No two properties are exactly alike; the appraiser must make many subjective adjustments to the sales prices of the comparable properties (comps) to reflect more clearly the subject property's worth. The reasons for the various differences in the sales prices of comps must be determined and their prices adjusted to reflect what they would have sold for had they more exactly matched the subject property.

For instance, the appraiser must be able to estimate what the sales price of a comp would be if it were the same age, condition, style, floor plan, size, location, and material as the subject property and also what price it would bring on the day of the appraisal, rather than at the time of its actual sale, six months or a year ago. The appraiser must make these adjustments, all of which involve judgments based on experience, in order to estimate the subject property's value more accurately. An appraiser's efforts depend on the magnitude of the loan and the degree of risk involved. These efforts can expand from a mere impression of value, as discerned by a drive-by examination of the subject property and a recollection of other similar properties recently sold, to a massive report based on 10, 15, or more comparables. Each comparable is adjusted for significant variables to reflect the subject's value. These comprehensive appraisals are made easier by the increasing use of computer technology.

* William L. Ventolo, Jr., and Martha R. Williams, 8th ed. (Chicago: Dearborn Real Estate Education ®, 2001.)

FOR EXAMPLE

The subject house is brick, 10 years old, in good condition, has 3 bedrooms and 1½ baths, has 1,800 square feet, and is located in a medium-quality neighborhood. Comparable "A" sold for $140,000 last week, is made of brick, 8 years old, in good condition, has 3 bedrooms and 1½ baths, has 1,500 square feet, and is in a good neighborhood. Comparable "B" sold for $160,000 two weeks ago, is a frame house, 10 years old, in good condition, has 4 bedrooms and only 1 bath, has 2,000 square feet, and is located in a good neighborhood.

	Subject House	Comp A	Comp B
Price		$140,000	$160,000
Material	Brick	0	+18,000
Age	10 years	– 5,600	0
Condition	Good	0	0
Bedrooms	3	0	–25,000
Baths	1 1/2	0	+10,000
Square Feet	1,800	+ 22,500	–15,000
Adjusted Price		$156,900	$138,000

Estimate of subject property's market value = $150,000

A combination of the drive-by appraisal and detailed computer research is often accepted today by Fannie Mae and Freddie Mac lenders.

Cost Approach

The cost approach method of estimating a property's value is based on the current value of its physical parts. In the **cost approach** an appraiser examines and evaluates the subject property, its improvements, amenities, and land value. This technique includes an estimation of the current cost to reproduce the improvements, an estimate of the improvements' depreciation, and an estimate of the land value as derived by using the direct sales comparison approach.

An appraiser accumulates data about the current cost of building the subject property. If the property is actually newly constructed, its plans and specifications are reviewed and analyzed to estimate its value. An older property requires an examination of its design and composition to estimate its current reproduction cost. Obviously, the cost approach works best with recently built properties or unique one-of-a-kind properties.

When used properties are appraised, a depreciation allowance must be applied to the costs of reproduction. This depreciation adjustment is based on the *rule of substitution* that states that no rational, economical person would pay the same price for a used property as for the same property when new.

Depreciation is defined as a lessening in value from physical deterioration, functional obsolescence, or economic obsolescence. An example of physical deterioration is the six-year-old roof that may need patching or replacement. Functional obsolescence describes a situation in which access to one bedroom is available only through an adjoining bedroom. An example of economic obsolescence is a location downwind from a sewage treatment plant. The appraiser must include in the adjustments a consideration of the present physical condition of the improvements, their functional utility, and the effects of forces outside the property on its value.

After the reproduction cost is calculated and adjusted to allow for depreciation of the improvements, the value of the land, as determined by the direct sales comparison approach, is added to the depreciated figure to arrive at an estimate of the total property value. The cost approach in formula form is as follows:

$$
\begin{array}{r}
\text{Current Replacement Cost of Improvements} \\
- \ \text{Depreciation} \\
\hline
\text{Estimate of Current Value of Improvements} \\
+ \ \text{Amenities and Land Value} \\
\hline
\text{Estimate of Current Value of Property}
\end{array}
$$

For EXAMPLE

If a 10-year-old house with an estimated 50-year life consists of 1,800 square feet, with a current reproduction cost factor of $75 per square foot, and the lot is worth $25,000, the estimate of property value using the cost approach is $133,000.

1,800	Square feet
× 75	Reproduction cost
135,000	Value of improvements when new
× 0.80	Straight-line depreciation reciprocal
108,000	Depreciated value of improvements
+ 25,000	Lot value
$133,000	Estimated property value

Income Capitalization Approach

The income approach measures the value of a property on the basis of its ability to generate income by capitalizing the net annual income using a current market *capitalization rate*. In other words, the **income approach** actually measures the present worth of a property's income stream based on an investor's required rate of return.

This method is best suited to estimating the value of apartments, stores, shopping centers, and office buildings. The first factor an appraiser determines is the property's annual *gross market income*. Although a subject property may have an established rental income, an appraiser must verify whether this income is based on market rents or rents that are higher or lower than the market rate. Thus, the direct sales comparison approach is first employed to locate similar properties and analyze their rental schedules.

After the gross annual rental income has been determined, an appropriate amount must be deducted for operating expenses such as property taxes, insurance, maintenance, vacancy allowances, management, utilities, pest control, snow removal, accounting services, and advertising. Although depreciation is not considered an operating expense per se, most appraisers will include an item called *reserves for replacements* or *reserves for major repairs*. An income property should be able to support itself in every way to substantiate its value.

A *net annual market rental income* is derived when the operating expenses are deducted from the gross annual market rent. This net rental income is the amount that is capitalized into an estimate of the property's value using the formula:

$$\text{Value} = \frac{\text{Net Income}}{\text{Capitalization Rate}}$$

*F*OR EXAMPLE

Consider an apartment house generating $250,000 gross annual income. Operating expenses, including vacancies, total 45% of this income. In a market that supports a 10% capitalization rate, this property is worth $1,375,000 using the income approach.

Gross Annual Income	$ 250,000
Operating Ratio Reciprocal	0.55
Net Operating Income	137,500
Capitalization Rate	÷ 0.10
Estimate of Value	$1,375,000

Gross Rent Multiplier (GRM)

When estimating the value of single-family homes, a **gross rent multiplier (GRM)** or gross income multiplier (GIM) is often used. The GRM is derived by locating comparable properties that have sold recently, then dividing their sales prices by a monthly market gross rent to derive the multiplier.

Selling price ÷ Sales price

*F*OR EXAMPLE

A property that sold for $60,000 and could be rented for $500 per month will develop a GRM of 120 ($60,000 ÷ $500 = 120). Likewise, when a property similar to the property being appraised is sold for $72,000 and could be rented for $600 per month, the GRM is also 120 ($72,000 ÷ $600 = 120). Therefore, if the subject property could be rented for $550 per month and the market GRM is 120, its estimated value is $66,000 ($550 × 120 = $66,000).

Reconciliation of Data and Opinion of Value

After applying the preceding approaches pertinent to the estimate of a particular property's value, an appraiser reviews the results, reconciles or correlates the different values derived, and renders a written opinion of the property's value. This opinion may place more emphasis on one approach than another. For instance, the cost approach is more reliable when appraising a newer property than an older one. The income approach is more valid with true income property rather than with houses or vacant land on which an appraiser must impute a fictitious "rent" before this approach can be applied. The direct sales comparison approach supplies the balancing aspect to an appraisal, frequently providing the middle value in a spectrum where the cost approach is invariably high and the income approach is usually low. The direct sales comparison approach is also an integral part of the other two approaches. It is used in the cost approach to determine the value of the land and in the income approach to help derive the net annual market rental income to be capitalized. One way of **reconciliation** is to apply the **weighted average** technique, which assigns percentages to illustrate the importance of one approach over another.

FOR EXAMPLE

If an appraiser finds that the market, cost, and income approaches indicate $80,000, $85,000, and $86,000 respectively, and the appraiser weights them 50%, 30%, and 20% respectively, the reconciliation will be $82,700.

$$
\begin{aligned}
\$80{,}000 \times 0.50 &= \$40{,}000 \\
85{,}000 \times 0.30 &= 25{,}500 \\
86{,}000 \times 0.20 &= \underline{17{,}200} \\
&\ \ \$82{,}700
\end{aligned}
$$

When an appraisal is completed, it is delivered to the loan officer to aid in the final loan decision. As noted previously, a loan amount is based on the *lesser* of either this appraised value or the sales price of the property.

QUALIFYING THE TITLE

This means who is recorded on the title?

Anticipating a new loan, the loan processor will secure a **title report** on the collateral property. The components of a title report are a survey, and a search of the records to determine all the interests in a property. Normally, property interests are perfected through the appropriate filing and recording of standard notices. A recorded deed notifies the world that a grantee has the legal fee title to the property. A recorded construction lien is notice of another's interest in a property. These forms of recording are described as **constructive notices,** an express revelation of a fact.

Another form of notice, one that is imputed by law, is described as an **actual notice.** Even if a buyer does not actually inspect the house that is in the process of being purchased, its occupants have displayed their claim to certain rights merely through their physical possession of the property, even if they have not recorded that interest. The buyer is presumed to know of the occupants' interest in the property, as this information is available through ordinary inquiry. Similarly, even if a person does not actually view the recorded information, it is presumed to be known by actual notice because it is there for the viewing.

At least three methods are employed for obtaining assurance of good title—the abstract and opinion, title insurance, and the Torrens system. Whichever method is used, the title report on the collateral provides the loan officer and the lender's attorney all recorded information relevant to the legal status of the subject property, as well as any interests revealed by actual notice. This title search requirement is yet another manifestation of a lender's efforts to protect the loan investment.

Abstract and Opinion of Title

An **abstract of title** is described as a synopsis of the current recorded condition of a property's title. Abstracting is the process of searching the records to accumulate information that is then distilled by the abstractor and presented as a formal report.

In the past, abstracts were given by the seller of a property to the new buyer after all transactions that occurred during the seller's ownership were added. These abstracts, in addition to the deed transferring fee title, were delivered to a buyer for approval before a transaction was closed. The attorney for the buyer indicated approval through an oral report, an informal note, or a formal written title opinion instrument. The reviewing attorney might be liable if anything had been overlooked that would result in a future loss to the buyer.

In current practice, an *abstract* is not considered an official document, because it makes no pretense of disclosing any hidden title hazards. The abstractor is responsible only for an accurate portrayal of documents *of record* pertinent to a property's title status. If the loan officer wants a more expert analysis of a title, a request is made for an opinion on the condition of the collateral's title from a lawyer. This opinion is based on the facts revealed in the abstract, and all defects in the title are brought to the loan officer's attention. However, neither the abstractor who searches the title nor the lawyer who renders an opinion of the title's condition issues a guarantee or insures against defects. If the lender requires additional protection against hidden defects or possible errors in the abstracting process, a title insurance policy must be secured.

Title Insurance

Title insurance is based on risk elimination rather than risk assumption. A title insurance policy insures the quality of title on real estate as it exists on the date of the policy, but it does not insure against future events. Consequently, most of the premium goes to investigating the history of the title (risk elimination).

Although the abstract together with an attorney's opinion is still used in some areas of the United States, the trend toward an expanded nationwide mortgage market has brought about the rapid growth of title insurance companies. These title companies combine the abstracting process with a program of insurance that guarantees the validity and accuracy of the title search. A purchaser of **title insurance** can rely on the assets of the insurance company to back up its guarantee of a property's marketable title. These guarantees are evidenced by policies of title insurance. Most financial fiduciaries now require that a title policy be issued to them for the full face amount of the loan.

When a title insurance policy is issued to a lender (the insured), it is usually in the *American Land Title Association (ALTA)* form. While a *standard* title policy insures against losses overlooked in the search of the recorded chain of title, an ALTA policy expands this standard coverage to include many unusual risks. Among these risks are forgeries, incompetency of parties involved in issuing documents pertaining to the transfer of ownership, legal status of parties involved in the specific loan negotiations, surveying errors, and other possible off-record defects. Some additional risks can be and usually are covered by special endorsements to an insurance policy. These might include protection against any unrecorded easements or liens, rights of parties in possession of the subject property, mining claims, water rights, and additional negotiated special items pertinent to the property involved. The expanded ALTA policy is usually required by participants in the secondary mortgage market—Fannie Mae, Freddie Mac, and GNMA—for the added protection it provides. Most practitioners use the phrase "an ALTA policy" when describing an extended coverage policy.

Title insurance companies are seeking to cut costs and offer faster services through new technology. Many companies are converting to automatic indexing systems that provide instant electronic transfer of information. This shortens the title search period and reduces personnel requirements. Some title companies are developing new earnings opportunities by forming real estate services subsidiaries such as offering property appraisals, flood plain certification, and credit reporting.

A new form of title insurance was developed in 2001 by the Radian Guaranty Inc., called the Radian Lien Protection (RLP) policy. (See www.radiangroupinc.com.) RLP is available at about half the cost of traditional title insurance but is used only for refinancing, second mortgages, and home equity loans. It insures only the lenders, not the borrowers, guaranteeing the lender's lien priority. The American Land Title Association is challenging Radian for offering title insurance without the required regulatory approvals or licensing.

Torrens System

The *Torrens system* of title guarantees is designed to shorten the time needed to search the title. It places the insurance process in the hands of the state. Essentially, under the Torrens plan, a title is searched only as far back as the previous search. It is assumed in the process that all transactions prior to the last search were accurate and legal and that any problems that might have been revealed were resolved satisfactorily. A **Torrens Certificate** is issued, which includes the state as guarantor of the title in the event of a claim arising under the Torrens system. A charge is made for this certificate to cover the costs of the search, and, in some states, an additional premium is charged to provide a reserve fund to cover any contingent losses.

The Torrens system has some advantages over the regular recording system, including saving time, eliminating the accumulation of large quantities of title evidence, and lowering the costs of title examining and insuring. Some states participating in its implementation include Colorado, Georgia, Hawaii, Illinois, Massachusetts, and Minnesota, New York, North Carolina, Ohio, Virginia, and Washington. Apparently, the significant cost of converting to the system has inhibited its adoption in the other states.

Title Faults

Whether the abstract and opinion, the title insurance policy, or the Torrens system is used, in all cases a property's title is searched by an experienced abstractor, who prepares a report of those recorded documents that clearly affect the quality of ownership. In addition, a survey is often required. If a fault is found, sometimes called a **cloud on the title**, the loan process will not continue until this cloud is cleared to the lender's satisfaction. Such a cloud could be an unsatisfied construction lien, an income tax lien, a property tax lien, an encroachment, or a zoning violation. Sometimes a borrower's name is not legally correct on the deed, or the deed has a faulty acknowledgment or lacks the appropriate signatures.

Because of the many complexities in a real estate transaction, there are innumerable possibilities for faults to appear in a title search and property survey. It is the abstractor's responsibility to discover and report them.

In certain instances where clouds are difficult to remove by ordinary means, they will need to be cleared by the seller of the property or by the borrower's filing a **suit to quiet title.** After appropriate evidence has been submitted, a judge removes or modifies an otherwise damaging fault in a title, and the loan process can continue. The assurance of good title is as essential to a loan's completion as the credit of the borrower and the value of the collateral. The sales of foreclosed properties create complexities that require scrupulous examination and careful documentation of the condition of the title.

Surveys

Although many loan closings require delivery of a plat to identify the location of buildings on the lot, some lenders may require a full **survey** of the collateral property as a condition for a new loan. Although many properties are part of subdivisions that have been engineered and described by licensed and registered surveyors and engineers, some owners might have enlarged their homes or added to the improvements since the original survey. These might not meet the various setback restrictions required in the local zoning laws. Some properties might have been resubdivided, while others might now have an encroachment problem.

Surveys often reveal errors in legal descriptions or discover encroachments and easement infractions. A few interesting lawsuits have developed as a result of the wrong property being encumbered by a new real estate loan.

SUMMARY

This chapter described the process of obtaining a real estate loan, including qualifying the borrowers, evaluating the collateral, and determining the status of the property's legal title.

Beginning with an application to secure a loan, the borrowers' credit is analyzed to determine their ability to honor debts and repay the loan as agreed. Current assets and employment are verified and a credit rating is obtained. Other basic criteria used to determine the applicants' creditworthiness include gross monthly earnings, adequate to meet the required monthly mortgage payment, stability of earnings, and a good prognosis for continued employment and advancement.

The value of the real estate to be pledged as collateral is analyzed by either a staff appraiser or an independent fee appraiser. A formal appraisal report offering the appraiser's opinion of the subject property's value is submitted to the loan processor. This estimate of value is derived from the appraiser's application of one or more of the three basic appraisal techniques—the direct sales comparison approach, the cost approach, and the income approach.

The direct sales comparison approach for estimating the value of real property matches the subject property to other, similar properties sold recently to make a value comparison. Because there are no perfect comparables, however, adjustments must be made to the sales price of those comparables that most closely resemble the subject property. These adjustments account for differences in size, age, location, condition, and any other significant factors. The adjusted sales prices for the comps then indicates the subject property's market value.

The cost approach examines the total worth of a property in terms of the current value of its component parts. The current prices of the bricks, lumber, plumbing fixtures, nails, roofing, electrical fixtures, and so on are added together to estimate the value of the building were it to be reproduced at the time of the appraisal as closely as possible to its present condition. If the property is not new, its reproduction cost is depreciated by an appropriate amount. This depreciated value for the improvements, when added to the market value of the lot, establishes an estimate of the total property value.

The income approach measures the value of a property on the basis of the amount and quality of its income stream. An appraiser using the income approach divides the net annual income from the property by a market capitalization rate to derive an estimate of the property's value.

After collecting all data pertinent to the subject property and deriving value estimates by using the various approaches, the appraiser reconciles these estimates and renders an opinion of the property's value. This appraised value is compared to the sales price; the loan is made on the basis of the lower figure.

After a borrower's credit and the collateral's value are verified, the current status of the property's title is examined carefully, usually by a trained abstractor. The abstract is delivered to the lender's attorney for an opinion of accuracy and validity. Because of the growing activity of the secondary mortgage market in the United States and its concurrent necessity for added protection, lenders usually require title insurance to guarantee the status of the title.

CHAPTER 12

Mon 3/14

Closing Real Estate Loans

▼ **KEY TERMS**

ad valorem
assignment
closing statements
escrow (funds)
hazard insurance

impound funds
improvement district
    bonds
mortgagee's title
    insurance

origination fee
owner's title insurance
points
prorations

Once the loan process has reached the point at which a borrower's credit has been approved, the collateral's value is acceptable, and the legal title to the collateral is clear, the loan underwriter approves the loan, and preparations for closing begin. An approved loan commitment is communicated to all interested parties, obligating the lender to issue the loan under the terms and conditions stipulated. This commitment remains in force for only a limited time, preventing any delay in the closing. In addition, the necessary legal documents for the transaction are prepared, an escrow is established if one is to be used for the closing, and the loan closing statements allocating the appropriate charges and credits are provided. All parties concerned are notified of the date and place of the closing, which varies throughout the United States. In the western United States closings are usually handled in escrow; in the middle and eastern sections, closings are done by a settlement attorney or title insurance company agent. After all documents have been signed, the deed has been transferred, the loan has been recorded, and the monies have been paid, the loan process is completed.

COSTS OF SECURING A LOAN

A number of costs are associated with securing a real estate loan. Those that are described in this chapter are not all included in each loan transaction. They do represent the normal charges a borrower will encounter when securing a mortgage loan.

The Real Estate Settlement Procedures Act of 1974 (RESPA) requires a loan/escrow officer to make a good faith estimate of a loan's closing costs and provide this estimate to borrowers within three business days of the loan application. This information informs the borrowers of the various costs involved and prepares them to arrange for the necessary funds to close. Figure 12.1 is a copy of the RESPA good faith estimate form. Notice that the borrowers must sign the form as testimony that they have received it in order to avoid any future claim of ignorance of the settlement costs. The lender must also provide the borrower with a truth-in-lending statement showing the true annual rate of interest received on the loan.

Points

Some real estate loans are offered for "7.75 percent interest and no points," while others are "7.5 percent interest and 1 point," or "7 percent interest and 2 points." A "point" is actually one percent of the loan amount so two points on a $100,000 loan equals $2,000. Discount points represent a sum of money paid to a lender at the inception of a loan that raises the yield on the loan without raising the interest rate. The number of **points** charged by a lender reflect

- the risk on the loan, the higher the risk (a borrower's weak credit), the higher the points; and
- the contract interest rate as compared to the market interest rates, the lower the contract rate, the higher the points.

Placement or Origination Fee

Most lenders charge the borrower a placement or **origination fee** to cover the costs of establishing a new loan. This charge pays for the services of the loan officer and others, as well as for the materials used in the loan process.

Impound Funds (Escrow Accounts)

As discussed in earlier chapters, the great majority of real estate loans are made on single-family, owner-occupied homes and condominiums. Invariably, lenders making these loans require borrowers to include proportionate amounts of money to be impounded monthly for payment of property taxes, insurance premiums, and any required property improvement assessments. These **impound funds**, or **escrow funds**, are deposited in a special escrow account held until needed. Lenders normally require that two month's taxes and insurance be left on deposit in the escrow account to offset possible tax or insurance premium increases. Regardless of the payment schedule chosen, escrow funds are collected in addition to the principal and interest and result in a total monthly payment that is familiarly labeled *PITI*—that is, principal, interest, taxes, and insurance.

Property Taxes

Property taxes are imposed on private property owners as a basic source of funds to pay for the various public services of state, county, city, school district, and other local

FIGURE 12.1 Good Faith Estimate

In accordance with the Real Estate Settlement Procedures Act (RESPA) of 1974, outlined below are your ESTIMATE costs in connection with the above referenced transaction.

DOWN PAYMENT . . . . $_____ $_____

CLOSING COSTS:
Broker's Commission . . . . $_____ $_____
FHA-VA Loan Discount or Points . . . . $_____ $_____
Origination Fee or Service Charge . . . . $_____ $_____
Initial Private Mortgage Insurance Premium . . . . $_____ $_____
Appraisal Fee . . . . $_____ $_____
Inspection Fee . . . . $_____ $_____
Escrow or Settlement Fee . . . . $_____ $_____
Owner's Title Policy . . . . $_____ $_____
Title Insurance—Lender's Coverage (ALTA) . . . . $_____ $_____
Recording Fees . . . . $_____ $_____
Credit Report Charges . . . . $_____ $_____
Tax Service Contract . . . . $_____ $_____
Document Preparation Fee . . . . $_____ $_____
Termite Inspection . . . . $_____ $_____
Buydown . . . . $_____ $_____
_____ $_____ $_____

TOTAL CLOSING COSTS . . . . $_____ $_____

IMPOUNDS OR PREPAID ITEMS:
First Year's Insurance Policy Plus _____ Months . . . . $_____ $_____
Taxes . . . . $_____ $_____
MIP or PMI . . . . $_____ $_____
Initial or Prepaid Interest from C.O.E. _____ to _____ . . . . $_____ $_____
_____ $_____ $_____

TOTAL IMPOUNDS . . . . $_____ $_____

TOTAL MOVE-IN COSTS
(Down Payment + Closing Costs + Impounds) . . . . $_____ $_____

ESTIMATED MONTHLY PAYMENT:
Principal and Interest . . . . $_____ $_____
MIP or PMI . . . . $_____ $_____
Taxes . . . . $_____ $_____
Insurance . . . . $_____ $_____
_____ $_____ $_____

TOTAL MONTHLY PAYMENT . . . . $_____ $_____

NOTE: This form does not necessarily cover all items you may be required to pay in cash at settlement. It does, however, ESTIMATE the amount you will likely pay to the best of our knowledge as of the date of application.

Provided that I qualify financially for a loan, I (we) understand that the terms of any commitment to make a loan which may be issued hereafter shall only be binding to lender as follows:

Funds shall be committed for a period of _____ days from the date the loan _____.
Interest rate and service charge shall be committed for a period of _____ days from the date the loan _____.

In the event the permanent real estate loan does not close within the time period referred to above, and lender is no longer accepting applications for this type of credit, I (we) understand that lender is under no obligation to extend its commitment to make my (our) loan. Should I (we) request lender to issue a new commitment to extend credit after the expiration date of this commitment, the terms of the loan shall be renegotiated and I (we) must requalify if deemed necessary. I (We) understand that if lender agrees to issue a new commitment to extend credit, lender may, at its option, require my (our) loan to be closed at lender's current market rate with such service charges as are in effect for my (our) particular category of loan at the time.

I (We) have received a copy of the Good Faith Estimate, HUD Booklet, Financial Privacy Notice and Consumer Handbook on Adjustable Rate Mortgages.

Agent/Processor _____   Signature _____

Phone _____ Date _____   Date _____

governmental jurisdictions. Liens for delinquent property taxes have priority over other liens, so lenders will often require the impounding of funds to pay property taxes to protect their position. How much each property owner contributes depends on two factors—the specific monetary requirements of the governmental bodies of the jurisdiction in which the property is located and the total market valuation of all the taxable properties within that jurisdiction.

The taxing process begins by determining the funds needed to satisfy the specific budgetary requirements of each governing body within the taxing district for the following fiscal year. At the same time, every county assessor must maintain a current inventory of the fair market value of all privately owned real property within the county's boundaries. Thus, the term coined for this form of taxation is *ad valorem*, that is, "according to value." Some counties use this *fair market value* when calculating the total valuation of taxable properties. Most counties, however, apply an assessor's factor to the fair market value, which reduces this amount to an *assessed valuation* of all taxable property within the county.

Ad Valorem = according to value

The tax rate to be applied to individual properties is derived by dividing the total budgetary requirements of the taxing district by the total value of the taxable property within the jurisdiction. The tax rate is usually expressed in terms of so many mills (thousandths of a cent) or dollars per thousand dollars of assessed value.

*F*OR EXAMPLE

A taxable property having a fair market value of $60,000 in a jurisdiction that applies a 35% assessor's factor would have a $21,000 assessed valuation. If the tax rate on this particular property is $100 per $1,000 of assessed value, also described as a $100-mill rate, the tax to be paid for the year is $2,100. This owner would pay $175 monthly for the property tax impound ($2,100 ÷ 12 = $175).

Insurance Premiums

Various insurance charges are included in each loan transaction. Borrowers will be charged for premiums for hazard insurance, title insurance and mortgage insurance.

Hazard Insurance. In addition to the property tax impound, a lender usually insists that a proportionate share of the hazard insurance premium be included in the monthly payment. Such insurance premiums are based on risk—the higher the risk, the higher the insurance premium. If a house were of wood-frame construction and located in a relatively isolated area far from any possible fire-fighting service, the insurance rate for this home would be higher than the rate for a brick home situated two blocks from a fire station. Also, if an area is vulnerable to hurricanes, tornadoes, excessive floods, or other natural disasters, insurance rates will reflect these risks.

Whatever method used to determine the insurance rate, one-twelfth of the annual premium will usually be included in a monthly payment. Thus, a hazard insurance policy with a $360 annual premium will require that an additional $30 per month be included in the payment.

Title Insurance. As discussed in Chapter 11, most lenders will require that title insurance be issued. When a new loan is concurrently part of a property sale, *two title insurance policies are required.* The first, for the full amount of the purchase price, is called an **owner's title insurance** policy and is issued in the name of the new owner. Depending on local custom, the seller or the buyer may be required to pay the premium to the title company to secure this owner's insurance policy. If, as in most of the eastern states, a *warranty deed* is issued by the seller-grantor in favor of the buyer-grantee, the *buyer* usually purchases a title policy. The seller is saying with a personal title warranty, as evidenced by the deed, that the title is clear of clouds and that, if the buyers wish to secure additional protection, they will have to pay that title insurance premium.

In most western states a somewhat different attitude prevails. Here the custom is for the *seller* to purchase a title insurance policy in favor of the buyer, because the deed generally used to transfer fee title is a *bargain and sale deed.* This deed does not warrant anything other than the fact that the seller has the legal right to transfer title of the property. Thus in exchange for not having any continuing personal responsibility to defend a buyer in the event of a future lawsuit over the legality of the property's title, a western seller customarily pays the title insurance premium and transfers that liability to the title insurance company.

In the middle United States, the custom is for both buyer and seller to share these costs. In all circumstances, however, the question of who pays the title insurance premiums (and other costs as well) is often a subject of negotiation between the parties to the loan transaction, the current local conditions of the real estate market being the final arbiter.

The second title insurance policy, called **mortgagee's title insurance,** is issued in favor of the lender. The premium for this policy is paid by the borrower. It usually is at a reduced rate because, when a loan is being secured as part of a property's purchase, the mortgagee's policy is issued simultaneously with an owner's policy and the coverage is only for the duration and amount of the loan.

The mortgagee's title insurance is usually issued as an ALTA policy covering the possibility of loss to the *lender,* not the property owner. If there is a claim under this insurance, the settlement generally is for the remaining balance of the loan.

All title insurance premiums are paid only once and guarantee the named beneficiaries as long as they own the property, or as long as a loan is in existence. Once a property is resold or a loan is repaid, new policies are issued to serve the new circumstances. Title insurance premiums vary from state to state because of local regulatory requirements.

Mortgage Insurance. When a conventional loan is insured or an FHA loan is created, there is a charge to the borrower for the insurance premium. Except for the funding fee, the VA has no insurance premium.

As examined in Chapter 4, there is a trend currently to try to eliminate or minimize mortgage insurance. A new method is to require a larger down payment, so some companies waive the private mortgage insurance on a conventional loan with at least a 10 percent down payment. Some lenders offering this opportunity adjust the interest rate upwards a bit to make up the loss in premiums.

Assessment Liens

Occasionally a property is charged with an assessment lien for off-site improvements, such as sewer installations or street paving. Assessment charges are calculated by dividing the total costs of the improvements by some common denominator—such as total front feet or total square feet to assess fairly those properties benefiting from the improvements. This rate is applied to the individual property, and either the charges are paid in cash or the lien goes to bond. Because these **improvement district bonds** are priority liens, a lender will insist that a proportionate monthly amount of the required assessment payment be impounded, along with the taxes and insurance.

Interest Adjustments

Most lenders arrange their mortgage payments for collection on the 1st day or 15th day of the month, based to some degree on a borrower's requirements. Mortgage payments are normally paid in arrears; that is, the payment on May 1 covers the principal due on that day and the interest is charged back for the month of April. Customarily these payments start a month or two after a loan's inception, depending on when during the month the loan is closed. As a result of varying closing dates and specific mortgage starting times, interest is usually adjusted from the closing date to the end of the month and is charged to the borrower to establish the appropriate payment pattern.

*F*OR EXAMPLE

Consider an $80,000 loan at 9% interest closed on April 15. The first payment is not due until June 1. The interest adjustment to be paid in advance at the loan closing is $320.

Principal	$80,000
Interest Rate	× 0.09
Annual Interest	7,200
Pro Rata Days	÷ 360
Daily Rate	20.00
Number of Days	× 16
Pro Rata Interest	$320.00

(Note: In those states not charging for the day of settlement, the charge would be $300 for 15 days.)

Under Regulation Z of the Federal Reserve, lenders are required to quote to the borrowers the true interest charges, called the annual percentage rate (APR). The APR includes the interest paid in the settlement plus service charges, points, fees, and other costs paid by the borrower.

Prepayment Penalties

Whenever an existing financial encumbrance that includes a prepayment penalty is satisfied prior to its normal time, the amount of the penalty is charged to the owner of the collateral property. Thus, if an existing loan is paid off when the seller receives funds from the buyer who has a new loan, the seller is charged the penalty. Few loans today other than Jumbo ARMs have prepayment penalties. Any that do must disclose this requirement in the truth-in-lending statement provided the borrower at the loan's inception.

Additional Charges and Requirements

Every real estate sale and/or loan closing will incur additional charges for services rendered. The seller usually is charged for the selling brokerage commission. However, buyer's brokers are becoming popular and if a transaction is structured as such, the buyer may be charged for all or a part of the commission.

Some states impose a transfer tax on real estate sales. These taxes vary but a typical charge could be one-half of 1 percent of the *new* money involved. Thus a $100,000 cash sale would require a tax of $500 ($100,000 × 0.005 = $500). The same sale structured with a $20,000 cash down payment to an assumed existing loan balance of $80,000 would require a transfer tax of $100 ($20,000 × 0.005 = $100). The seller usually pays the transfer tax.

The borrower would be charged with the costs for securing a credit report, an appraisal, and, if necessary, a survey. If an attorney's opinion is required, the borrower and seller would pay their respective costs. All parties would pay their share of the escrow and recording fees. Often new houses or remodeled houses in urban renewal areas will need documents indicating that they have met the housing code and are ready for occupancy. Also, in those parts of the country exposed to possible flooding from lakes or rivers, the Army Corps of Engineers has designated certain lands as flood areas. To secure financing for houses in these flood plains, borrowers must purchase flood insurance.

Prorations

When closing a real estate transaction, the escrow agent prorates certain items to allocate the costs and credits to the appropriate parties. Included in the items subject to proration analysis are interest to date on existing loans, property taxes, hazard insurance premiums, rents, assessments, and homeowner's fees. **Prorations** are usually computed on a 360-day year and a 30-day month. However, FHA and VA loans continue to have 365-day prorations. All prorations are *through* the day of closing with the seller held responsible for that day. However, some areas, like Florida and Virginia, hold the buyer responsible for the closing day. Responsibility should be specified in the sales contract or the escrow instructions.

Interest. When a buyer assumes an existing loan, the interest owed to the date of settlement is charged to the seller.

FOR EXAMPLE

Consider a loan with a balance of $63,759.84 and an interest rate of 9%. Settlement is on the 21st day with the payment having been made on the 1st day of the settlement month.

Mortgage Balance	$63,759.84
Interest Rate	× 0.09
Year's Interest	5,738.38
Pro Rata Days	÷ 360
Daily Rate	15.94
Number of Days	× 21
Pro Rata Amount	$334.74 Charge seller, credit buyer

When a new loan is created, the interest is prorated to the date of the first payment and charged to the borrower.

FOR EXAMPLE

Consider a $100,000 VA or FHA loan at 7½% interest beginning on May 15 with the first payment due on July 1.

Mortgage Amount	$100,000.00
Interest Rate	× 0.075
Year's Interest	7,500.00
Pro Rata Days	÷ 365
Daily Rate	20.55
Number of Days	× 46
Pro Rata Amount	945.30 Charge borrower

Property Taxes. Because property taxes are paid in arrears, when a buyer assumes an existing loan, the taxes are prorated to the settlement date, charged to the seller, and credited to the buyer.

FOR EXAMPLE

Consider a property with a tax of $1,650 for the year. The settlement date is May 1 and the taxes have been paid to December 31 the previous year.

Property Taxes	$1,650.00
Pro Rata Days	÷ 360
Daily Rate	4.58
Number of Days	× 120
Pro Rata Amount	$549.60 Charge seller, credit buyer

When a new loan is created, the borrower is required to deposit two months' taxes in advance into the escrow collection account and is charged this amount in the settlement.

*F*OR EXAMPLE

Consider a property with a tax of $1,650 for the year and a two-month advance charge.

Property Taxes	$1,650.00
Pro Rata Months	÷ 12
Monthly Rate	137.50
Number of Months	× 2
Pro Rata Amount	$275.00

Insurance Premiums. In a sale of real estate, the existing hazard insurance policy is usually canceled by the seller and replaced with a new policy by the buyer. Less frequently, the existing policy is assumed by the buyer. Property insurance premiums generally are paid in advance. Thus, when a policy is assumed, the seller receives a credit for the unused portion of the premium. When a new policy is required, the buyer will pay for a full year's premium in advance and an additional two months for the escrow collection account.

*F*OR EXAMPLE

Consider an assumption of an insurance premium of $225 for the year and a six-month proration.

Insurance Premium	$225.00
Pro Rata Months	÷ 12
Monthly Rate	18.75
Number of Months	× 6
Credit Seller/Charge Buyer	$112.50

*F*OR EXAMPLE

Consider a new loan and a premium of $225 for insurance for the year and a two-month advance charge.

Insurance Premium	$225.00
Pro Rata Months	÷ 12
Monthly Rate	18.75
Number of Prepaid Months	× 2
Charge Borrower for Impounds	$37.50

Additional Prorations. When an income property is sold, additional care must be taken in the closing to allocate the proper credits and charges for rents and deposits due and collected in advance. In addition, utility charges must be accounted for or handled outside of escrow. Sometimes a property has an outstanding balance due from an improvement district assessment. This is prorated and the proper charges and credits allocated to the appropriate parties. Also, any homeowner's association or recreational association fees and dues need to be prorated and charged or credited accordingly.

Closing Statements

The final step in the loan process is for the escrow officer to prepare the **closing statements,** using the HUD-1 Form as required by RESPA, allocating the appropriate charges and credits. Once this is completed, the parties are notified of the closing date. After all the proper documents have been signed and recorded, the final settlement of funds is made and all monies are paid to the appropriate parties.

FOR EXAMPLE

Consider the sale of a $100,000 house. The buyer makes a $5,000 deposit and secures a conventional uninsured loan for $80,000 at 7% percent interest. The first payment is due on August 1. There are two loans to be satisfied: a first mortgage with a balance of $59,575 at 12% interest paid to May 1 and a second mortgage of $5,000 at 18% interest paid to May 1. The settlement date is May 15. Property taxes are $2,400 for the year paid to January 1 of this year. The hazard insurance premium for a new policy is $360. The new lender is charging a 1% origination fee, a 2% discount, a $150 appraisal fee, a $75 credit report fee, an interest adjustment amount of $875 and a loan collection establishment fee of $100. The title company is charging a mortgagee's title insurance premium of $390, an owner's title insurance premium of $250 (the seller agreed to pay this cost) and an escrow fee of $200, to be shared equally. The broker is charging the seller a 5% commission. Additional costs include recording fees to the buyer of $16 and to the seller of $20, and two sellers' charges of $100 each for termite and roof inspection.

A HUD-1 settlement statement illustrating the treatment of these numbers is shown in Figure 12.2.

SERVICING THE LOAN

Once the loan has been closed, arrangements must be made to service it. Principal and interest payments need to be collected in a timely manner and accurate records must be kept. Some loan payments include amounts for property taxes and insurance. The servicing agent not only must place these funds in a proper escrow account, but also must take responsibility for their payment, promptly and in the proper amounts. These activities are repetitive and continuing, usually on a monthly basis for many years.

Servicing duties are usually accepted by most lenders as part of the loan closing. In fact, the costs of setting up these collection escrows, as well as the monies required to prime the tax and insurance accounts, are built into a loan's closing statement. A few weeks after

FIGURE 12.2　HUD-1 Settlement Statement

A. **Settlement Statement**	U.S. Department of Housing and Urban Development	OMB Approval No. 2502-0265

B. Type of Loan

1. ☐ FHA　2. ☐ FmHA　3. ☒ Conv. Unins.	6. File Number:	7. Loan Number:	8. Mortgage Insurance Case Number:
4. ☐ VA　5. ☐ Conv. Ins.			

C. Note: This form is furnished to give you a statement of actual settlement costs. Amounts paid to and by the settlement agent are shown. Items marked "(p.o.c.)" were paid outside the closing; they are shown here for informational purposes and are not included in the totals.

D. Name & Address of Borrower: Ted Smith	E. Name & Address of Seller: Edyth Jones	F. Name & Address of Lender: Friendly Loan Co.

G. Property Location: 225 Mockingbird Lane Fairview, Alabama	H. Settlement Agent: John Thomas	
	Place of Settlement: Efficient Title Co.	I. Settlement Date: 5/15

J.　Summary of Borrower's Transaction		K.　Summary of Seller's Transaction	
100.　Gross Amount Due From Borrower		**400.　Gross Amount Due To Seller**	
101.　Contract sales price	100,000	401.　Contract sales price	100,000
102.　Personal property		402.　Personal property	
103.　Settlement charges to borrower (line 1400)	4,926	403.	
104.		404.	
105.		405.	
Adjustments for items paid by seller in advance		**Adjustments for items paid by seller in advance**	
106.　City/town taxes　　to		406.　City/town taxes　　to	
107.　County taxes　　to		407.　County taxes　　to	
108.　Assessments　　to		408.　Assessments　　to	
109.		409.	
110.		410.	
111.		411.	
112.		412.	
120.　Gross Amount Due From Borrower	104,926	**420.　Gross Amount Due To Seller**	100,000
200.　Amounts Paid By Or In Behalf Of Borrower		**500.　Reductions In Amount Due To Seller**	
201.　Deposit or earnest money	5,000	501.　Excess deposit (see instructions)	
202.　Principal amount of new loan(s)	80,000	502.　Settlement charges to seller (line 1400)	5,570
203.　Existing loan(s) taken subject to		503.　Existing loan(s) taken subject to	
204.		504.　Payoff of first mortgage loan	59,575
205.		505.　Payoff of second mortgage loan	5,000
206.		506.	
207.		507.	
208.		508.	
209.		509.	
Adjustments for items unpaid by seller		**Adjustments for items unpaid by seller**	
210.　City/town taxes　　1/1 to 5/15	900	510.　City/town taxes　　1/1 to 5/15	900
211.　County taxes　　to		511.　County taxes　　to	
212.　Assessments　　to		512.　Assessments　　to	
213.		513.　Interest 1st mtg. 5/1 to 5/15	297
214.		514.　Interest 2nd mtg. 5/1 to 5/15	37
215.		515.	
216.		516.	
217.		517.	
218.		518.	
219.		519.	
220.　Total Paid By/For Borrower	85,900	**520.　Total Reduction Amount Due Seller**	71,379
300.　Cash At Settlement From/To Borrower		**600.　Cash At Settlement To/From Seller**	
301.　Gross Amount due from borrower (line 120)	104,926	601.　Gross amount due to seller (line 420)	100,000
302.　Less amounts paid by/for borrower (line 220)	(85,900)	602.　Less reductions in amt. due seller (line 520)	(71,379)
303.　Cash ☒ From ☐ To Borrower	19,026	**603.　Cash** ☒ To ☐ From Seller	71,379

Section 5 of the Real Estate Settlement Procedures Act (RESPA) requires the following: • HUD must develop a Special Information Booklet to help persons borrowing money to finance the purchase of residential real estate to better understand the nature and costs of real estate settlement services; • Each lender must provide the booklet to all applicants from whom it receives or for whom it prepares a written application to borrow money to finance the purchase of residential real estate; • Lenders must prepare and distribute with the Booklet a Good Faith Estimate of the settlement costs that the borrower is likely to incur in connection with the settlement. These disclosures are manadatory.

Section 4(a) of RESPA mandates that HUD develop and prescribe this standard form to be used at the time of loan settlement to provide full disclosure of all charges imposed upon the borrower and seller. These are third party disclosures that are designed to provide the borrower with pertinent information during the settlement process in order to be a better shopper.

The Public Reporting Burden for this collection of information is estimated to average one hour per response, including the time for reviewing instructions, searching existing data sources, gathering and maintaining the data needed, and completing and reviewing the collection of information.

This agency may not collect this information, and you are not required to complete this form, unless it displays a currently valid OMB control number.

The information requested does not lend itself to confidentiality.

FIGURE 12.2 HUD-1 Settlement Statement (continued)

L. Settlement Charges			Paid From Borrowers Funds at Settlement	Paid From Seller's Funds at Settlement
700. Total Sales/Broker's Commission based on price $ ___ @ ___ % =				
Division of Commission (line 700) as follows:				
701. $ 5,000	to Dynamic Realty			
702. $	to			
703. Commission paid at Settlement				5,000
704.				
800. Items Payable In Connection With Loan				
801. Loan Origination Fee	1 %		800	
802. Loan Discount	2 %		1,600	
803. Appraisal Fee	to		150	
804. Credit Report	to		75	
805. Lender's Inspection Fee				
806. Mortgage Insurance Application Fee to				
807. Assumption Fee				
808. Collection Escrow Establishment Fee			100	
809.				
810.				
811.				
900. Items Required By Lender To Be Paid In Advance				
901. Interest from 5/15 to 7/1 @$ 19.44	/day		875	
902. Mortgage Insurance Premium for	months to			
903. Hazard Insurance Premium for	1 years to Hazard Ins. Co.		360	
904.	years to			
905.				
1000. Reserves Deposited With Lender				
1001. Hazard insurance	2 months@$ 30	per month	60	
1002. Mortgage insurance	months@$	per month		
1003. City property taxes	months@$	per month		
1004. County property taxes	2 months@$ 200	per month	400	
1005. Annual assessments	months@$	per month		
1006.	months@$	per month		
1007.	months@$	per month		
1008.	months@$	per month		
1100. Title Charges				
1101. Settlement or closing fee	to Efficient Title Co.		100	100
1102. Abstract or title search	to			
1103. Title examination	to			
1104. Title insurance binder	to			
1105. Document preparation	to			
1106. Notary fees	to			
1107. Attorney's fees	to			
(includes above items numbers:	)			
1108. Title insurance	to Efficient Title Co.		390	250
(includes above items numbers:	)			
1109. Lender's coverage	$			
1110. Owner's coverage	$			
1111.				
1112.				
1113.				
1200. Government Recording and Transfer Charges				
1201. Recording fees: Deed $ 6 ; Mortgage $ 10 ; Releases $ 20			16	20
1202. City/county tax/stamps: Deed $; Mortgage $				
1203. State tax/stamps: Deed $; Mortgage $				
1204.				
1205.				
1300. Additional Settlement Charges				
1301. Survey to				
1302. Pest inspection to Clean Up Termite Co.				100
1303. Roof inspection to Guaranteed Roofing Co.				100
1304.				
1305.				
1400. Total Settlement Charges (enter on lines 103, Section J and 502, Section K)			4,926	5,570

closing, the borrowers usually receive information as to how and where to make the payments. A coupon booklet is often included, in which the borrower is instructed to send the appropriate coupon for each specific month's payment along with the check. The coupon indicates two payment amounts on its face, one amount if paid by the required date, a higher amount if paid late.

ASSIGNMENT OF THE LOAN

For many years, the servicing of real estate loans by financial institutions was the task of the lending institutions, because they maintained ownership of the securities. This relationship changed over time as the originators of the loans found it more expedient to sell these securities in the secondary market.

Now most of these loans are sold (assigned) in the secondary market, but the loan originators often retain the servicing responsibility under a contract with the new owners. For their fee, ranging from 0.25 percent to 0.625 percent or more, the loan originators can build up a substantial loan collection business. In fact, servicing fees are an important part of mortgage bankers' profits.

These servicing companies collect the payments and keep records for borrowers and lenders. They provide a property tax service, checking the records of the county for the amounts due and paying the taxes on time. Servicing companies are also billed directly by insurance companies for premiums due on the various policies placed on the collateral properties. Probably most important, they maintain a watchful eye on the timely receipt of loan payments.

When a payment is late, the collection manager is alerted to watch for the check. If it is not forthcoming, a letter is sent to the borrowers that notifies them of the consequences of a default. If no payments are received, the manager notifies the investors and proceeds to follow their directions to foreclose on the property.

When loan collection portfolios are sold, notices must be sent to borrowers to mail payments to the new owners of the securities. Under the loan servicing transfer provisions of the October 27, 1990, Federal Housing Law:

- lenders must give 15-day advance notice, by a Loan Transfer Disclosure statement, that the loan is changing hands;
- both the old and the new lenders must give toll-free phone numbers and the name of the person empowered to handle borrower inquiries or complaints; and
- waivers of up to 60 days after the loan assignment must be given for late fees if the borrower sent a payment on time but to the wrong lender.

SUMMARY

After a loan application has been approved, the collateral property's value established, and the legal title cleared, the escrow officer prepares the required closing documents and secures the necessary signatures to close the loan.

The various costs associated with establishing a loan are derived for accountability. Included in these costs are: points reflecting the risks on the loan; origination or placement fees; impound funds composed of portions of the property taxes, hazard insurance premiums, and assessment liens, if any; interest adjustments; prepayment penalties if paying off an existing loan; title insurance premiums; and mortgage insurance premiums.

When the amounts of these costs have been determined, the escrow officer prorates them and allocates the debits and credits to the appropriate parties. A closing statement is prepared for approval by the parties involved. With the delivery of the funds to the seller and the recordation of the necessary papers transferring title, the loan transaction is completed. After a loan is closed, it is serviced directly by the lender or indirectly by a loan servicing company. In either case, the borrower usually receives a booklet with coupons to send in each month with the payment check.

CHAPTER 13

Contemporary Real Estate Finance

Know this well

▼ KEY TERMS

adjusted book basis
balloon payment
blanket mortgage
blends
boot
bridge loan
completion bond
condominium
construction mortgage
construction/permanent
   loan
convertible loan
cooperative
credit loan
draws
exchange

hard-money mortgage
installment sale
Internal Revenue Code
   Section 1031
joint venture
kicker
leasehold mortgages
lease-option
mobile home loans
mortgage participation
open-end mortgage
option
package mortgage
purchase-money
   mortgage

realized capital gain
recognized capital gain
recognition clause
reverse annuity
   mortgage (RAM)
right-of-first-refusal
sale-leaseback
sale-leaseback-buyback
security agreements
split-fee financing
stop date
term loan
two-step mortgage
wraparound
   encumbrance

Real estate loans can be as flexible and adaptable as needed to satisfy market demands. Contemporary financing techniques offer an opportunity to provide for most contingencies by varying one or more of the four basic characteristics of a real estate loan—the principal amount, the interest rate, the payment schedule, and the repayment terms. Each loan lends itself to a number of variations, limited only by the imaginations of those involved. This chapter examines the alternative lending techniques once thought innovative that today are accepted as standard.

INTEREST

From a borrower's point of view, *interest* can be described as *rent paid* for the use of money. A lender views interest as money received or *earned* from a loan investment. Thus, just as rent is paid and received for the use of an apartment, house, office, or store under the special conditions of a lease, real estate finance can be considered the process by which interest and principal are paid and received under the terms and conditions of a loan agreement. Money is borrowed (leased) at a certain interest rate (rent) for a specified time period during which the amount borrowed is repaid.

The amount of rent that a landlord can charge for the use of property depends on the rental market for that particular type of real estate. Similarly, the rate of interest that a lender can charge depends on the money market as it affects that particular type of loan. A rational borrower will not pay a lender more interest than the lowest interest rate available on a specific loan at a particular time.

Simple Interest

Most loans made on real estate are established at a simple rate of interest. *Simple interest* is "rent" that is paid only for the amount of principal still owed. When money is repaid to the lender, rent for that money stops.

The formula for computing simple interest is

$$I = PRT$$

where

$$I = \text{interest}$$
$$P = \text{principal}$$
$$R = \text{rate}$$
$$T = \text{time}$$

*F*OR EXAMPLE

Using this formula, the interest on a $1,000 loan to be repaid in one year at 8% is $80.

$I = PRT$
$I = \$1,000 \times 0.8 \times 1$
$I = \$80$

This simple interest formula is incorporated into the following types of repayment plans.

Term Loan. Also known as a straight loan or bullet loan, a **term loan** requires payments of interest only with the entire principal being repaid at a specified time, called the **stop date.** The loan is then paid in full with a **balloon payment** of the principal plus any interest still owed.

FOR EXAMPLE

Consider a term loan of $10,000 at 8% per annum, payable interest only monthly, to be paid in full in three years.

Loan Amount	$ 10,000
Interest Rate	× .08
Annual Interest	800
Pro Rata Months	÷ 12
Monthly Interest Payment	66.66
Final Principal Payment	10,000
Balloon Payment	$10,066.66

Amortization. The most common payment format for a real estate loan is a system of regular payments made over a specified period. These payments include portions for both principal and interest, the process is called *amortization*. Amortization tables are available that have the level monthly payments precalculated when the loan is established under a fixed rate of interest (see Table 13.1).

FOR EXAMPLE

Consider a term loan of $90,000 at 7% for 30 years. The monthly payment of principal and interest is $599.40.

Number of Thousands	$ 90
Payment Factor (Table 13.1)	× 6.66
Monthly Payment P & I	$599.40

Note that there may be a few pennies difference in various amortization tables due to rounding.

Distribution of Principal and Interest. Intrinsic in the amortization design is the distribution of the level payments into proportionate amounts of principal and interest.

TABLE 13.1   Monthly Payment Required to Amortize a $1,000 Loan

Years	5%	5.5%	6%	6.5%	7%	7.5%	8%
5	18.88	19.11	19.34	19.57	19.81	20.04	20.28
10	10.61	10.86	11.11	11.36	11.62	11.88	12.14
15	7.91	8.18	8.44	8.72	8.99	9.28	9.56
25	5.85	6.15	6.45	6.76	7.07	7.39	7.72
30	5.37	5.68	6.00	6.33	6.66	7.00	7.34

To compute the monthly principal and interest, multiply the number of thousands in the loan by the appropriate factor.

FOR EXAMPLE

Consider the $90,000 loan at 7% interest for 30 years with a monthly principal and interest payment of $599.40.

Payment No.	Balance	Interest	Principal
1	$90,000.00	$525.00	$74.40
2	89,925.60	524.57	74.83
3	89,850.77	524.13	75.27
4	89,775.50	523.69	75.71
180	66,686.82	389.01	210.39
etc. to 360			

The schedule in the example can be extended for the full period of 360 months to show the complete distribution of principal and interest and the remaining balance of the loan at any time. These amortization schedules can be prepared on computer printouts and are often presented by lenders to borrowers so they can follow the progress of their payments.

VARIATIONS IN PAYMENTS AND INTEREST RATES

In a fixed-rate (standard) mortgage instrument two basic characteristics do *not* change throughout the life of the loan: the interest rate and the repayment term. In addition to the principal and interest the lender often collects monthly an amount needed to pay annual taxes and insurance. This amount, sometimes referred to as *impound funds* or *escrow funds,* is determined by dividing the total amount due each year by 12. Although the principal plus interest payment remains constant over the life of the loan, the amount needed to pay the taxes and insurance may vary, resulting in a change in the total monthly payment. The accrued interest due on the loan is always paid first, with the balance of the payment allocated to principal, taxes, and insurance accordingly. The result of this standard payment format is that the borrower begins to build an equity with the first monthly payment.

Traditionally most loans are fairly standard in their payment schedules, requiring a certain sum to be paid at regular intervals over a prescribed time period. However, some real estate loans are designed to vary the required payments and interest to reflect more accurately the financial capabilities of a borrower, as well as the current state of the economy.

These alternative mortgage instruments allow a lender's return to keep pace with prevailing interest rates while simultaneously providing a borrower the opportunity to qualify for larger mortgage amounts.

Graduated-Payment Mortgage (GPM)

A graduated-payment mortgage is designed with lower payments in the early years of a loan. These payments increase gradually until they are sufficient to amortize the loan fully. Thus, buyers are able to obtain home loans with affordable payments while the lenders earn the desired interest rate over the loan term. A GPM may specify less-than-interest-only early payments. This results in *negative amortization* or *deferred interest,* and the principal amount owed increases over time by the amount of the deficiency. As the monthly payments are increased each year, however, the situation is reversed and the loan is amortized. Two deferred-interest plans are the FHA 245 program and the Department of Veterans Affairs graduated-payment plan.

Adjustable-Rate Mortgage (ARM)

In an adjustable-rate mortgage (ARM) the interest rate is adjusted in accordance with a prearranged index. The ARM usually includes an annual interest rate cap to protect the borrower from volatile interest rate fluctuations. In addition, there usually is an overall interest rate cap over the entire term of the loan.

Fannie Mae continuously revises its ARM plans. These plans are designed to give the consumer the protective features they desire. Consider the following when selecting an adjustable-rate or variable-rate mortgage:

Adjustment Periods. This indicates the frequency of interest rate adjustments with concomitant payments. For example, the interest of a one-year ARM will change every year, while the interest of a three-year ARM will change every three years.

Initial Rate. Sometimes called the "teaser rate," it will always be well below market rate in order to attract borrowers to this type of loan.

Note Rate. The note rate or the calculated rate is the adjusted rate, index plus margin, imposed from time to time at the adjustment period.

Qualifying Rate. Because ARM interest rates fluctuate from time to time, the rate at which to qualify a borrower often creates problems. If the initial loan rate is low but is expected to increase in the near future, the borrower may not be able to make the higher payments. Freddie Mac has an underwriting rule concerning the method by which borrowers can qualify for an ARM. Those with a less than 20 percent down payment must qualify at the maximum second-year rate. However, all interest rate adjustments on the loan will be made from the initial loan rate.

Borrowers should be cautious about incentives offered by some lenders. Lenders sometimes advertise below-market rates for a limited time period. At the end of the initial period, the interest rate is automatically increased. For example, an initial rate of 5 percent results in monthly payments of $429.46 on an $80,000, 30-year loan, but payments will increase to $702.06 at 10 percent.

Index. The index is the starting point to adjust a borrower's applicable interest rate. Lenders must use an index that is readily available to the borrower but beyond the control of the lender. Some indexes are more volatile than others. Those most frequently used are

- the six-month, three-year, and five-year Treasury rates;
- the Eleventh District Federal Home Loan Bank cost of funds;
- the national average contract interest rate on conventional home loans;
- the national median cost of funds to federally insured savings institutions;
- the new CD-ARMs by Fannie Mae tied to the average certificate of deposit interest rate; and
- the London Interbank (LIBOR) interest rates.

Margin. Each lender adds a certain margin percentage amount to the index at every adjustment period to derive the new rate. Individual lenders set different margins based on their estimated expenses and profit goals. Fannie Mae's interest rate adjustments for its ARMs fall between 1.5 and 3.0 percent, depending on the market. Thus, an initial rate of 6.0 percent will increase to 9.0 percent with an index adjustment of 1.0 percent and a margin of 2.0 percent.

Interest Rate Caps. Most variable rate loans include an *annual cap* applied to the adjusted interest rate. This cap limits interest rate increases or decreases over a stated period of time and varies from lender to lender and ranges from one to two percentage points per year. Some lenders also include a *life-of-the-loan* interest cap ranging up to six percent. This combination of caps provides the borrower protection against debilitating payment increases.

Payment Caps. Some lenders will use annual *payment caps* instead of *interest rate caps*. The most common payment cap is 7.5 percent of the initial payment. This is equivalent to 1 percent change in the interest rate. This means a payment of $750 per month, principal and interest, could not vary up or down more than $56.25 per month in one year's time. These payment caps are also combined with life-of-the-loan caps in some plans.

Most variable-rate loans do not need to include a prepayment penalty. Without this penalty, a borrower can more easily refinance to a fixed-rate mortgage. Some lenders also include a **convertible loan** feature that allows a variable-rate loan to be changed to a fixed-rate loan after the initial adjustment periods have been completed. A copy of the Fannie Mae adjustable-rate note appears in Figure 13.1.

All ARM originations from federally insured lending institutions must comply with disclosure regulations. Under an amendment to Regulation Z, the borrower must receive

- a descriptive ARM brochure;
- details of the specific loan program; and
- an illustrative example, based on a $10,000 loan, showing how the payments and loan balance have been affected by historical changes in the index.

INNOVATIVE PAYMENT PLANS

In addition to varying the payments and interest in a real estate loan, alternative types of loans can be arranged to satisfy the borrower's specific needs. Following are a few new popular alternative loan plans.

Buydown Mortgage

The buydown mortgage allows the homeseller, builder, buyer, buyer's parents, or any other third party or combination of parties to make a lump-sum payment to the mortgage lender at the time the loan is originated. These funds are used to reduce the interest rate and thus the buyer's monthly payments during the early years of the mortgage. Under the Fannie Mae buydown program, the reduced payments may have a term of no less than one year or more than five years. The maximum interest rate reduction on fixed-rate loans is 3 percent.

A stepped-rate plan may also be used. Here the interest rate is brought down to the lower rate in the first year of the buydown term and then increased gradually each year. The borrower's monthly payments cannot be increased by more than 7.5 percent per year.

FIGURE 13.1 Adjustable-Rate Note

ADJUSTABLE RATE NOTE
(1 Year Treasury Index -- Rate Caps)

THIS NOTE CONTAINS PROVISIONS ALLOWING FOR CHANGES IN MY INTEREST RATE AND MY MONTHLY PAYMENT. THIS NOTE LIMITS THE AMOUNT MY INTEREST RATE CAN CHANGE AT ANY ONE TIME AND THE MAXIMUM RATE I MUST PAY.

_____, _____   _____, _____
       [Date]   [City]   [State]

_____
[Property Address]

1. BORROWER'S PROMISE TO PAY

In return for a loan that I have received, I promise to pay U.S. $_____ (this amount is called "principal"), plus interest, to the order of the Lender. The Lender is _____ _____. I will make all payments under this Note in the form of cash, check or money order.

I understand that the Lender may transfer this Note. The Lender or anyone who takes this Note by transfer and who is entitled to receive payments under this Note is called the "Note Holder."

2. INTEREST

Interest will be charged on unpaid principal until the full amount of principal has been paid. I will pay interest at a yearly rate of _____%. The interest rate I will pay will change in accordance with Section 4 of this Note.

The interest rate required by this Section 2 and Section 4 of this Note is the rate I will pay both before and after any default described in Section 7(B) of this Note.

3. PAYMENTS

(A) Time and Place of Payments

I will pay principal and interest by making a payment every month.

I will make my monthly payment on the first day of each month beginning on _____, _____. I will make these payments every month until I have paid all of the principal and interest and any other charges described below that I may owe under this Note. Each monthly payment will be applied as of its scheduled due date and will be applied to interest before principal. If, on _____, 20___, I still owe amounts under this Note, I will pay those amounts in full on that date, which is called the "maturity date."

I will make my monthly payments at _____ _____ or at a different place if required by the Note Holder.

(B) Amount of My Initial Monthly Payments

Each of my initial monthly payments will be in the amount of U.S. $_____. This amount may change.

(C) Monthly Payment Changes

Changes in my monthly payment will reflect changes in the unpaid principal of my loan and in the interest rate that I must pay. The Note Holder will determine my new interest rate and the changed amount of my monthly payment in accordance with Section 4 of this Note.

4. INTEREST RATE AND MONTHLY PAYMENT CHANGES

(A) Change Dates

The interest rate I will pay may change on the first day of _____, _____, and on that day every 12th month thereafter. Each date on which my interest rate could change is called a "Change Date."

(B) The Index

Beginning with the first Change Date, my interest rate will be based on an Index. The "Index" is the weekly average yield on United States Treasury securities adjusted to a constant maturity of 1 year, as made available by the Federal Reserve Board. The most recent Index figure available as of the date 45 days before each Change Date is called the "Current Index."

If the Index is no longer available, the Note Holder will choose a new index which is based upon comparable information. The Note Holder will give me notice of this choice.

FIGURE 13.1   Adjustable-Rate Note (continued)

(C) Calculation of Changes

Before each Change Date, the Note Holder will calculate my new interest rate by adding _____ _____ percentage points (_____%) to the Current Index. The Note Holder will then round the result of this addition to the nearest one-eighth of one percentage point (0.125%). Subject to the limits stated in Section 4(D) below, this rounded amount will be my new interest rate until the next Change Date.

The Note Holder will then determine the amount of the monthly payment that would be sufficient to repay the unpaid principal that I am expected to owe at the Change Date in full on the maturity date at my new interest rate in substantially equal payments. The result of this calculation will be the new amount of my monthly payment.

(D) Limits on Interest Rate Changes

The interest rate I am required to pay at the first Change Date will not be greater than _____% or less than _____%. Thereafter, my interest rate will never be increased or decreased on any single Change Date by more than one percentage point (1.0%) from the rate of interest I have been paying for the preceding twelve months. My interest rate will never be greater than _____%.

(E) Effective Date of Changes

My new interest rate will become effective on each Change Date. I will pay the amount of my new monthly payment beginning on the first monthly payment date after the Change Date until the amount of my monthly payment changes again.

(F) Notice of Changes

The Note Holder will deliver or mail to me a notice of any changes in my interest rate and the amount of my monthly payment before the effective date of any change. The notice will include information required by law to be given me and also the title and telephone number of a person who will answer any question I may have regarding the notice.

5. BORROWER'S RIGHT TO PREPAY

I have the right to make payments of principal at any time before they are due. A payment of principal only is known as a "prepayment." When I make a prepayment, I will tell the Note Holder in writing that I am doing so. I may not designate a payment as a prepayment if I have not made all the monthly payments due under the Note.

I may make a full prepayment or partial prepayments without paying a prepayment charge. The Note Holder will use my prepayments to reduce the amount of principal that I owe under this Note. However, the Note Holder may apply my prepayment to the accrued and unpaid interest on the prepayment amount, before applying my prepayment to reduce the principal amount of the Note. If I make a partial prepayment, there will be no changes in the due dates of my monthly payment unless the Note Holder agrees in writing to those changes. My partial prepayment may reduce the amount of my monthly payments after the first Change Date following my partial prepayment. However, any reduction due to my partial prepayment may be offset by an interest rate increase.

6. LOAN CHARGES

If a law, which applies to this loan and which sets maximum loan charges, is finally interpreted so that the interest or other loan charges collected or to be collected in connection with this loan exceed the permitted limits, then: (i) any such loan charge shall be reduced by the amount necessary to reduce the charge to the permitted limit; and (ii) any sums already collected from me which exceeded permitted limits will be refunded to me. The Note Holder may choose to make this refund by reducing the principal I owe under this Note or by making a direct payment to me. If a refund reduces principal, the reduction will be treated as a partial prepayment.

7. BORROWER'S FAILURE TO PAY AS REQUIRED

(A) Late Charges for Overdue Payments

If the Note Holder has not received the full amount of any monthly payment by the end of _____ calendar days after the date it is due, I will pay a late charge to the Note Holder. The amount of the charge will be _____% of my overdue payment of principal and interest. I will pay this late charge promptly but only once on each late payment.

(B) Default

If I do not pay the full amount of each monthly payment on the date it is due, I will be in default.

(C) Notice of Default

If I am in default, the Note Holder may send me a written notice telling me that if I do not pay the overdue amount by a certain date, the Note Holder may require me to pay immediately the full amount of principal which has not been paid and all the interest that I owe on that amount. That date must be at least 30 days after the date on which the notice is mailed to me or delivered by other means.

(D) No Waiver By Note Holder

Even if, at a time when I am in default, the Note Holder does not require me to pay immediately in full as described above, the Note Holder will still have the right to do so if I am in default at a later time.

(E) Payment of Note Holder's Costs and Expenses

If the Note Holder has required me to pay immediately in full as described above, the Note Holder will have the right

FIGURE 13.1 Adjustable-Rate Note (continued)

to be paid back by me for all of its costs and expenses in enforcing this Note to the extent not prohibited by applicable law. Those expenses include, for example, reasonable attorneys' fees.

8. GIVING OF NOTICES

Unless applicable law requires a different method, any notice that must be given to me under this Note will be given by delivering it or by mailing it by first class mail to me at the Property Address above or at a different address if I give the Note Holder a notice of my different address.

Any notice that must be given to the Note Holder under this Note will be given by delivering it or by mailing it by first class mail to the Note Holder at the address stated in Section 3(A) above or at a different address if I am given a notice of that different address.

9. OBLIGATIONS OF PERSONS UNDER THIS NOTE

If more than one person signs this Note, each person is fully and personally obligated to keep all of the promises made in this Note, including the promise to pay the full amount owed. Any person who is a guarantor, surety or endorser of this Note is also obligated to do these things. Any person who takes over these obligations, including the obligations of a guarantor, surety or endorser of this Note, is also obligated to keep all of the promises made in this Note. The Note Holder may enforce its rights under this Note against each person individually or against all of us together. This means that any one of us may be required to pay all of the amounts owed under this Note.

10. WAIVERS

I and any other person who has obligations under this Note waive the rights of presentment and notice of dishonor. "Presentment" means the right to require the Note Holder to demand payment of amounts due. "Notice of dishonor" means the right to require the Note Holder to give notice to other persons that amounts due have not been paid.

11. UNIFORM SECURED NOTE

This Note is a uniform instrument with limited variations in some jurisdictions. In addition to the protections given to the Note Holder under this Note, a Mortgage, Deed of Trust or Security Deed (the "Security Instrument"), dated the same date as this Note, protects the Note Holder from possible losses which might result if I do not keep the promises which I make in this Note. That Security Instrument describes how and under what conditions I may be required to make immediate payment in full of all amounts I owe under this Note. Some of those conditions are described as follows:

If all or any part of the Property or any Interest in the Property is sold or transferred (or if Borrower is not a natural person and a beneficial interest in Borrower is sold or transferred) without Lender's prior written consent, Lender may require immediate payment in full of all sums secured by this Security Instrument. However, this option shall not be exercised by Lender if such exercise is prohibited by federal law. Lender also shall not exercise this option if: (a) Borrower causes to be submitted to Lender information required by Lender to evaluate the intended transferee as if a new loan were being made to the transferee; and (b) Lender reasonably determines that Lender's security will not be impaired by the loan assumption and that the risk of a breach of any covenant or agreement in this Security Instrument is acceptable to Lender.

To the extent permitted by Applicable Law, Lender may charge a reasonable fee as a condition to Lender's consent to the loan assumption. Lender may also require the transferee to sign an assumption agreement that is acceptable to Lender and that obligates the transferee to keep all the promises and agreements made in the Note and in this Security Instrument. Borrower will continue to be obligated under the Note and this Security Instrument unless Lender releases Borrower in writing.

FIGURE 13.1 Adjustable-Rate Note (continued)

If Lender exercises the option to require immediate payment in full, Lender shall give Borrower notice of acceleration. The notice shall provide a period of not less than 30 days from the date the notice is given in accordance with Section 15 within which Borrower must pay all sums secured by this Security Instrument. If Borrower fails to pay these sums prior to the expiration of this period, Lender may invoke any remedies permitted by this Security Instrument without further notice or demand on Borrower.

WITNESS THE HAND(S) AND SEAL(S) OF THE UNDERSIGNED.

_____ (Seal)
                                                                -Borrower

_____(Seal)
                                                                -Borrower

_____(Seal)
                                                                -Borrower

[Sign Original Only]

MULTISTATE ADJUSTABLE RATE NOTE--ARM 5-1--Single Family--Fannie Mae/Freddie Mac UNIFORM INSTRUMENT   Form 3501 3/99 *(page 4 of 4 pages)*

15-Year Mortgage. The 15-year mortgage has become very popular. It comprises about 33 percent of Freddie Mac's loan portfolio. The attraction of this relatively short-term real estate loan is the amount of interest that can be saved when compared with a 30-year loan. The major inhibiting quality of the 15-year loan is the higher amount required for monthly principal and interest.

Reverse Annuity Mortgage (RAM)

This plan is based on a borrower's ability to capitalize on accumulated equity and is designed to enhance the income of the elderly. Many senior citizens own their homes free and clear but often face the problem that their incomes are fixed and relatively low. Thus, the **reverse annuity mortgage (RAM)** allows them to utilize their equities, with the *lender* paying the *borrower* a fixed annuity.

The property is pledged as collateral to a lender, who may provide funds to the borrower in one of three ways:

1. Regular monthly checks to the borrower until a stipulated balance has been achieved with no cash payment of interest involved. The increase in the loan balance each month represents the cash advanced, plus interest on the outstanding balance.
2. An initial lump-sum payment.
3. A line-of-credit on which checks may be drawn. When the maximum loan amount is reached, the borrower is obligated to start repayment. In some cases this requires the sale of the property.

FOR EXAMPLE

An eligible couple has a $37,500 house, which they own free and clear, but they need additional money to supplement retirement income. With a RAM, a lender could make monthly payments of $147 to the couple for 10 years. At the end of the term the couple would have received a total of $17,607 and would owe $30,000. If the couple lived beyond the 10-year period, they could sell their home and move to other living quarters. Most participants in RAMs anticipate the need for a change in housing by the time the repayment requirements mature.

Under the HUD reverse mortgage program the monthly payments continue for as long as the borrowers live in the home with no repayment required until the property is sold. Any remaining value is distributed to the homeowners or their survivors. If there is any shortfall, HUD pays the lender. The size of the reverse mortgage loan is determined by several factors: the age of the borrower (must be at least 62); the interest rate, and the value of the property. There are no asset or income limitations on the HUD RAM.

HUD will insure loans taken out by owners 62 years of age or older and offers three mortgage plans: (1) a *tenure mortgage,* under which the lender makes monthly payments as long as the owner occupies the residence; (2) a *term mortgage,* under which the payments are made for a specific number of years; and (3) a *line-of-credit mortgage,* under which the owner can draw against the credit as long as the cumulative draws plus accrued interest are less than the principal loan limit.

IN PRACTICE . . .

Sam and Sarah Jones are both in their late 70s. They have lived in their home for 35 years and paid off the original mortgage loan many years ago. Unfortunately, Sam's health has been deteriorating over the past two years and he is no longer able to tend his rather extensive garden. The garden not only provided Sam with a great deal of pleasure but it provided an extra source of income during the spring and summer months. Sarah has been famous for years for her scrumptious baked goods. During the long winter months she filled the house with the smells of her breads and muffins, which she delivered to local restaurants—in exchange for cash to supplement their Social Security checks.

Although Sam's condition does not require him to be hospitalized, he cannot work in the garden anymore, nor can he deliver Sarah's baked goods to the restaurants. In fact, Sarah finds that with the additional care Sam needs, she really does not have the time (or the energy) to spend long hours in the kitchen baking. The loss of this additional income has made it very difficult for the Joneses. They realize, sadly, they will probably have to sell their home of 35 years and move into a small apartment. Is there a better solution for Sam and Sarah?

Fortunately, Sam noticed an article in the *AARP Modern Maturity* magazine about the benefits of a reverse annuity mortgage (RAM). He contacted a local lender and learned that under this plan, the Joneses will be able to secure a mortgage on the house where the bank sends them a check every month. The loan will be repaid when the property is eventually sold, the Jones will have enough cash to meet their monthly expenses, and most important—Sam and Sarah can stay in the home they love!

Fannie Mae Senior Housing Opportunities Program

Fannie Mae has a special program available to Americans 62 years old or older that offers four financing options:

1. an accessory apartment, which is a private living unit in a single-family home, allowing independence and privacy with an assurance of help nearby;
2. a cottage housing opportunity, which is a separate, self-contained unit built on the lot of an existing home, generally the home of a relative, offering privacy and nearness;
3. home sharing within a single-family home converted into up to four living units according to Fannie Mae standards;
4. a sale-leaseback arrangement allowing a senior the opportunity to sell the home to an investor, perhaps a member of the family, and then lease it back.

To qualify, a regular salary is not essential, but income from part-time work, pensions, Social Security, interest, dividends, and other sources must be sufficient to meet Fannie Mae's usual requirements. The monthly mortgage payments must not exceed 28 percent of the borrower's monthly gross income and the borrower's total debt, including monthly payments, may not exceed 36 percent of the gross income.

Fannie Mae's Two-Step Mortgage Plan

Fannie Mae, in its continuous efforts to introduce new products to enhance its activities, has available a **two-step mortgage,** a hybrid between a fixed-rate and an adjustable-rate loan. The two-step requires a 10 percent down payment and offers interest rates at least three eighths of one percent lower than the market rates for a 30-year fixed-rate loan. The lower rate remains in effect for 7 years and is then adjusted automatically *once* for the balance of the loan period. The new rate is based on the 10-year Treasury bond rate but has a maximum six percent cap. No additional fees are charged when the two-step is converted.

VARIATIONS IN FORMATS

The deed of trust; note and mortgage; and contract for deed are flexible and therefore adaptable to many situations by using creative design. Almost every realty financing contingency can be solved to the satisfaction of all the participants. Not only can specific terms and conditions be designed to meet particular requirements, but special forms of these three lending instruments can also be developed to finance unique real estate situations. Descriptions of some alternative forms for the basic financing instruments follow.

Open-End Mortgage

An **open-end mortgage,** also known as a *mortgage for future advances,* allows a borrower to secure additional funds from a lender under terms specified in the original mortgage. Thus, an open-end mortgagee can advance funds to a mortgagor on an existing mortgage—funds that, in many instances, represent the principal already paid by the borrower. This allows a mortgage to stay alive for a longer period of time and can in some cases save the borrower the time and much of the expense of refinancing. The funds advanced by this process are repaid by either extending the term of the mortgage loan or increasing the monthly payments by the amount appropriate to maintain the original amortization schedule. The interest rate can also be adjusted accordingly, and appropriate fees can be charged.

Open-end mortgages have become useful financial tools for single-family home loans. Mortgagors are allowed to borrow funds for personal property purchases made after the original loan is recorded. These amounts are added to the principal owed, and the payments are increased to accommodate the new balance. If the personal property becomes part of the loan's collateral, along with the real property, the open-end mortgage is converted into a package mortgage, which will be described later in this chapter.

Open-end mortgages are often utilized by farmers to raise funds to meet their seasonal operating expenses. Similarly, builders use the open-end mortgage for their construction loans in which advances are made periodically while the building is being completed. In addition, many private loan companies are offering customers an opportunity to draw down on a line of credit backed by the collateral of their home equity.

A basic legal problem associated with open-end financing is one of securing future advances under an already existing debt instrument and, at the same time, preserving its priority against any possible intervening liens. In most states an obligatory future advance under the terms of an existing mortgage is interpreted as having priority over intervening liens. For example, an advance made under a construction mortgage that sets forth a specific pattern of draws is interpreted to have priority over a construction (mechanic's) lien that may have been filed in the period prior to the last advance.

On the other hand, nonobligatory future advances do not have priority over intervening liens, according to most state laws. In other words, the legal security of the advances to be made in the future under an already existing mortgage may not be enforceable against debts incurred by a borrower in the intervening time period.

If the terms of a mortgage do not obligate a mortgagee to make *specific* future advances, the mortgagee is well advised to protect the priority of the lien by searching the record for intervening liens prior to making any advances. Prevailing practice does not require a title search, but merely binds a mortgagee to any liens of which there has been outside notice. A few states require a title search, and actually reduce the mortgagee to a junior position against any recorded intervening liens. A search of the records can only be to the advantage of the original mortgagee.

In addition, under the laws of those states that have adopted the Uniform Commercial Code, any personal property **security agreements** for the purchase of goods that become fixtures on the collateral property have a priority lien over future advances made under an original mortgage. Suppose a homeowner signs a financing contract with the ABC Appliance Company to purchase and install a central air-conditioning system in June, and the agreement is recorded. In December the owners secure an advance on their open-end mortgage to build an addition to their home. Because the central air-conditioning system is now a fixture, the appliance company's lien will take priority over any future advances made by the original mortgagee.

Not all states allow open-end mortgages. Texas, for example, does not allow open-end mortgages or lines of credit loans for residential properties under their Home Equity Loan Legislation.

Construction Mortgage

A **construction mortgage,** also called an interim financing instrument, is a unique form of open-end mortgage. It is a loan to finance the costs of labor and materials as they are used during the course of constructing a new building. An interim mortgage usually covers the period from the commencement of a project until the loan is replaced by a more permanent form of financing at the completion of construction. This financial format is unique because the building pledged as part of the collateral for the loan is *not in existence* at the time that the mortgage is created. The value of the land is the only available collateral at the loan's inception, a condition that requires the lender to seek some form of extra protection.

The procedure for protecting the lender is both logical and practical. Although the full amount to be loaned is committed at the start of construction, the funds are distributed in installments as the building progresses, not as a lump sum in advance. The outstanding loan balance is matched to the value of the collateral as it grows.

Application and Requirements. To obtain a construction loan, the borrower submits plans and specifications for a building to be constructed on a specific site to a loan officer for analysis. Based on the total value of the land and the building to be constructed thereon, a lender will make a commitment for a construction loan, usually at the rate of 75 percent of the property's total value.

Hence a $100,000 project would be eligible for a $75,000 construction loan. This amount normally would be adequate to cover most, if not all, of the costs of construction, with the $25,000, or 25 percent equity, representing the value of the free and clear lot. Because construction mortgages usually are secured from financial fiduciaries, these institutions normally require that the lot be lien-free in order to preserve the first priority position of the construction loan. In a case where the lot is encumbered by an existing mortgage or lease, the mortgagee or the landlord must subordinate that interest to the lien of the construction mortgage before the loan can be granted.

Construction loans are available for projects of all sizes, from the smallest home to the largest shopping center, and the basic loan format is similar in each case. The charges imposed for securing a construction loan are usually based on a one-time 1 percent placement fee paid at the loan's inception, plus interest at about two points above the prime rate charged to AAA-rated borrowers. Thus, based on a prime rate of 8 percent and a 2 percent overcharge, a $75,000 construction loan would be placed for a front-end fee of $750 plus 10 percent interest on the funds disbursed from time to time. Interest rates and placement fees fluctuate as a function of business cycles, borrowers' credit ratings, and individual situations.

Pattern of Disbursements. Disbursement of funds under a construction loan usually follows either of two basic patterns. A construction loan may be designed to include a schedule for disbursing funds in a series of **draws** as construction progresses. In a five-stage plan, an interim financier distributes 20 percent of the funds each time the building reaches another one-fifth of completion.

In the $75,000 example, $15,000 is distributed to the builder when the first stage is accomplished, with subsequent $15,000 draws until completion, when the final draw is paid. This final $15,000 might be withheld pending the full payment of all labor and materials as evidenced by lien waivers from each of the contractors and subcontractors of the job, receipt of a *certificate of completion and approval for occupancy* issued by a building inspector, or expiration of the statutory time to file a construction lien.

Interest is charged on these monies only after they are disbursed following each inspection of the work's progress. Careful records are kept of the interest as it begins from each disbursement date, and the accumulated interest charges and the entire construction loan principal are paid in full within some relatively short period of time after the completion of the project. Usually a construction loan is replaced by a permanent, long-term senior encumbrance for which the builder has arranged in advance.

Another pattern of disbursement under a construction loan requires the borrower to submit all bills for subcontracted labor and materials to the lender, who then pays these bills and charges the loan account accordingly. This plan gives the lender greater control over the possibility of intervening construction liens.

The pattern of disbursement, in the form of either draws to the builder or direct payments from the lender, effectively matches the value of the collateral to the amount of the loan outstanding at a particular time. If there is a default at any point during construction, the lender can foreclose and recover the collateral in its unfinished condition. It can then be sold *as is* or completed to recover the investment.

Lender Protection. There are no insurance plans for guaranteeing the payments on construction loans. As additional protection, many construction financiers insist their borrowers-builders secure a **completion bond** from an insurance company, naming the lender as the primary beneficiary. The bond is drawn in the amount of the total construction cost and is exercised only if the builder is unable to complete the construction. Under this circumstance the lender can step in and use the bond proceeds to pursue the completion and subsequent sale of the property to recover the interim loan funds. Often small building companies cannot qualify for bonding and must pledge other assets as additional collateral for a construction loan.

Construction loans are drawn for relatively short time periods—six months to a year for a house and up to three years for larger projects. The interim lender needs to be paid in full at the end of these periods and is vitally concerned with making provisions *in advance* for the security and satisfaction of the construction loan. The borrower is equally concerned with this payback and is eager to be relieved of the heavy interest burden imposed during the loan period. Therefore, provisions for a permanent, long-term mortgage are made prior to the origination of the construction loan, to satisfy or take out the interim financier at the completion of construction.

In most cases the standby commitment for a takeout permanent loan will be exercised after the construction is completed to the satisfaction of this final lender. The builder must submit a set of plans and specifications to the long-term lender. When the application is approved, a written agreement of the standby commitment is delivered to the interim financier, enabling the construction loan to be placed. The interim lender can then rely on being paid in full at the expiration of the contract.

Sources of Funds. The relatively short-term nature of construction loans closely matches the investment profile of commercial banks, which take an active role in this form of financing. However, some fiduciaries that generally deal in long-term loans also participate in interim financing. For example, some lenders will provide money for construction and then simply convert these interim mortgages to permanent mortgages for eligible borrowers. In other words, these lenders have created an in-house loan package, called a **construction/permanent loan.**

While construction loans are tailored to the investment needs of commercial banks, permanent long-term takeout loans match the investment designs of thrift institutions and life insurance companies. Thus, all types of investment groups can participate in the various stages of construction financing.

An expedient way to orchestrate the activities of these various participants is through the services of a mortgage banking company, which often has all of these various lenders as investors. A developer can have a mortgage banker process the entire construction procedure in a "one stop loan shop."

Blanket Mortgage

Depending on the terms of a specific transaction, a lender may require a borrower to pledge *more than one* parcel of property as collateral to back up a mortgage. The debt instrument used in this situation is called a **blanket mortgage** and can take any of the financing forms discussed previously. On occasion the federal government secures a *blan-*

ket lien against all of the properties of a person who has failed to pay income tax. When the properties encumbered by a blanket mortgage or federal blanket lien are located in more than one county, the debt instrument must be reproduced and recorded at the courthouse in each county where a subject property is located.

Release Clauses. When two or more properties are pledged as collateral for one loan, it is often necessary to provide some means for relinquishing an individual parcel as payments are made. Such a tool is called a *release clause*. In exchange for some action, such as a designated amount of repayment, a specific property or portion of a property can be freed from the lien of a blanket mortgage.

Blanket mortgages are often used to purchase large tracts of land for development, and a release clause usually is incorporated into these financing instruments. The absence of a release clause requires the payment in full of the entire balance due before any portion of the land can be sold lien free. The alternative is to sell a portion of the land *without* satisfying the underlying blanket mortgage or contract for deed. This latter technique could create many difficulties for the buyer of a small parcel. If the payments on the underlying encumbrance are not made on time by the developer, the small parcel owner may be wiped out in a foreclosure. Unfortunately, some land promotion developments in this country were designed on this nonrelease basis, with concurrent losses to individual buyers.

Recognition Clause. Most responsible land developers secure a special **recognition clause** from their underlying financiers that protects individual small parcel owners. This clause specifies that in the event of a default and a resultant foreclosure the underlying financier will recognize and protect the rights of each individual lot owner. Many states require not only full disclosure of the physical attributes of the land involved in such a development but also a description of all financing terms. These state disclosure laws closely parallel those of the federal government for interstate land sale promotions.

Mortgage Participation

There are three types of mortgage participation. One is a partnership among several mortgagees, a second includes the teaming of several mortgagors, and a third establishes a partnership between a mortgagee and a mortgagor.

Partnership of Mortgagees. In the first type, a **mortgage participation** involves more than one mortgagee as the owner of the instrument designed to finance a real estate project. It is used in large project financing. Several mortgagees join together, each advancing a proportionate share of the monies required and receiving a commensurate share of the mortgage payments.

The format of the GNMA mortgage pooling operation is in contrast to a simple partnership involving two or more mortgagees in a single mortgage. Many individual investors, large and small, may purchase shares in a designated group, or pool, of mortgages, and GNMA guarantees the repayment of principal and interest on these shares. Here we see that mortgage-backed securities are in reality a form of mortgage participation.

In addition to the private partnerships among several mortgagees on a single loan and the GNMA mortgage-backed securities program, real estate mortgage trusts (REMTs) also offer opportunities for mortgage partnerships. Trusts are formed where investors purchase beneficial shares under special terms. Using the pool of monies acquired by the sale of these beneficial interests, mortgage trust managers invest in real estate mortgages and distribute the profits according to a prearranged formula. The private ownership quality of REMTs allows them to invest in high-risk loans such as junior loans or construction financing. Sometimes, as a result of adverse financial conditions, REMTs are inadvertently converted to REITs (real estate investment trusts) when they foreclose on their delinquent mortgagors and end up *owning* the properties they financed.

Partnership of mortgagors. The second type of mortgage participation involves several mortgagors sharing responsibility for a single mortgage on a multifamily property, called a **cooperative.**

A cooperative vests ownership in a corporation that issues stock to all purchasers, giving them the right to lease a unit from "their" corporation. This proprietary lease is drawn subject to the rules and restrictions established by the corporation, and management is in the hands of a board of directors elected by the stockholders. The major weakness of the cooperative form of mortgage participation is that each cooperative participant is dependent on the other owners to prevent a default of the mortgage. A financially irresponsible tenant or units that remain unsold for long periods create a financial strain on the remaining tenants who are still liable for making the total mortgage payments.

The **condominium** has replaced the cooperative in most states. The condominium is designed to have each unit owner pay cash or get an individual mortgage loan eliminating any reliance on other owners in the condominium project.

Partnership of Mortgagees and Mortgagors. The third type of participation, called a *participation mortgage,* is engendered when a mortgagee becomes a partner in the ownership of a project on which a loan will be placed. When a developer requests a commitment for a participation mortgage on a substantial commercial real estate project, a lender may accept a higher loan-to-value ratio, lower the interest rate, or make other concessions in return for a percentage of the project's ownership as a condition for issuing the loan commitment. These mortgagee ownerships range from 5 to 50 percent or more and simultaneously make the lender a partner in the development as well as its financier.

Leasehold Mortgage

Tenants are able to pledge their leasehold interests as collateral for **leasehold mortgages.** Some of these mortgages are eligible for FHA and VA insurance and guarantees, and national banks have been authorized to make such loans provided that the lease term extends for a sufficient interval after the expiration of the leasehold mortgage. For instance, the VA guarantees leasehold loans that will be repaid 15 years prior to the expiration of the ground lease, and the FHA insures leasehold mortgages issued on 99-year leases.

The major sources of funds for leasehold mortgages are life insurance companies, mutual savings banks, and commercial banks. Any fiduciary lender must be in first priority lien position so that full title to the collateral property may be secured in the event of a default. Thus a leasehold mortgage arrangement usually includes the *landlord's pledge* of the legal fee in the property as well as the *tenant's pledge* of the improvements as collateral for the loan. The landlord's pledge of the fee simple legal rights in the land is called *subordination*.

As a consequence, if a loan default occurs that necessitates a foreclosure action, a lender will be protected by having the legal right to recover *both* the land and the building. Most leasehold mortgages are designed to include both land and buildings as collateral, requiring the landlord's subordination of the legal fee to the new lien.

Credit Loans. There are some rare exceptions to the landlord's pledging the land or subordinating the legal fee to the lender. Such exceptions involve tenant-developers whose credit is strong enough to make consideration of the collateral's value almost incidental to the loan transaction. If a company such as Target or J.C. Penney wants to secure financing to construct stores or warehouses, it could obtain any needed funds simply through its signature alone and the pledge of the leasehold interests if the company was building on leased land. The landowner would not be required to participate in such a financial arrangement. This form of finance, in which a mortgage is issued strictly on the financial strength of a borrower without much regard for the value of the collateral, is called a **credit loan.**

Package Mortgage

Often real estate purchases include items of personal property in the transaction. Generally expensive items of personal property are encumbered by a security agreement. The security agreement format involves filing a financing statement with the secretary of state in which the personal property purchase takes place. Some local filing may also be required at a county recorder's office for special types of collateral, such as farm equipment or crops. Subsequent filings must also be made properly at the place or places of the original filing to provide proper notice on a continuing basis. Such documents could include statements of continuation, termination, release, assignment, and amendment. A financing statement is effective for a specified period of time, usually five years, and must be renewed if necessary, or it will automatically lapse.

When personal property is included with the sale of real estate, however, it is possible to use a single financing instrument. This form of financing is called a **package mortgage.** It includes as collateral not only the real estate but certain fixtures attached to the property and/or other items of personal property described in the mortgage document. Most installations, such as heating units, plumbing fixtures, and central air systems, when attached to the real estate become real property and are automatically included under the lien. However, other fixtures not normally considered real property, such as ranges, ovens, refrigerators, freezers, dishwashers, carpets, and draperies, may be included in a home purchase financing agreement to attract buyers. This inclusion will enable homebuyers to stretch the payments for these items over the entire term of the mortgage, as opposed to the shorter term of a consumer installment loan.

The use of the package mortgage is increasing in popularity throughout the United States because it offers the added attraction to the buyer of not making separate cash down payments for these items. Moreover, having the payments for these purchases lowered substantially from the relatively high interest rate structure of the usual short-term personal property financing pattern is another attraction. An additional incentive to use the package loan is that the interest on a home loan is tax deductible whereas the interest on a consumer loan is not. Many commercial rental properties, including condominiums, apartment rentals, office buildings, and clinics, are specifically designed to include package financing.

Mobile Home Mortgage

The problem in describing the unique quality of a loan for a mobile home is not in the nature of the instrument itself, which can assume any of the forms previously discussed, but in the definition of the collateral. Is a mobile home real property or personal property? This definition determines the type of finance instrument necessary.

There is little doubt that a travel trailer attached by a hitch to an automobile or set onto the bed of a pickup truck or a van-type travel home is clearly identifiable as personal property. They pose no problem of definition and are financed by a personal property debt instrument. However, some difficulty arises in classifying trailers that are larger than travel units but also attach easily to a hitch and are parked temporarily at rental trailer parks. These smaller mobile homes are also generally financed as personal property.

More pertinent to real estate finance are the larger mobile homes manufactured as factory-built housing units. Many are legally transportable only by professional mobile home movers. These units are permanently attached to lots in rental parks that cater to long-term tenancies or are installed on property purchased by the mobile home owner. When long-term leases are involved or a mobile home owner has title to the lot on which the unit is permanently affixed, real estate financing is possible.

All forms of financial instruments are applicable to both a mobile home and its lot, but the repayment terms of these encumbrances would normally be for a shorter period of time than for other forms of real estate. Although the quality of the construction of most mobile homes is increasingly more durable, the lending institutions are still reluctant to place long-term loans on this type of collateral. The depreciation on mobile homes is severe in the first few years of their lives, and, as a result, **mobile home loans** are usually established for a 15-year period, as compared to conventional home loans of up to 30 years' duration. Nevertheless, some of the larger double-wide units are now being financed for up to 20 years. Many of these loans are eligible for FHA or VA financing.

Purchase-Money Mortgage

A **purchase-money mortgage** is created when a seller carries back a portion or all of the sales price as a loan to a buyer. A purchase-money mortgage can be either a senior or junior lien on the property. If executed simultaneously with a deed conveying title, it acquires the highest legal lien priority possible.

Hard Money Mortgage (Equity Mortgage)

Unlike a mortgage given to finance a specific real estate *sale,* a **hard money mortgage** is one given by a borrower in exchange for actual money received, "cash out." A first mortgage executed in exchange for cash funds is described as a hard money mortgage. Frequently a hard money mortgage will take the form of a junior loan given to a private mortgage company in exchange for cash needed by the borrower to purchase an item of personal property or solve some personal financial crisis. The borrower usually will pledge the equity in the property as collateral for this hard money mortgage.

Bridge Loan

A **bridge loan** is an equity loan designed to serve a specific purpose, usually for a relatively short period of time. For example, owners of one property wishing to purchase another might seek a short-term bridge loan on their equity to be able to close the purchase. This loan would be satisfied when the old property was sold or at a specified time, whichever came first. The bridge loan is usually an interest-only term loan, requiring a balloon payment at its conclusion.

Wraparound Encumbrance (Wrap)

A **wraparound encumbrance,** also known as an *all-inclusive encumbrance,* is a special instrument created as a junior financing tool that encompasses an existing debt. Adopting any of the three basic financing forms, these encumbrances are used in circumstances where existing financing cannot be prepaid easily due to a lock-in clause or a high prepayment penalty. They are also used where the low interest rate on the existing mortgage allows a lender to secure a higher yield by making a wrap loan.

*F*OR *EXAMPLE*

The sale of a $60,000 property with a $10,000 cash down payment and an assumable first mortgage balance of $40,000 can be financed by a seller who would carry back a new wraparound loan for $50,000. This wraparound would require the purchaser-mortgagor to make payments on the $50,000, while the seller-wraparound-mortgagee would retain responsibility for making the required payments on the undisturbed existing $40,000 first mortgage.

The use of the wrap has diminished dramatically as most of the existing real estate loans cannot be easily assumed. Nevertheless, some individuals still use this type of financing to sell their properties. Lenders also use the wrap to enhance their yields. For example, some lenders offer their borrowers an opportunity to secure additional funds on the equities in their properties at less-than-market interest rates by arranging to wrap the existing loans at a one-point or two-point override. These loans are also known in some areas as **blends.**

TAX-FREE MORTGAGE LENDING

In addition to the variations in mortgage payment formats discussed to this point, there are special aspects of real estate that can be served through creative finance. Included are the more esoteric arrangements that provide participants with extra cash, tax free, by capitalizing in a number of ways on equities that accumulate on properties through growth in value and the paydown of existing loan balances.

Refinancing

One effective tool for acquiring additional funds while postponing any income tax impact is to *refinance* property that has developed an increased equity through a rise in property value, the amortization of its existing loan, or both. Refinancing involves securing a new loan to replace an old loan. Logically the new loan should be of sufficient quantity not only to satisfy the balance of the existing loan, but also to pay all of the placement costs involved and to generate new cash for the borrower to use. Any money acquired by refinancing is not subject to income tax, even if these funds exceed the original purchase price of the specific property or its **adjusted book basis.** This money is considered borrowed money and, as such, is not taxable.

In this regard and germane to our discussion of income tax impacts is the distinction between two types of capital gains income. **Realized capital gain** is the actual profit derived from a transaction, such as the money received from refinancing, while **recognized capital gain** is the profit that is subject to being taxed. In the case of refinancing, only when the realized capital gain becomes recognized gain on the *sale* of the property will there be any capital gains income subject to taxation. In the meantime, real property can be financed and refinanced over time to generate tax-free cash.

Most refinancing decisions are governed by balancing the possible gains to be made against the known costs to be incurred. For instance, to refinance an existing 9 percent interest loan with one at 15 percent interest is not practical unless the borrower can earn more than 15 percent on a reinvestment of the new monies secured. Otherwise the best alternative is to leave the existing financial arrangement alone. In other words, a refinancing decision should be based on the alternative investment opportunities as a measurement of opportunity costs. And these measurements, like so many others in real estate finance, include subjective as well as objective inputs.

Installment Sales

A special financing tool designed to postpone capital gains income taxes on properties that do *not* qualify for special exemptions available under the income tax laws is called an **installment sale** plan.

A gain on an installment sale is computed in the same manner as is the net capital gain on a cash sale: gross sales price minus costs of sale minus adjusted book basis equals net capital gain. However, under an installment sale the seller can elect either to pay the total tax due in the year of the sale or to spread the tax obligation over the length of the installment contract.

The installment sale provision in the tax law was originally intended as a relief provision for owners who could sell their property only by agreeing to accept payments in installments. Such a seller might receive less cash in the year of the sale than the tax required on the total gain. The law allows tax payments to be made as installment payments are received.

Sellers soon realized that under a progressive tax system the total tax could well be less if paid in installments, because much of the gain could be paid later when the seller would be in a lower tax bracket and also because of the time value of money. Thus, an installment sale became a desirable end in itself.

FOR EXAMPLE

Consider a property that is sold for $100,000 net. The buyer pays $40,000 cash and assumes an existing loan balance of $60,000. The adjusted book basis on the date of the sale is $80,000. Given these facts, a cash transaction would result in a 28% bracket taxpayer paying $5,600 tax on this property in the year of the sale ($100,000 − $80,000 = $20,000 capital gain × 0.28 = $5,600).

An installment sale can be designed to postpone portions of the seller's tax liability. For instance, the sale can be structured to require $8,000 as a cash down payment and $32,000 as a junior loan back to the seller. The buyer then assumes the $60,000 existing loan. The installment contract is payable in four equal annual principal payments plus interest at an agreed rate.

Computation of the seller's tax liability under the installment contract first requires a determination of the *installment factor* (gain divided by equity) to identify what portion is return of the equity buildup.

FOR EXAMPLE

In this case the seller's gain is $20,000 ($100,000 − $80,000) while the equity is $40,000 ($100,000 − $60,000). Therefore, the installment factor is 50% ($20,000 gain ÷ $40,000 equity = 0.50).

The seller's annual tax liability is $1,120 ($8,000 × 0.50 = $4,000 × 0.28 = $1,120), for a total of $5,600 over five years ($1,120 × 5 = $5,600). This is exactly the same total tax that would be paid if the property were sold for cash. The installment treatment allows the seller to pay this sum over the term of the contract as the principal is received. All interest received by the seller is declared as portfolio income. The computations are as follows:

Sale Price	$100,000	Sale Price	$100,000
Down Payment	− 8,000	Adjusted Basis	− 80,000
	92,000	Capital Gain	20,000
Second Mortgage	− 60,000		
First Mortgage	32,000		
		Sale Price	100,000
		First Mortgage	− 60,000
		Equity	40,000

(continued)

F**OR EXAMPLE** (continued)

Taxes (28 Percent Bracket)
Sale Year:

$$\text{Gain} \div \text{Equity} = \frac{20,000}{40,000} = 0.50$$

$8,000 × 0.50 =	$4,000
$4,000 × 0.28 =	1,120
Years 2 Through 5:	
$4,000 × 0.28 × 4 =	4,480
Total Tax	$5,600

The installment plan allows a seller to pay tax in amounts proportionate to the gain collected each year. A seller whose tax bracket *decreases* over the term of an installment contract will pay *less* tax than if he or she had elected to pay the full tax in the year of the sale. This arrangement is particularly advantageous to a seller nearing retirement age who will enter a lower tax bracket during the term of the installment contract. On the other hand, there is the possibility that a seller's tax bracket could rise over the installment term, which would lead to the payment of *more* tax. Consequently, a seller is allowed to pay the full amount of tax due on a capital gain whenever it becomes expedient during the installment contract period.

Option to Buy

Although the **option** and the installment sale are quite different in legal form, they can have the same economic effect. In the *installment sale,* the seller takes back a purchase-money loan to be paid off, with interest, over several years. Normally, if the buyer defaults, the seller can foreclose. Likewise, an *option* gives the buyer, also known as the optionee, the absolute right (but not the obligation) to acquire certain real estate during the option period, provided the option payments are kept current. One tax difference between the two forms is that the installment seller must treat a portion of each payment as taxable capital gains income (except interest-only payments), whereas option payments received by the owner are not recognized as income until the option is exercised or lapses.

A significant difference exists between the two forms in the event of the death of the property owner prior to the transaction's completion—that is, before the installment contract is satisfied or before the option is exercised. In the former situation, the estate is taxed twice, once as unpaid income under the installment sale and again as a capital gain when the heirs secure the payoff (IRS Code Section 691). In the latter situation, because title did not change hands under the option, the impact of tax is felt only at the estate level. The heirs receive a stepped-up basis to shelter the capital gain at payoff.

Lease with Option to Buy

A variation of the option to buy is a **lease-option** to buy. In this case, the buyer agrees to purchase the property at a price negotiated within the lease. Often, a portion of the rent is applied to the purchase price as an incentive for closing the transaction. It is rare for these agreements to be completed as written. More often, new negotiations are entered into at the time of the lease expiration, primarily as a result of changing economic circumstances. Contemporary lease-options include a **right-of-first-refusal** clause instead of an outright option. Here, the price is not fixed at the outset; market conditions dictate the final value to be accepted by both parties.

Exchanges

Another method often employed to postpone tax on capital gains is the property **exchange** technique. **Internal Revenue Code Section 1031** provides for the recognition of gain to be postponed under the following conditions:

- Properties to be exchanged must be held for productive use in a trade or business or for investment.
- Properties to be exchanged must be of like kind to each other; that is, their nature or character must be similar. "Like kind" is only limited to another income-producing property. A rental condo could be exchanged for a delicatessen, a rental townhouse could be exchanged for a gas station or marina. One property may be exchanged for several properties; it is not limited to one.
- Properties must actually be exchanged.

Property held for productive use in a trade or business may include machinery, automobiles, factories, and rental apartments. Property held for investment may include vacant land and antiques. Like kind includes a machine for a machine or real estate for real estate. Improvements on the land are considered to be differences in the *quality* of the real estate, not in the type. Thus, a vacant lot can be exchanged for a store property. Often unlike property, called **boot,** is included in an exchange and must be accounted for separately.

There are at least six basic mathematical computations involved in the exchange process:

1. Balancing the equities
2. Deriving realized gains
3. Deriving recognized gains
4. Determining tax impacts
5. Reestablishing book basis
6. Allocation of new basis

These computations are illustrated by the two-party exchange recorded in Table 13.2.

It is rare to make a straight two-party exchange. More frequently, there are three-party exchanges or more, as well as "delayed" (Starker) exchanges requiring definite time limits, 45 days to select and 180 days to settle.

Generally, the investor who is trading up benefits by not being required to pay taxes, while the downside exchanger is taxed on gains. A prudent investment program provides for trading up during an investor's acquisition years and trading down after retirement, when tax brackets are lower.

TABLE 13.2 Two-Party Exchange

STEP 1. Balancing Equities

	Property A		Property B
	$100,000	EXCHANGE PRICE	$150,000
	− 60,000	EXISTING MORTGAGE	− 80,000
	40,000	OWNER'S EQUITY	$ 70,000
	+ 30,000	CASH REQUIRED	
	$ 70,000		

STEP 2. Deriving Realized Gain

	$100,000	EXCHANGE PRICE	$150,000
	− 70,000	ADJUSTED BASIS	− 90,000
	$ 30,000	REALIZED GAIN	$ 60,000

STEP 3. Deriving Recognized Gain
(Recognized gain equals the sum of unlike properties.)

	−0−	CASH RECEIVED	$30,000
	−0−	BOOT	−0−
	−0−	MORTGAGE RELIEF	+20,000
	−0−	RECOGNIZED GAIN	$50,000

STEP 4. Determining Tax Impact
(Taxable income is the realized gain or the recognized gain whichever is *less.*)

	$30,000	REALIZED GAIN	$60,000
	−0−	RECOGNIZED GAIN	50,000
	−0−	TAXABLE GAIN	$50,000

(Note: B will pay income tax on $50,000. A will pay no tax.)

STEP 5. Reestablishing Book Basis

	A	B
Old Basis	$ 70,000	$ 90,000
New Mortgage	80,000	60,000
Cash and Boot Paid	30,000	−0−
Recognized Gain	+ −0−	+ 50,000
Total:	$180,000	$200,000

Less

	A	B
Old Mortgage	$ 60,000	$ 80,000
Cash and Boot Received	+ −0−	+ 30,000
Total:	$ 60,000	$110,000

New Basis	$120,000	$ 90,000

STEP 6. Allocating New Basis

Each party will decide which portions of his or her new basis to allocate to land and to improvements in order to establish new depreciation schedules

SALE-LEASEBACK

A useful tool of real estate finance, the **sale-leaseback,** is used primarily for larger projects. In this situation the owner of the property sells it to an investor and leases it back at the same time. This financing arrangement is utilized when companies with considerable cash tied up in their real estate want to free this capital for more speculative ventures. The lease utilized for this method is usually a fully net lease that extends over a period long enough for the investor to recover invested funds and to make a fair profit on the investment.

The sale-leaseback approach to real estate finance is generally applied to commercial properties, because rents paid by businesses and professional persons are deductible expenses in the year in which they are incurred. Using this approach, a seller-lessee enjoys many benefits:

- the seller-lessee retains possession of the property while obtaining the full sales price, in some cases keeping the right to repurchase the property at the end of the lease, in effect freeing capital frozen in equity;
- the seller-lessee maintains an appreciable interest in realty that can be capitalized by subleasing or by mortgaging the leasehold; and
- the seller-lessee gets a tax deduction for the full amount of the rent, equivalent to being able to take depreciation deductions for both the building *and* the land.

The cash secured from the sale might be utilized for plant expansion, remodeling, or investing in other opportunities. In addition, a lease appears as an indirect liability on a firm's balance sheet, whereas a mortgage shows up as a direct liability and adversely affects the firm's debt ratio in terms of obtaining future financing.

The advantages to the investor-landlord in this type of arrangement include a fair return *on* and *of* the investment in the form of rent during the lease term and ownership of a depreciable asset already occupied by a "good" tenant. In other words, the investor is buying a guaranteed income stream that can mostly be sheltered through the proper use of interest and depreciation allowances. When determining the rent to be paid on the lease, the investor can actually manage the risk by the amount of rent received. The rent for a quality tenant will normally be lower than the rent for a high-risk tenant.

When the lease includes an option for the tenant to repurchase the property at the end of the lease term, it is called a **sale-leaseback-buyback.** However, care must be taken to establish the buyback price for the fair market value at the time of sale. Otherwise the arrangement is considered a long-term installment mortgage, and any income tax benefits that might have been enjoyed during the term of the lease will be disallowed by the Internal Revenue Service.

SELLER REFINANCES PRIOR TO SALE

When selling real property, if a *buyer* cannot qualify for a new first mortgage, the *seller* may be able to refinance the property and get a mortgage that can be assumed by the buyer. Such a situation might arise if the buyer has a prior bankruptcy or divorce or is newly employed or in other similar circumstances limiting credit ability. At the same time, the seller wishes to acquire as much cash as possible from the sale to secure a new mortgage, and requires the buyer to pay cash for the difference and assume the new loan, completing the transaction.

A variation of this technique is used when a seller refinances a property and accepts a carry-back wraparound contract for deed from the buyer after receiving an agreed-upon down payment. Seller refinancing has been made more difficult as most new real estate loans made today are not easily assumable.

TRADING ON SELLER'S EQUITY

Reversing the approach above, in which the seller refinances prior to the sale, a buyer can secure a sizable cash amount to be paid to a seller by refinancing the subject property instead of assuming the existing mortgage balance. By arranging the offer accordingly, a buyer might be able to leverage 100 percent and still be able to develop cash for the seller.

For EXAMPLE

Assume a $50,000 property with an existing first mortgage balance of $30,000 and a seller who is willing to accept a second mortgage for $10,000 and a $10,000 cash down payment if the buyer assumes the first mortgage.

An enterprising buyer could offer to secure a new first mortgage for $40,000, based on the property's value of $50,000; satisfy the $30,000 existing mortgage; give the seller the $10,000 cash difference; and execute a $10,000 second purchase-money mortgage to the seller as required. In effect, the seller will be securing the $10,000 cash plus the second mortgage for $10,000 as agreed, but the cash down payment would be acquired by capitalizing on the seller's own equity. Under this arrangement the seller is relieved of any liability for the mortgage debt on the property, which would not have been the case had the buyer assumed the existing mortgage. The buyer, on the other hand, has leveraged 100%.

The weakness in this format from the seller's point of view is the fact that the buyer has no cash invested and that the second mortgage is now behind a larger first mortgage, increasing the seller's risks on both counts. However, these risks can be offset with a higher interest rate on the second mortgage, possibly a higher sales price, a wrap as the junior financing alternative, and/or strict forfeiture provisions in the junior lien.

EQUITY PARTICIPATION

Lenders sometimes can expand their earning possibilities by participating in a real estate transaction as both owners and financiers. In addition to the Shared Appreciation Mortgage (SAM), where the lender reduces the initial interest rate in exchange for a share of the property's future increased value, there are other variations of this type of participation financing.

Sale-Buyback (Sale-Contract Back)

Under this variation of the sale-leaseback technique, a lender, usually a life insurance company or a pension fund, agrees to purchase a completed project from the developer and sell it right back on an installment sale contract for deed. The lender retains legal title to the property and profits by including a **kicker** in the payment to cover a participation return *of* the investment as well as regular interest *on* the investment. The developer profits through 100 percent financing and the depreciation shelter that comes with gaining equitable title to the property.

These contracts are usually designed to extend 10 years longer than a normal mortgage term, with the payments made during the time of an average mortgage loan being sufficient to repay the purchase price. The additional 10 years of payments are added compensation to the lender-participator. If a contract runs for 30 years, it might include payments for 20 years, sufficient to amortize the sales price, then continue for an additional 10 years at a higher interest rate to satisfy the kicker requirement.

Splitting Ownership

A more common form of lender participation than the sale-buyback form is **split-fee financing.** In this plan, the lender purchases the *land* and leases it to the developer while financing the improvements to be constructed on the leasehold as well.

The land lease payments can be established at an agreed-upon base rate plus a percentage of the tenant's income above a specified point. Under this arrangement, the lender-investor benefits by receiving a fixed return on the investment plus possible overages, while maintaining residual property rights through ownership of the fee. The developer has the advantage of high leverage and a fully depreciable asset, because he or she owns the leasehold improvements but not the land.

Joint Ventures

Probably the most complete form of equity participation is the **joint venture,** in which the lender puts 100 percent of the funds needed for a development "up front" in exchange for the expertise and time of the developer. The lender then becomes an investor in full partnership with the developer.

Some joint venture partnerships are expanded to include the landowner, the construction company, the financier, and the developer, who supervises the entire project from its inception until it is completely rented and sometimes even beyond as a permanent manager. Passive investors in joint venture partnerships cannot use a loss from passive investment to protect their active income.

SUMMARY

The scope of activities in the real estate finance market is broadened by many modern variations on loans. Variable-rate mortgage loans (VRMs) and variable-payment-plan loans, such as a graduated-payment mortgage (GPM), allow lenders and borrowers to tailor specific interest and payment variations to meet their needs.

Under a reverse annuity mortgage (RAM) a borrower, usually a senior citizen, pledges a property as collateral and secures monthly payments from the lender until a maximum amount has been reached. Then the loan must be repaid. A convertible loan allows a borrower to switch from an adjustable-rate loan to a fixed-rate loan to offset fears of an unaffordable high payment.

An open-end mortgage is designed to allow for future advances under terms specified in the original contract. The construction mortgage is the most commonly used open-end form.

A construction loan is designed to finance the cost of labor and materials during the course of constructing a building. It matches the amount of money loaned to the growing value of the collateral building. A system of draws is scheduled, with the builder collecting proportionate sums from the lender during the various stages of construction.

Blanket mortgages include more than one property as collateral. Release clauses are incorporated into the format to allow portions of the collateral to be released as needed. One type of partnership financing establishes ownership between two or more mortgagees in a single mortgage. Another involves several mortgagors sharing the responsibility for a single mortgage, such as in a cooperative apartment structure. Participation finance is created when a mortgagee acts as financier and receives part ownership at the same time. Leasehold mortgages include the pledging of a tenant's leasehold interest in a property in exchange for financing the improvements to be built thereon.

A mobile home loan can be insured by the FHA or guaranteed by the VA. A purchase-money mortgage is created when a seller carries back a portion of a property's sales price as a loan to the buyer. A hard-money mortgage is a cash loan to a borrower. Usually a property owner pledges equity as collateral to a private mortgage company for a second mortgage and receives cash needed to purchase some item of personal property. A wraparound encumbrance is a special form of junior financing designed to encompass an already existing financial instrument.

A major source of tax-free dollars is available through the refinancing of the equity accumulated in real property. A property's growth in value over time and the increased equity resulting from the amortization of an existing encumbrance often provide a base for securing new funds. As borrowed money, refinancing proceeds are not taxable income, even when these funds exceed the original price paid for the property. However, any gains will be taxed when the property is sold.

When real property must be sold, a taxpayer has various alternatives to postpone taxes on the net gain. Property sellers may defer their taxes by using an installment sale financing technique or by "trading up" through an exchange.

A useful commercial property financing arrangement is the sale-leaseback technique. This plan involves selling real estate to an investor and, at the same time, leasing it back. The buyer benefits from a return *on* the investment plus a return *of* the investment. The seller-tenant benefits from the immediate cash proceeds of the sale, plus tax deductions for the full amount of the rent and continued possession of the premises. When the sale-leaseback includes a buyback option at a fair market value upon the lease's completion, the seller-tenant can continue to control the property far into the future.

Sometimes sellers will refinance prior to a sale in order to cash out their equity. They must seek to obtain a new mortgage that can be assumed by a buyer.

CHAPTER 14

Defaults and Foreclosures

▼ KEY TERMS

acceleration clause
auction
deed in lieu of
  foreclosure
default
deficiency judgment
delinquency
equitable redemption
  period

eviction
forbearance
foreclosure
grace period
judgment decree
judicial foreclosure
late payment charge
lis pendens
moratoriums

recast
statutory redemption
  period
strict forfeiture
subrogation
voluntary transfer of
  deed
workouts

The basic responsibilities of the parties to a real estate financial contract are relatively clear-cut. In exchange for money loaned, a borrower is obligated to repay the loan according to conditions stipulated in the contract as well as preserve the value of the collateral and the priority lien position of the lender. In the event the borrower breaches these obligations, the lender can exercise its power of acceleration and insist that the loan balance, accrued interest, and costs incurred be paid immediately and in full.

In the vast majority of real estate financing arrangements, a comfortable rhythm of lending and repayment is established between the participants, with few unusual circumstances occurring to cause a breach in the loan agreement. Financial fiduciaries are bound by law and company policy to display the highest ethical responsibility in granting real estate loans. A lender will establish a real estate loan on the basis of availability of funds, general economic conditions, local economic stability, and competitive lenders' actions, as well as the borrower's financial position and the property's value.

Except for infrequent periods in U.S. economic history when severe depressions or recessions created serious financial difficulties, a borrower who pledges realty as security for a loan generally enjoys the benefits of a steady inflation in the economy that usually increases the value of the property. At the same time, the balance owed on the loan is being paid down. The interaction between this growth in value and the lessening of the loan balance increases the protection against risk for the lender. The subtle, slow, and steady increase of an equity position locks the borrower into continued payments on the loan to protect the growing investment. Even a borrower on a 100 percent loan soon develops some measurable equity in property and a commensurate desire to protect it. The equity position inures to the advantage of the lender by lowering the incidences of mortgage defaults. In fact, foreclosures in this country historically represent a very low percentage of the total loans made, even in times of distress.

When a real estate loan does fail, it is often the result of events that are beyond the control of the parties to the loan. As always, there are circumstances under which individuals and companies suffer personal or financial setbacks that may jeopardize their ability to maintain normal payment patterns. Some of the more readily recognized problems include loss of employment, illness, divorce, bankruptcy, loss of tenants' rent as a result of local economic setbacks (overbuilding of income properties, for example), or ordinary mismanagement. Under such conditions, real estate loan payments usually cannot be met. Defaults and foreclosures result.

DEFAULTS

A **default** is the breach of one or more of the conditions or terms of a loan agreement. When a default occurs, the **acceleration clause** contained in all loan contracts is activated, allowing the lender to declare the full amount of the debt immediately due and payable. If the borrower cannot or will not meet this requirement, the lender may foreclose against the collateral to recover any loss. Although legally any default in a loan contract enables the lender to accelerate the debt, most lenders seek to avoid foreclosure and arrange a plan with the borrower to protect the interests of both parties and avoid costly, time-consuming court procedures. These efforts are called **workouts** and take the form of payment waivers, refinancing, or other arrangements designed to avoid a foreclosure. HUD has trained housing counselors to help financially troubled families avoid the loss of their homes.

However, in an irreconcilable situation between a defaulted borrower and the lender, acceleration and ultimate foreclosure are the lender's last resort. It is generally accepted that most lenders do not want to own the real estate that is pledged as collateral for their loans. However, defaults do occur, even though lenders will expend every effort to qualify their borrowers in order to ensure the success of their loans.

Delinquencies

Most loan defaults occur when the borrower falls behind in making payments, in paying taxes, insurance premiums, or other lien payments.

Principal and Interest. The most common form of default occurs when the payment of principal and interest is not made when due, called **delinquency.**

Loan agreements stipulate that the regular payment is due "on or before" a specified date, but most lenders will allow a reasonable **grace period,** usually up to 15 days, in which to receive the regular payment. Many loan arrangements include a **late payment charge** of some specific amount that is applied if the borrower exceeds the grace period. This late

IN PRACTICE . . .

Bob Brown has made some poor choices on the stock market and now finds himself two months behind on his mortgage payment with no hope of catching up, or even being able to continue the regular payment, at least until he is able to sell his beach house and SUV.

He is tempted to just lock the door and walk away but he has always had a good credit rating in the past and believes that this would create such a black mark on his credit that he would never be able to get another loan for any reason! A friend who is a real estate agent encourages him to contact his lender immediately to discuss his situation and look for any possible solution other than foreclosure.

Bob is pleasantly surprised to learn that the bank is willing to work with him, and that they, in fact, are not at all interested in having to foreclose! They just want their money. Bob's agent friend had suggested giving the bank the keys and the deed to the property (in lieu of foreclosure), but the bank is not interested in having to sell the house. Instead they suggest a three-month moratorium where no payment would be required. This should give Bob time to sell the beach house and SUV, giving him the funds to make the loan current. If for some reason this does not work, they will consider extending the term of the loan by the extra three months, with Bob resuming regular payments at the end of the moratorium period. As a last resort, they might consider recasting the loan for a new period of time, resulting in a lower monthly payment. The important issue here is that Bob contacted the lender as soon as he realized he was in trouble. Too often people wait until it really is too late to avoid foreclosure, a no-win situation for both borrower and lender.

payment fee is imposed to encourage promptness and offset the extra bookkeeping costs that delinquent accounts entail. Most lenders are not disturbed by payments made within grace periods, but they will take remedial action when an account consistently incurs late charges or when a borrower exceeds a 30-day delinquency period.

Property Taxes. Another cause for default is the nonpayment or late payment of property taxes. Although this situation is not too prevalent with residential loans because of the effectiveness of the impounding technique, it becomes a more serious problem with commercial real estate financing, in which impounds generally are not required.

The nonpayment of property taxes is a technical default under a real estate loan. Property taxes represent a priority lien over most existing liens on real estate. If a tax lien is imposed, the lender's position as priority lienholder is jeopardized. If a lender is unaware of a property tax delinquency and thus is not protected, the collateral property may be sold for taxes, *eliminating the safe lien position.* As a consequence, all realty loan agreements include a clause stipulating a borrower's responsibility to pay property taxes in the amount and on the date required. Otherwise the lender is notified by the county treasurer, and the loan goes into default and may be accelerated.

Other Liens. Defaults may also occur when a borrower allows other liens that have priority over the loan to vest against the collateral property. Such liens might be imposed for nonpayment of federal or state income taxes or city taxes. In some jurisdictions, construction and materialmen's liens can take priority over any preexisting liens. Under these circumstances, a lender may consider a loan in default and pursue appropriate legal remedies.

Hazard Insurance. Another cause for default is the nonpayment of *hazard insurance* premiums required by the lender for the protection of the value of the improvements on the collateral property. Again the impounding technique prevents most of the possible difficulties in this area. However, some realty loan arrangements allow the borrower to pay insurance premiums outside the framework of the regular payment structure, contingent on the mortgagee's prior approval of the insurance carrier and the terms of the policy. Where this independent payment flexibility is granted, the borrower is obligated to make the premium payments on time to prevent any lapse of coverage and is usually required to provide the lender with a copy of the paid invoice as evidence of this accomplishment.

The lender is named in the hazard insurance policy as a coinsured along with the borrower-property owner. If any losses are incurred by reason of fire, windstorm, or other insurable circumstance, the lender's collateral position must be preserved. The damages will be repaired to the lender's satisfaction, or the insurance proceeds will be applied to reduce the balance of the loan to match the reduced value of the collateral.

Poor Property Management

Often lenders include a provision in a formal real estate loan agreement that requires a borrower to maintain the collateral property in such a manner that its value will not diminish to the point of undermining the lender's security position. A breach of this covenant creates a technical default of the terms of the loan. It is rather difficult to assess the amount of "waste" that creates such a defaulting situation, especially as its discovery would depend on constant inspection by a lender, an impractical task where many loans are being serviced. Usually a lender will rely on a borrower's pride of ownership to protect the collateral, but a serious violation can result in a loan default and acceleration of the debt.

ADJUSTMENTS

A final foreclosure action is studiously avoided whenever possible. Before a lender decides to foreclose, full consideration is taken of the amount of the borrower's equity in the property, the general state of the current real estate market, and the positions of any junior lienholders. The lender also judiciously weighs the circumstances that caused the default and the attitude of the borrower concerning the repair of the breach in the contract.

The only time a foreclosure should *ever* be considered is when the current market value of the collateral property is actually *less* than the balance of the indebtedness *and* the borrower can no longer make the payment that has been adjusted to meet the emergency situation. Even under these extreme circumstances, a borrower should be aware that a foreclosure is *not* mandatory and that a *deed in lieu of foreclosure* from the borrower to the lender will end their relationship in an amicable, efficient, and legal manner, if the lender will accept it. However, a deed in lieu of foreclosure will still have a negative impact on the borrower's total credit rating.

The greatest risk to a lender's making a real estate loan is that a property pledged as collateral will be abandoned by the borrower. Although this risk is considerably less when unimproved land is the collateral, any improved property left vacant becomes an immediate and irritating source of concern for a lender.

An abandoned property may well indicate the complete and total frustration that borrowers have experienced in trying to solve their problems. A borrower is logically the first person to know of trouble and should attempt to solve the problem with the help of the lender. Failing in this attempt, the borrower should seek to sell the property at a profit. If this is not possible because of market conditions, the borrower should try to recover the equity or, at the very least, try to *give the property away* to someone who will assume the mortgage.

Only when a borrower has made this final effort to give the property away and failed, and when payments can no longer be made, should abandonment be considered. At this point, frustration may cause a borrower blindly to seek retaliation and perhaps even physically damage the collateral. A knowledgeable lender is aware of this possibility. Even if an abandoned property is left in good condition, a vacant building is often an invitation for vandalism. In some areas an abandoned property is considered fair game for the stripping of any valuable parts. When investigating their delinquent accounts, many lenders have discovered empty shells of buildings. The wrecking of abandoned properties often is quite vicious, the apparent motivation just plain, wanton destructiveness. An abandoned property is anathema to a lender. To perfect a fee in the collateral, quick legal action must be taken to gain immediate possession of the real estate so that it may be protected during the foreclosure procedure.

In the final analysis most borrowers have more power than they realize and should be able to negotiate with their lenders from positions of strength rather than weakness. And increasingly, lenders *are* making every effort to cooperate and prevent a foreclosure action. These efforts include a variety of adjustments to the terms and conditions of the real estate loan contract to reflect emergency needs.

Moratoriums and Recasting

As discussed earlier, the most common default on real estate loans is delinquent payments. These payment delinquencies can occur because of overextension of credit, loss of job, loss of earnings due to sickness or injury, personal tragedies, and other problems.

When a loan becomes a problem, the person charged with the responsibility for supervising the collection of delinquent accounts will contact the borrower to discover the cause. Most lenders will attempt to cooperate with those borrowers who have legitimate excuses for failing to make payments. Sometimes a lender will waive a portion of the payment, usually the principal amount, to help a delinquent borrower regain financial balance. At other times the interest portion of the payment is waived as well and added to the balance owed toward that time when the borrower regains financial stability. Frequently the entire payment is waived for some reasonable length of time.

These partial or full payment waivers, described as **forbearance** or **moratoriums,** originated during the Great Depression monetary crises. A lender expects that during the moratorium period the borrower can solve the problems by securing a new job, selling the property to a buyer qualified to make the loan payments, or finding some other acceptable solution.

Granting a moratorium on payments can create peripheral problems for the borrower because these postponed amounts must eventually be paid sometime during the remaining life of the loan. Therefore a forbearance arrangement will usually require that a borrower add extra money to the regular payments when they are reinstated. These extra monies will be applied to satisfy the bubble of principal and interest that accrued during the moratorium.

Both Fannie Mae and Freddie Mac are aggressively seeking to identify and assist delinquent borrowers who are on the "fast track" to foreclosure. For financial situations that are short-term or curable, both companies are now far more likely to approve modification of loan terms.

For a defaulted borrower just recovering sound economic footing, an increase in payments may present too great an additional burden. In order to offset any possible hardships that these extra payments might create, a lender may choose to extend the term of the loan by a time interval equal to the moratorium period. Then the borrower can continue to make regularly scheduled monthly payments at the same amount, but for a longer period of time. Another alternative is for the lender to require one balloon payment for all the monies accrued during the moratorium, to be payable at the loan's scheduled expiration date.

Delinquent loans can also be **recast** to lower the payments to suit a borrower's damaged financial position. When a loan has been paid down over a period of time, say, five years, and a default is imminent as a result of a borrower's financial crisis, the lender may redesign the balance still owed into a new loan extending the original time period or even longer, if feasible. This recasting would effectively reduce the payments required and relieve the pressure on the borrower.

Recasting invariably requires a new title search to discover if any intervening liens or second encumbrances have been recorded. This is especially necessary in the case of a delinquent borrower who might have sought aid from other sources. A lender may also require additional collateral and/or cosigners for the new financing agreement.

Voluntary Conveyance of Deed

When all efforts at adjusting the terms of a loan to solve a borrower's problems have failed and the property cannot be sold to a buyer willing and able to assume the loan's balance, a lender often will seek to secure a **voluntary transfer of deed** from the borrower. This action prevents the costly and time-consuming process of foreclosure. By executing either a quitclaim deed or a regular deed, a borrower can eliminate the stigma of a foreclosure, maintain a respectable credit rating, and avoid the possibility of a deficiency judgment. On some applications for a new loan, the borrowers are asked if they have ever executed a voluntary **deed in lieu of foreclosure**.

A deed in lieu of foreclosure is a mutual agreement in which the delinquent owners of a property deed it to the lender in return for various considerations, usually a release from liability under the terms of the loan. It can be completed quickly, without the cost of a foreclosure, and the rights of third parties having interests in the property are left undisturbed.

The efficiency of this technique for avoiding a foreclosure is sometimes offset by its being disallowed if it has been used to avoid the inclusion of the asset in a bankruptcy. It is necessary to verify that the borrower was solvent at the time of the voluntary transfer. Also, as already mentioned, the rights of third parties must be protected; hence, the borrower may still be liable for junior encumbrances not cleared prior to the transfer.

Lenders are fully aware of the difficulties with evictions as well as the costs and time involved in a full foreclosure process. Most often a lender encourages a hopelessly defaulted borrower to transfer a deed voluntarily. However, the lender must take care to be protected against any future claims of fraud or duress by the borrower. Note: Some lenders consider a voluntary conveyance of deed a blot on a borrower's credit rating and consider it as bad as a regular foreclosure.

The Housing Act of 1964

Under the 1964 Housing Act, the FHA required that lenders provide relief in situations in which default is beyond a borrower's control. For example, a lender might recast or extend the mortgage of a borrower who has defaulted because of unemployment during a serious illness. The VA also requires leniency in the case of a borrower who is willing but unable to pay. The VA itself may pay for such delinquencies in order to keep a loan current for a veteran, although these payments do not reduce the debtor's obligation. The VA retains the right to collect these advances at a future date.

FORECLOSURES

When all else has failed, a lender pursues foreclosure to recover the collateral in order to sell it and recoup the investment. By definition, to foreclose means to shut out, exclude, bar, or deprive one of the right to redeem a mortgage, deed of trust, or land contract. **Foreclosure,** then, is not only a process to recover a lender's collateral but also a procedure whereby a borrower's rights of redemption are eliminated, and all interests in the subject property are removed.

Under old English law a borrower had few, if any, rights in property beyond possession. If the borrower did not pay on time and in the amount called for, any property rights were immediately forfeited, and full ownership was vested in the lender.

This instantaneous and often capricious deprivation of property rights aroused widespread criticism and eventually was brought before the monarch, who assigned the adjudication of these grievances to a court of equity. Certain hardship cases were ruled on according to their merit, rather than on legal technicalities. Gradually a system developed wherein a distressed borrower was allowed extra time to raise the funds necessary to protect property rights. This relief was called an **equitable redemption period.** Under this ruling a borrower could secure a certain period beyond the default time in order to redeem the property. This could be accomplished by either bringing the payments current or repaying the total amount of the principal due in addition to interest owed and any court costs incurred.

As time passed, borrowers began to abuse their equitable redemption rights. Some defaulted borrowers remained in possession of their property beyond the redemption period and otherwise created great difficulties for lenders trying to reclaim the forfeited collateral. Complaints to the court of equity resulted in the decree of foreclosure, a legal process whereby the equitable period of redemption could be terminated under appropriate conditions. This became known as *strict foreclosure* or **strict forfeiture**.

Our present-day redemption and foreclosure processes have evolved from these medieval court decisions. However, during the 1800s, when the U.S. economy was still basically agrarian, many states expanded the strict foreclosure procedure to include additional protection for borrowers' equity interests in anticipation of better harvests in the following year. At the end of the equitable redemption period the mortgagee was directed to sell the property at *public auction* rather than automatically take title to the collateral. It was hoped that the foreclosure sale would obtain a fair market value for the property and save part of the borrower's equity. In addition, the defaulted borrower was given another redemption period *after the sale* to recover the property before title to the collateral was transferred.

This additional time period is termed the **statutory redemption period** because it came into being as a result of the enactment of state statutes. During the entire redemption period the defaulted borrower is allowed to retain possession of the property. The foreclosure methods and redemption periods vary from state to state.

Lenders are concerned not only with maintaining the integrity of their collateral but with the disposition of the income generated by the property. Therefore, in certain cases lenders can petition the courts for the right of possession to protect the collateral. If possession is granted, and it invariably is in the case of abandoned property, the lender must maintain accurate records of the distribution of income from the property during the statutory redemption period. Any balance left after deductions for the required payments and property maintenance must be credited to the reduction of the debt.

A new trend is emerging in some states to have the statutory redemption period run *prior* to the foreclosure sale. In Illinois there is a decree of foreclosure, *then* a 90-day redemption period, *then* the sale.

Judicial Foreclosure and Sale

A common foreclosure procedure, called the **judicial foreclosure** and sale process, involves the use of the courts and the consequent sale of the collateral at public auction. This foreclosure procedure is used with conventional mortgages, conventional insured mortgages, FHA-insured mortgages, VA-guaranteed mortgages, and junior mortgages.

Conventional Mortgages. Before a lender forecloses on a conventional first mortgage, the delinquent mortgagor is notified of the default and the reasons for it. An immediate solution is required, and all efforts must be expended to solve the problem as soon as possible. However, if all attempts fail, a complaint is filed by the mortgagee in the court for the county in which the property is located, and a summons is issued to the mortgagor, initiating the foreclosure action.

Simultaneous with this activity, a title search is made to determine the identities of all parties having an interest in the collateral property, and a **lis pendens** is filed with the court, giving notice to the world of the pending foreclosure action. Notice is sent to all parties having an interest in the property, requesting that they appear to defend their interests, or else they will be *foreclosed* from any future rights by judgment of the court. It is vitally important for the complainant-mortgagee to notify *all* junior lienholders of the foreclosure action lest they be omitted from participation in the property auction and thus acquire the right to file suit on their own at some future time.

Depending on the number of days required by the jurisdiction for public notice to inform any and all persons having an *unrecorded* interest in the subject property that a foreclosure suit is imminent, and depending on the availability of a court date, the complaint is eventually aired before a presiding judge. In most instances the defendant-mortgagor does not appear in court unless special circumstances are presented in defense of the default. Those creditors who do appear to present their claims are recognized and noted, and a sale of the property at public auction by a court-appointed referee or sheriff is ordered by means of a **judgment decree.**

A public sale is necessary so the actual market value of the subject property can be established. The auction will probably not generate any bids in excess of the balance of the mortgage debt, because it is assumed that the mortgagor made every effort to recover those monies prior to the foreclosure. Basically a lender sues for foreclosure under the terms of the *mortgage*. If the proceeds from the auction sale are not sufficient to recover the outstanding loan balance plus costs, then a mortgagee may, in most states, also sue on the *note* for the deficiency. However, to establish this suit on a note, a lender *does not bid* at the auction.

If a mortgagee does not anticipate pursuing a deficiency, and most do not because of the apparent financial straits of the defaulted mortgagor, the mortgagee makes the opening bid at the auction. This bid is usually an amount equal to the loan balance plus interest to date and court costs, and then the lender hopes that someone else will bid at least one dollar more to "bail the lender out." If there are any junior lienholders or other creditors who look to the property as collateral for *their* loans, they now have the opportunity to step in and bid to protect their priority positions. Their bids obligate them to repay the first mortgagee. When no junior lienholders or creditors enter a bid, the auction closes at the first mortgagee's bid price. Any interests that these junior creditors may have in the property are effectively eliminated. However, if any other person bids an amount above the first mortgage, after the first lien is paid the excess funds are distributed to the junior lienholders in order of their priority, with any money left over going to the defaulted mortgagor.

Conventional Insured Mortgages. Under the terms of the insurance policies of most private mortgage insurance companies, a default is interpreted to be nonpayment for four months. Within ten days of default, the mortgagee is required to notify the insurer, who then decides whether to instruct the mortgagee to foreclose.

When a conventional insured mortgage is foreclosed, the first mortgagee is the original bidder at the public auction of the collateral property. Under these circumstances the successful bidder-mortgagee files notice with the insurance company within 60 days after the legal proceedings have transpired. If the insurance company is confident of recovering the losses by purchasing the collateral property from the mortgagee and then reselling it, it will reimburse the mortgagee for the total amount of the bid and secure title to the property. If, however, the company does not foresee any possibility for this recovery, it may elect to only pay the mortgagee the agreed-upon specific amount of insurance, and the mortgagee will retain ownership of the property. The collateral is then sold to recover any balance still unpaid.

In any cases of judicial foreclosure and sale, any ownership rights acquired by the successful bidder at the foreclosure auction are still subject to any redemption rights of the defaulted mortgagor. A full fee simple absolute title cannot vest in the bidder until these redemption rights have expired.

FHA-Insured Mortgages. Foreclosures on FHA-insured mortgages originate with the filing of Form 2068, Notice of Default, which must be given to the local FHA administrative office within 60 days of default. This notice describes the reasons for the mortgagor's delinquency, such as death, illness, marital difficulties, income depletion, excessive obligations, employment transfers, or military service.

In many cases involving delinquent FHA-insured mortgages, counselors from the local FHA offices will attempt to design an agreement between the mortgagee and the mortgagor for adjustments to the loan conditions in order to prevent foreclosure. The most common technique used in circumstances where a default is beyond the mortgagor's control but deemed curable is forbearance of foreclosure.

If the problems causing the default are solved within a one-year period, the mortgagee informs the local FHA office of the solution. If not, a default status report is filed, and the mortgagee must initiate foreclosure proceedings. If the bids at the auction are less than the unpaid balance, the mortgagee is expected to bid the debt, take title, and present it to the FHA along with a claim for insurance, which may be paid in cash or in government debentures. In some cases, with prior FHA approval, the mortgagee may assign the defaulted mortgage directly to the FHA before the final foreclosure action in exchange for insurance benefits. In any case, if the property can be sold easily at a price that will repay the loan in full, the mortgagee simply will sell the property after bidding at the auction and will not apply for FHA compensation. If the FHA ends up as the owner of the property, the collateral will be resold "as is" or repaired, refurbished, and resold at a higher price to help minimize the losses to the FHA.

VA-Guaranteed Mortgages. Unlike the FHA-insured mortgages, whereby a lender's entire risk is recovered from the insurance benefits, a VA loan is similar to a privately insured loan in that a lender receives only the *top portion* of the outstanding loan balance. In the event of a delinquency of more than three months on a VA loan, the mortgagee must file proper notification with the local VA office, which may then elect to bring the loan current if it wishes, with **subrogation** rights to the mortgagee against the mortgagor for the amount advanced. This means that the VA claim against the defaulted veteran takes priority over the rights of the mortgagee to these funds.

Much like the FHA, VA lenders are required to make every effort to offset a foreclosure through forbearance, payment adjustments, sale of the property, deed in lieu of foreclosure, or other acceptable solutions. Actual foreclosure is considered only as a last resort.

In the event of a foreclosure, the mortgagee is usually the original bidder at the auction and submits a claim for losses to the local VA office. The VA then has the option either to pay the unpaid balance, interest, and court costs and take title to the collateral or to require that the mortgagee retain the property and the VA will pay only the difference between the determined value of the property on the date of foreclosure and the mortgage balance. The latter alternative is usually chosen when the property is badly deteriorated, accenting the importance for a mortgagee to properly supervise the collateral.

Junior Mortgages. Defaults of junior mortgages are handled in exactly the same manner as senior mortgages. Here, however, the relationship is usually between two individuals rather than between an institutional lender and an individual borrower.

A junior lender usually seeks the counsel of an attorney to manage the foreclosure process. The delinquent borrower is requested to cure the problem within a certain time period. If a cure cannot be accomplished, notice is given to all persons having an interest in the property, and the attorney then files for foreclosure.

The junior lender is generally the bidder at the public sale and secures ownership of the collateral property subject to the balance of the existing senior loan. This loan is usually required to be paid in full because the foreclosure triggers the due-on-sale clause, unless other solutions are negotiated ahead of time.

Power-of-Sale Foreclosure

An alternative to the judicial foreclosure process is the *power-of-sale method* of collateral recovery. Under this form a lender or the trustee has the right to sell the collateral property upon default without being required to spend the time and money involved in a court foreclosure suit. In fact, under this form of lender control a borrower's redemption time frame is shortened considerably by the elimination of the statutory redemption period granted in the judicial process.

Deeds of Trust. The most common application of the power-of-sale foreclosure process is by exercise of the trustee's responsibility created in a deed of trust. In the event of a default, the beneficiary (lender) notifies the trustee in writing of the trustor's (borrower's) delinquency and instructs the trustee to begin the foreclosure by sale process.

Notice of default is recorded by the trustee at the county recorder's office within the jurisdiction's designated time period, usually 90 days, to give notice to the public of the intended auction. This official notice is accompanied by advertisements in public newspapers that state the total amount due and the date of the public sale. Unlike the notice given in the judicial process, notice need not be given to each individual junior lienholder when the power-of-sale process is enforced. However, the trustor-borrowers must be given special notice of the situation so they have full benefit of the redemption period.

During the equitable redemption period preceding the auction, the trustors or any junior lienholders may cure the default by making up any delinquent payments together with interest and costs to date. However, if such payments are not made, the property is placed for sale at public auction shortly after the expiration of the redemption period, and absolute title passes to the successful bidder.

Mortgages. The power-of-sale foreclosure process may be incorporated into the standard *mortgage* contract in approximately one-third of the states where the trust deed is not in use.

The procedure for foreclosing a mortgage under a power of sale is essentially the same as the one used to foreclose a deed of trust, except that in most states allowing this foreclosure format, the mortgagee is prohibited from bidding at the sale. In addition, the amount that the mortgagee may recover by suing for a deficiency judgment on the note is limited. Some states actually prohibit any deficiency judgments in cases of mortgage power-of-sale proceedings. The purchaser at a mortgagee's sale acquires the same type of title that would be acquired at a judicial auction and steps into the mortgagor's interest in the property. Because of the limitations imposed on this form of foreclosure, the mortgage power of sale is not widely used.

Strict Foreclosure

Although the judicial foreclosure procedure and statutory redemption periods are the prevailing practices, in some states it is still possible for a lender to recover the collateral through a strict foreclosure process. After appropriate notice has been given to the delin-

FIGURE 14.1 Strict Foreclosure or Strict Foreclosure Clause

Should the Seller elect to enforce a forfeiture hereunder, it may do so as follows: By depositing in the United States mail, postage prepaid, a written declaration of forfeiture addressed to the Buyers at their last known address. Upon such declaration of forfeiture being made by the Seller as provided herein, all rights, estates, and interest hereby created or then existing in favor of the Buyers or any one claiming under them, shall cease, terminate, and become null and void, and the right of possession and all equitable and legal interest and estates on the premises herein described, and all improvements, and all other appurtenances, together with all sums of money theretofore paid by the Buyers hereunder, shall revert to and be vested in and become the sole property of the Seller in fee and the Buyers shall have no right either at law or in equity to reclaim or recover any compensation for moneys paid, services performed or improvements placed upon said land, and the money paid and the improvements erected shall be forfeited to and retained by and become the sole property of said Seller as liquidated damages for such default, and not as a penalty, and also as consideration for the execution of this agreement. The Seller shall have the right, immediately upon any declaration of forfeiture in the manner herein provided, to enter upon said premises and take exclusive possession thereof, with or without process of law. Provided, however, that no forfeiture hereunder shall be enforced until and after the expiration; after such default of the following periods, to wit:

Where the Buyer has paid less than 20% of the purchase price	30 days
Where the Buyer has paid 20%, or more, but less than 30% of the purchase price	60 days
Where the Buyer has paid 30%, or more, but less than 50% of the purchase price	120 days
Where the Buyer has paid 50%, or more of the purchase price	9 months

In computing the above percentages, the amount of any agreement for sale or mortgage agreed to be paid by the Buyers shall be treated as payment to the extent of principal actually paid thereon by the Buyer.

quent borrower and the proper papers have been filed and processed, the court establishes a specific time period during which the balance of the defaulted debt must be paid in full by the borrower. If this is not done, the borrower's equitable and statutory redemption rights are eliminated, depending on the special circumstances of the case, and full legal title is awarded to the lender.

Using strict foreclosure, it is possible for a lender to secure ownership to a property with a value in excess of the loan's balance. The basic fault with the strict foreclosure process, and the one that brought about the system of judicial foreclosure and sale proceedings, is that there is no clearly established value for the collateral because there is no public auction. Thus, a lender's losses cannot be determined, and as a result no deficiency judgments are permitted under the strict foreclosure method. Because of the possible inequities that might arise from the foreclosure of a property when no value is established, the strict foreclosure method is seldom utilized and, in fact, has been abolished by statute in some states.

The only effective surviving use of the strict foreclosure method still allowed in many states is under the contract for deed form of financing. By wording a land contract appropriately and carefully observing and following all of the legal steps required for adequate notice to the errant vendee and to the public, a vendor may exercise a strict foreclosure in certain low-equity loan arrangements. A typical strict forfeiture or strict foreclosure clause that can be included in any loan document is shown in Figure 14.1

FIGURE 14.2   Summary of Foreclosure Process

Judicial	**Power of Sale**	**Strict Foreclosure**
Notice	Notice	Notice
Lis pendens	Publication	Redemption period
Hearing	Public sale	Repossession
Decree	No redemption	
Public sale		
Redemption period		

By Advertisement	**Entry and Possession**	**Writ of Entry**
Notification	Court petition	Court petition
Public sale	Repossession	Eviction
Ownership certificate	Eviction	
Eviction		

Other Foreclosure Processes

As with a number of laws concerning real estate, many states have established their own unique methods for foreclosing on defaulted mortgages, most of which are variations of the strict foreclosure procedure.

By Advertisement.   Foreclosure by advertisement is a method whereby a mortgagee notifies the mortgagor of default and advertises that the property will be sold at public auction. The successful purchaser at the auction is awarded an ownership certificate rather than legal possession of the property. To gain possession of the newly acquired property, in most states recognizing this foreclosure process, the successful bidder has to bring an *action for ejectment* or **eviction,** which legally dispossesses a defaulted borrower from the premises after a court hearing. The extra cost and trouble associated with this foreclosure procedure keep it from being a popular form for recovering a mortgagee's collateral.

By Entry and Possession.   Maine, Massachusetts, New Hampshire, and Rhode Island recognize the power of a mortgagee to petition the court for the right to take actual physical possession of the collateral pledged on a defaulted loan. The entry for possession *must* be peaceable, made before witnesses, and attested to by a certificate filed with the court. Full legal ownership vests in the mortgagee after a period of time during which the mortgagor may redeem the property by repaying the mortgage lien plus costs.

By Writ of Entry.   Maine, Massachusetts and New Hampshire also allow a mortgagee to initiate a court action whereby a writ of *entry only* is granted. The writ specifies the delinquent amounts due from the mortgagor and the time in which such funds must be paid. If the debt is not paid in accordance with these requirements, the mortgagee receives full legal title to the property. A summary of foreclosure processes is shown in Figure 14.2.

DEFICIENCY JUDGMENTS

If a lender receives less money than the entire loan balance, interest to date, and costs incurred as a consequence of a default after the delinquency, default, and foreclosure processes have been completed, the lender may pursue the borrower for these losses. The lender sues on the note and secures a **deficiency judgment** from the court, including an unsecured blanket lien, which may be perfected *against any property* currently owned or acquired in the future by the foreclosed borrower or any other signatories to the note. As mentioned previously, in most cases a defaulted borrower does not have any assets to make up this deficiency; otherwise they would have been put to use to prevent the default in the first place. Therefore, deficiency judgments are practically unenforceable.

Recognizing this fact, Nebraska and South Dakota have eliminated deficiency judgments, except those from a specific court determination. California, North Carolina, Montana, and Oregon have eliminated deficiency judgments on encumbrances drawn between individuals for financing any portion of the purchase price in a real estate sale. And, as noted earlier, when the power-of-sale procedure for foreclosure is used, the lender's rights to deficiency judgments are severely restricted.

The current trend is to rely less on deficiencies and more on limiting a borrower's personal liability on a realty loan to the equity in the collateral property. Most commercial real estate loans are designed to include an *exculpatory clause,* which defines this limitation.

One reason given for this shift away from the use of deficiency judgments is that they tend to protect the dishonest borrower and penalize those borrowers who strive to make good their debts, frequently by extreme self-denial. The possibility of a deficiency judgment does little to change the spending habits of an unscrupulous debtor, because such judgments can become liens only against property the borrower holds or may acquire in the future. Dishonest debtors may avoid payment by making certain they do not own any property in their own names.

No deficiency judgments are allowed by the FHA, and although it is possible to obtain a deficiency judgment under a VA-guaranteed loan, the VA frowns on this practice. In general, then, there is little evidence that deficiency judgments as a means for recovering a lender's losses will become widespread. In fact, they may actually be eliminated by more states in the future.

TAX IMPACTS OF FORECLOSURE

In a foreclosure, there may be an unexpected tax consequence for the person or entity that has borrowed the money. In the normal course of events, paying off a real estate loan has no tax consequences. When the last payment is made, all principal borrowed has been returned, plus interest. However, in a foreclosure the loan is retired without being paid in full.

A tax is due when the property's adjusted book value is *less* than the balance of the loan. As far as the IRS is concerned, a foreclosure is considered a sale; if the amount of the defaulted loan exceeds the tax basis of the property, the IRS considers that a gain has been made.

*F*OR EXAMPLE

Owners of a property who have depreciated the improvements but who still have a remaining book value of $100,000 and default on a $500,000 loan would be obligated to pay income tax on $400,000.

*F*OR EXAMPLE

A limited partnership purchases a million-dollar property with $200,000 cash and an $800,000 loan. Assuming an interest-only payment, if the loan is foreclosed at a later date, say, when the book basis is reduced to $750,000, the individual investors would be obligated to pay income tax on the gain of $50,000.

Example 1 represents an extreme case, used to illustrate the problem. However, it is possible that the value of such a property would have dropped below the balance on the loan, and the owners could decide to offer the lender a deed in lieu of foreclosure. Then the tax obligation would impact. Example 2 is more realistic. It behooves every borrower to be aware of the tax consequences in a foreclosure.

AUCTIONS

The use of an **auction** to dispose of foreclosed properties is not a new concept, having been used extensively for years in farm and ranch finance. The major reason for the use of auctions is the pressure of the carrying costs for holding defaulted properties. Auctions often allow them to be sold quickly.

Carrying costs include those for mortgage insurance, maintenance, management, property taxes, and other related expenses. Usually, these costs will not be recouped in the form of a higher selling price. Add to these costs the interest rates in the current market, and you can see that holding foreclosed properties creates an enormous burden on lenders.

SUMMARY

This chapter summarized the consequences of defaults in real estate finance. By far the greatest number of realty financing arrangements do not result in problems leading to foreclosure. Rising property values coupled with the systematic repayment of loans invariably create measurable equity positions for the borrower, equity "cushions" that usually inhibit the loss of property because of loan default. A troubled borrower can, in most problem situations, arrange to dispose of assets and thus maintain financial equilibrium. Occasionally, however, misfortune cannot be averted and foreclosure develops as the sole remedy. Such a situation is most clearly recognized when property pledged as collateral is abandoned by a borrower. Here a lender's only recourse is to pursue immediately the acquisition of the property by appropriate legal means.

Under less dramatic circumstances, a lender usually attempts to adjust the conditions of a loan in order to help a troubled borrower over short-term difficulties. Delinquent loan payments are the most common cause for a default, although the nonpayment of taxes or hazard insurance premiums, lack of adequate maintenance, and allowing priority liens to vest are also defaultable conditions. To offset the possibility of a foreclosure on delinquent loans, many lenders exercise forbearance and waive the principal portion of a loan payment for a given period or even extend a limited moratorium on the full payments. Other adjustments in the terms of a delinquent loan that might aid the defaulted borrower include an extension of time or a recasting of the loan to reflect the borrower's current ability to pay under circumstances of financial stress.

Only if there are no alternatives is a loan foreclosed. Under a judicial foreclosure proceeding, the lender notifies the defaulting borrower and arranges the advertisement necessary to inform the public that the foreclosure is in process so that all creditors having an interest may be alerted. At the foreclosure sale the lender usually bids the outstanding balance hoping that someone will bid one dollar more and repay the loan. Invariably, however, there is no value in the defaulted property above the mortgage balance, and the lender becomes the property's owner after a judgment decree is issued.

When the defaulted mortgage is a conventional loan, the lender assumes the risks of ownership and attempts to sell the property to minimize losses. When the defaulted loan is FHA-insured, the lender recovers any balance owed from the FHA insurance benefits. When the loan is VA-guaranteed or privately insured, the lender will recover the top portion of the loan up to the insured amount and will sell the property to recover the balance.

The foreclosure process is designed to eliminate a borrower's rights in the collateral property. However, the laws of redemption grant the delinquent borrower certain specified times during which the property may be redeemed. Not until the redemption periods expire does the new buyer of the property receive title to it.

A junior lender follows essentially the same procedures in foreclosing a delinquent loan, except that the integrity of the existing senior lender's priority position must be maintained by seeing that the first-mortgage payments, property taxes, and insurance premiums are paid.

Some mortgages and all deeds of trust contain a power-of-sale provision that allows a lender to pursue a somewhat faster foreclosure process than under the judicial process. Under a power of sale a trustee is entitled to sell a defaulted collateral property with reduced redemption times allotted to the borrower. This is a relatively effective foreclosure tool that must follow definitive notification and advertisement procedures to be legally valid.

Strict foreclosure proceedings are used only rarely, mostly with contracts for deed. In fact, many states have declared this foreclosure process illegal in their jurisdictions. In effect the strict foreclosure process quickly eliminates a defaulted borrower's total redemption rights in property.

Other unique foreclosure processes are used in a few states. Foreclosure by advertisement, by entry and possession, and by writ of entry are additional means enabling lenders to recover their collateral.

After all the various processes have been exhausted and a lender sells the collateral, but does not accumulate funds in an amount adequate to cover the investment and costs, the borrower may be sued under the note, and the lender can secure a deficiency judgment for the amount of the loss. Some states have eliminated or reduced the impact of a deficiency judgment. Often it is a practical impossibility to actually secure these funds, and in the event of a foreclosure most lenders will look to the sale of the collateral property as their ultimate security.